ABOUT THIS PUBLICATION

FOR SERVICE ASSISTANCE

Customer Service
1.704.898.0770

North Carolina General Statues is published by The Muliti-Media Group of Greater Charlotte in Charlotte, North Carolina. Copyright 2015 by the Multi-Media Group of Greater Charlotte. This book or parts thereof may not be reproduced in any form, stored in a retrieval system, or transmitted in any form by any means—electronic, mechanical, photocopy, recording or otherwise—without prior written permission of the publisher, except as provided by United States of America copyright law.

The records required by U.S. Code 2257(a) through (c) and the pertinent regulations 28 C.F.R. Cli. 1, Part 75 with respect to this publication and all materials associated with such records are maintained by The Multi-Media Group of Greater Charlotte, Publisher and available for review by Attorney General.

www.visionbooks.org

Copyright © 2015 by MMGGC
All rights reserved!

TID: 5061591
ISBN (10) digit: 1502914336
ISBN (13) digit: 978-1502914330

123-4-56789-01239-Paperback
123-4-56789-01239-Hardback

First Edition

090520140547

Printed in the United States of America

1

2015 EDITION

North Carolina Criminal Law And Procedure-Pamphlet # 44

Printed In conjunction with the Administration of the Courts

North Carolina Criminal Law and Procedure
Pamphlet Reference Guide

Chapters	Pamphlet
Chapter 1 Civil Procedure	1
Chapter 1 Civil Procedure (Continue)	2
Chapter 1A Rules of Civil Procedure	2
Chapter 1B Contribution.	2
Chapter 1C Enforcement of Judgments.	2
Chapter 1D Punitive Damages.	2
Chapter 1E Eastern Band of Cherokee Indians.	2
Chapter 1F North Carolina Uniform Interstate Depositions and Discovery Act.	2
Chapter 2 - Clerk of Superior Court [Repealed and Transferred.]	3
Chapter 3 - Commissioners of Affidavits and Deeds [Repealed.]	3
Chapter 4 - Common Law	3
Chapter 5 - Contempt [Repealed.]	3
Chapter 5A - Contempt	3
Chapter 6 - Liability for Court Costs	3
Chapter 7 - Courts [Repealed and Transferred.]	3
Chapter 7A – Judicial Department	3
Chapter 7A – Continuation (Judicial Department)	4
Chapter 7A – Continuation (Judicial Department)	5
Chapter 7B - Juvenile Code	5
Chapter 8 - Evidence	6
Chapter 8A - Interpreters for Deaf Persons [Recodified.]	6
Chapter 8B - Interpreters for Deaf Persons	6
Chapter 8C - Evidence Code	6
Chapter 9 - Jurors	6
Chapter 10 - Notaries [Repealed.]	6
Chapter 10A - Notaries [Recodified.]	6
Chapter 10B - Notaries	6
Chapter 11 - Oaths	6
Chapter 12 - Statutory Construction	6
Chapter 13 - Citizenship Restored	6
Chapter 14 - Criminal Law	7
Chapter 14 –Criminal Law (Continuation)	8
Chapter 15 - Criminal Procedure	9
Chapter 15A - Criminal Procedure Act (Continuation)	10
Chapter 15A - Criminal Procedure Act (Continuation)	11
Chapter 15B - Victims Compensation	11
Chapter 15C - Address Confidentiality Program	11
Chapter 16 - Gaming Contracts and Futures	11
Chapter 17 - Habeas Corpus	11

Chapter 17A - Law-Enforcement Officers [Recodified.]	11
Chapter 17B - North Carolina Criminal Justice Education and Training System [Recodified.] Chapter 17C - North Carolina Criminal Justice Education and Training Standards Commission	11
	11
Chapter 17D - North Carolina Justice Academy	11
Chapter 17E - North Carolina Sheriffs' Education and Training Standards Commission	11
Chapter 18 - Regulation of Intoxicating Liquors [Repealed.]	12
Chapter 18A - Regulation of Intoxicating Liquors [Repealed.]	12
Chapter 18B - Regulation of Alcoholic Beverages	12
Chapter 18C - North Carolina State Lottery	12
Chapter 19 - Offenses against Public Morals	12
Chapter 19A - Protection of Animals	12
Chapter 20 - Motor Vehicles	13
Chapter 20 - Motor Vehicles (Continuation)	14
Chapter 20 - Motor Vehicles (Continuation)	15
Chapter 20 - Motor Vehicles (Continuation)	16
Chapter 21 - Bills of Lading	17
Chapter 22 - Contracts Requiring Writing	17
Chapter 22A - Signatures	17
Chapter 22B - Contracts Against Public Policy	17
Chapter 22C - Payments to Subcontractors	17
Chapter 23 - Debtor and Creditor	17
Chapter 24 – Interest	17
Chapter 25 – Uniform Commercial Code	18
Chapter 25 – Uniform Commercial Code (Continuation)	19
Chapter 25A – Retail Installment Sales Act	20
Chapter 25B - Credit	20
Chapter 25C - Sales of Artwork	20
Chapter 26 - Suretyship	20
Chapter 27 - Warehouse Receipts [Repealed.]	20
Chapter 28 - Administration [Repealed.]	20
Chapter 28A - Administration of Decedents' Estates	20
Chapter 28B - Estates of Absentees in Military Service	20
Chapter 28C - Estates of Missing Persons	20
Chapter 29 - Intestate Succession	21
Chapter 30 - Surviving Spouses	21
Chapter 31 - Wills	21
Chapter 31A - Acts Barring Property Rights	21
Chapter 31B - Renunciation of Property and Renunciation of Fiduciary Powers Act	21
Chapter 31C - Uniform Disposition of Community Property Rights at Death Act	21
Chapter 32 - Fiduciaries	21
Chapter 32A - Powers of Attorney	21
Chapter 33 - Guardian and Ward [Repealed and Recodified.]	21

Chapter 33A - North Carolina Uniform Transfers to Minors Act	21
Chapter 33B - North Carolina Uniform Custodial Trust Act	21
Chapter 34 - Veterans' Guardianship Act	22
Chapter 35 - Sterilization Procedures	22
Chapter 35A - Incompetency and Guardianship	22
Chapter 36 - Trusts and Trustees [Repealed.]	22
Chapter 36A - Trusts and Trustees	22
Chapter 36B - Uniform Management of Institutional Funds Act [Repealed.]	22
Chapter 36C - North Carolina Uniform Trust Code	22
Chapter 36D - North Carolina Community Third Party Trusts, Pooled Trusts	23
Chapter 36E - Uniform Prudent Management of Institutional Funds Act	23
Chapter 37 - Allocation of Principal and Income [Repealed.]	23
Chapter 37A - Uniform Principal and Income Act	23
Chapter 38 - Boundaries	23
Chapter 38A - Landowner Liability	23
Chapter 39 - Conveyances	23
Chapter 39A - Transfer Fee Covenants Prohibited	23
Chapter 40 - Eminent Domain [Repealed.]	23
Chapter 40A - Eminent Domain	23
Chapter 41 - Estates	23
Chapter 41A - State Fair Housing Act	23
Chapter 42 - Landlord and Tenant	23
Chapter 42A - Vacation Rental Act	23
Chapter 43 - Land Registration	23
Chapter 44 - Liens	24
Chapter 44A - Statutory Liens and Charges	24
Chapter 45 - Mortgages and Deeds of Trust	24
Chapter 45A - Good Funds Settlement Act	24
Chapter 46 - Partition	24
Chapter 47 - Probate and Registration	25
Chapter 47A - Unit Ownership	25
Chapter 47B - Real Property Marketable Title Act	25
Chapter 47C - North Carolina Condominium Act	25
Chapter 47D - Notice of Settlement Act [Expired.]	25
Chapter 47E - Residential Property Disclosure Act	25
Chapter 47F - North Carolina Planned Community Act	25
Chapter 47G - Option to Purchase Contracts	25
Chapter 47H - Contracts for Deed	25
Chapter 48 - Adoptions +	26
Chapter 48A - Minors	26
Chapter 49 - Bastardy	26
Chapter 49A - Rights of Children	26
Chapter 50 - Divorce and Alimony	26
Chapter 50A - Uniform Child-Custody Jurisdiction and	

Enforcement Act	26
Chapter 50B - Domestic Violence	26
Chapter 50C - Civil No-Contact Orders	26
Chapter 51 - Marriage	26
Chapter 52 - Powers and Liabilities of Married Persons	27
Chapter 52A - Uniform Reciprocal Enforcement of Support Act [Repealed.]	27
Chapter 52B - Uniform Premarital Agreement Act	27
Chapter 52C - Uniform Interstate Family Support Act	27
Chapter 53 - Banks	27
Chapter 53A - Business Development Corporations and North Carolina Capital Resource Corporations	28
Chapter 53B - Financial Privacy Act	28
Chapter 54 - Cooperative Organizations	28
Chapter 54A - Capital Stock Savings and Loan Associations [Repealed.]	28
Chapter 54B - Savings and Loan Associations	29
Chapter 54C - Savings Banks	29
Chapter 55 - North Carolina Business Corporation Act	30
Chapter 55A - North Carolina Nonprofit Corporation Act	31
Chapter 55B - Professional Corporation Act	31
Chapter 55C - Foreign Trade Zones	31
Chapter 55D - Filings, Names, and Registered Agents for Corporations, Nonprofit Corporations, and Partnerships	31
Chapter 56 - Electric, Telegraph and Power Companies [Repealed.]	31
Chapter 57 - Hospital, Medical and Dental Service Corporations [Recodified.]	31
Chapter 57A - Health Maintenance Organization Act [Recodified.]	31
Chapter 57B - Health Maintenance Organization Act [Recodified.]	31
Chapter 57C - North Carolina Limited Liability Company Act.	31
Chapter 58 - Insurance.	32
Chapter 58 - Insurance (Continuation)	33
Chapter 58 - Insurance (Continuation)	34
Chapter 58 - Insurance (Continuation)	35
Chapter 58 - Insurance (Continuation)	36
Chapter 58 - Insurance (Continuation)	37
Chapter 58 - Insurance (Continuation)	38
Chapter 58A - North Carolina Health Insurance Trust Commission [Recodified.]	38
Chapter 59 - Partnership.	39
Chapter 59B - Uniform Unincorporated Nonprofit Association Act.	39
Chapter 60 - Railroads and Other Carriers [Repealed and Transferred.]	39
Chapter 61 - Religious Societies	39
Chapter 62 - Public Utilities	39

Chapter 62 - Public Utilities (Continuation)	40
Chapter 62A - Public Safety Telephone Service And Wireless Telephone Service	40
Chapter 63 - Aeronautics	40
Chapter 63A - North Carolina Global TransPark Authority	40
Chapter 64 - Aliens	40
Chapter 65 – Cemeteries	40
Chapter 66 - Commerce and Business	41
Chapter 67 - Dogs	41
Chapter 68 - Fences and Stock Law	41
Chapter 69 - Fire Protection	41
Chapter 70 - Indian Antiquities, Archaeological Resources and Unmarked Human Skeletal Remains Protection	42
Chapter 71 - Indians [Repealed.]	42
Chapter 71A - Indians	42
Chapter 72 - Inns, Hotels and Restaurants	42
Chapter 73 - Mills	42
Chapter 74 - Mines and Quarries	42
Chapter 74A - Company Police [Repealed.]	42
Chapter 74B - Private Protective Services Act [Repealed.]	42
Chapter 74C - Private Protective Services	42
Chapter 74D - Alarm Systems	42
Chapter 74E - Company Police Act	42
Chapter 74F - Locksmith Licensing Act	42
Chapter 74G - Campus Police Act	42
Chapter 75 - Monopolies, Trusts and Consumer Protection	42
Chapter 75A - Boating and Water Safety	43
Chapter 75B - Discrimination in Business	43
Chapter 75C - Motion Picture Fair Competition Act	43
Chapter 75D - Racketeer Influenced and Corrupt Organizations	43
Chapter 75E - Unlawful Activities in Connection With Certain Corporate Transactions	43
Chapter 76 - Navigation	43
Chapter 76A - Navigation and Pilotage Commissions	43
Chapter 77 - Rivers, Creeks, and Coastal Waters	43
Chapter 78 - Securities Law [Repealed.]	43
Chapter 78A - North Carolina Securities Act	43
Chapter 78B - Tender Offer Disclosure Act [Repealed.]	43
Chapter 78C - Investment Advisers	43
Chapter 78D - Commodities Act	43
Chapter 79 - Strays [Repealed.]	43
Chapter 80 - Trademarks, Brands, etc.	44
Chapter 81 - Weights and Measures [Recodified.]	44
Chapter 81A - Weights and Measures Act of 1975.	44
Chapter 82 - Wrecks [Repealed.]	44
Chapter 83 - Architects [Recodified.]	44

Chapter 83A - Architects	44
Chapter 84 - Attorneys-at-Law	44
Chapter 84A - Foreign Legal Consultants	44
Chapter 85 - Auctions and Auctioneers [Repealed.]	44
Chapter 85A - Bail Bondsmen and Runners [Recodified.]	44
Chapter 85B - Auctions and Auctioneers	44
Chapter 85C - Bail Bondsmen and Runners [Recodified.]	44
Chapter 86 - Barbers [Recodified.]	44
Chapter 86A - Barbers	44
Chapter 87 - Contractors	44
Chapter 88 - Cosmetic Art [Repealed.]	44
Chapter 88A - Electrolysis Practice Act	44
Chapter 88B - Cosmetic Art	45
Chapter 89 - Engineering and Land Surveying [Recodified.]	45
Chapter 89A - Landscape Architects	45
Chapter 89B - Foresters	45
Chapter 89C - Engineering and Land Surveying	45
Chapter 89D - Landscape Contractors	45
Chapter 89E - Geologists Licensing Act	45
Chapter 89F - North Carolina Soil Scientist Licensing Act	45
Chapter 89G - Irrigation Contractors	45
Chapter 90 - Medicine and Allied Occupations	45
Chapter 90 - Medicine and Allied Occupations (Continuation)	46
Chapter 90 - Medicine and Allied Occupations (Continuation)	47
Chapter 90 - Medicine and Allied Occupations (Continuation)	48
Chapter 90A - Sanitarians and Water and Wastewater Treatment Facility Operators	48
Chapter 90B - Social Worker Certification and Licensure Act	48
Chapter 90C - North Carolina Recreational Therapy Licensure Act	48
Chapter 90D - Interpreters and Transliterators	48
Chapter 91 - Pawnbrokers [Repealed.]	48
Chapter 91A - Pawnbrokers Modernization Act of 1989	48
Chapter 92 - Photographers [Deleted.]	48
Chapter 93 - Certified Public Accountants	48
Chapter 93A - Real Estate License Law	49
Chapter 93B - Occupational Licensing Boards	49
Chapter 93C - Watchmakers [Repealed.]	49
Chapter 93D - North Carolina State Hearing Aid Dealers and Fitters Board.	49
Chapter 93E - North Carolina Appraisers Act	49
Chapter 94 - Apprenticeship	49
Chapter 95 - Department of Labor and Labor Regulations	49
Chapter 95 - Department of Labor and Labor Regulations (Continuation)	50
Chapter 96 - Employment Security	50
Chapter 97 - Workers' Compensation Act	50
Chapter 97 - Workers' Compensation Act (Continuation)	51

Chapter 98 - Burnt and Lost Records	51
Chapter 99 - Libel and Slander	51
Chapter 99A - Civil Remedies for Criminal Actions	51
Chapter 99B - Products Liability	51
Chapter 99C - Actions Relating to Winter Sports Safety and Accidents	51
Chapter 99D - Civil Rights	51
Chapter 99E - Special Liability Provisions	51
Chapter 100 - Monuments, Memorials and Parks	51
Chapter 101 - Names of Persons	51
Chapter 102 - Official Survey Base	51
Chapter 103 - Sundays, Holidays and Special Days	51
Chapter 104 - United States Lands	51
Chapter 104A - Degrees of Kinship	51
Chapter 104B - Hurricanes or Other Acts of Nature	51
Chapter 104C - Atomic Energy, Radioactivity and Ionizing Radiation [Repealed and Recodified.]	51
Chapter 104D - Southern States Energy Compact	51
Chapter 104E - North Carolina Radiation Protection Act	51
Chapter 104F - Southeast Interstate Low-Level Radioactive Waste Management Compact [Repealed]	51
Chapter 104G - North Carolina Low-Level Radioactive Waste Management Authority Act of 1987 [Repealed]	51
Chapter 105 - Taxation	51
Chapter 105 - Taxation (Continuation)	52
Chapter 105 - Taxation (Continuation)	53
Chapter 105 - Taxation (Continuation)	54
Chapter 105A - Setoff Debt Collection Act	55
Chapter 105B - Defaulted Student Loan Recovery Act	55
Chapter 106 - Agriculture	55
Chapter 106 - Agriculture (Continue)	56
Chapter 106 - Agriculture (Continue)	57
Chapter 107 - Agricultural Development Districts [Repealed.]	57
Chapter 108 - Social Services [Repealed and Recodified.]	57
Chapter 108A - Social Services	57
Chapter 108B - Community Action Programs	58
Chapter 108C Medicaid and Health Choice Provider Requirements.	58
Chapter 108D Medicaid Managed Care for Behavioral Health Services.	58
Chapter 109 - Bonds [Recodified.]	58
Chapter 110 - Child Welfare	58
Chapter 111 - Aid to the Blind	58
Chapter 112 - Confederate Homes and Pensions [Repealed.]	58
Chapter 113 - Conservation and Development	58
Chapter 113 - Conservation and Development (Continuation)	59

Chapter 113A - Pollution Control and Environment	59
Chapter 113A - Pollution Control and Environment (Continuation)	60
Chapter 113B - North Carolina Energy Policy Act of 1975	60
Chapter 114 - Department of Justice	60
Chapter 115 - Elementary and Secondary Education [Repealed.]	60
Chapter 115A - Community Colleges, Technical Institutes, and Industrial Education Centers [Repealed.]	60
Chapter 115B - Tuition and Fee Waivers	60
Chapter 115C - Elementary and Secondary Education	60
Chapter 115C - Elementary and Secondary Education (Continuation)	61
Chapter 115C - Elementary and Secondary Education (Continuation)	62
Chapter 115C - Elementary and Secondary Education (Continuation)	63
Chapter 115D - Community Colleges	63
Chapter 115E - Private Educational Facilities Finance Act [Recodified]	63
Chapter 116 - Higher Education	63
Chapter 116 - Higher Education (Continuation)	63
Chapter 116A - Escheats and Abandoned Property [Repealed.]	64
Chapter 116B - Escheats and Abandoned Property	64
Chapter 116C - Continuum of Education Programs	64
Chapter 116D - Higher Education Bonds	64
Chapter 117 - Electrification	64
Chapter 118 - Firemen's and Rescue Squad Workers' Relief and Pension Funds [Recodified.]	64
Chapter 118A - Firemen's Death Benefit Act [Repealed.]	64
Chapter 118B - Members of a Rescue Squad Death Benefit Act [Repealed.]	64
Chapter 119 - Gasoline and Oil Inspection and Regulation	64
Chapter 120 - General Assembly	65
Chapter 120 - General Assembly (Continuation)	66
Chapter 120 - General Assembly (Continuation)	67
Chapter 120C - Lobbying	67
Chapter 121 - Archives and History	67
Chapter 122 - Hospitals for the Mentally Disordered [Repealed.]	67
Chapter 122A - North Carolina Housing Finance Agency	67
Chapter 122B - North Carolina Agricultural Facilities Finance Act [Repealed.]	67
Chapter 122C - Mental Health, Developmental Disabilities, and Substance Abuse Act of 1985	67
Chapter 122C - Mental Health, Developmental Disabilities, and Substance Abuse Act of 1985 (Continuation)	68
Chapter 122D - North Carolina Agricultural Finance Act	68

Chapter 122E - North Carolina Housing Trust and Oil Overcharge Act	68
Chapter 123 - Impeachment	69
Chapter 123A - Industrial Development [Repealed.]	69
Chapter 124 - Internal Improvements	69
Chapter 125 - Libraries	69
Chapter 126 - State Personnel System	69
Chapter 127 - Militia [Repealed.]	69
Chapter 127A - Militia	69
Chapter 127B - Military Affairs	69
Chapter 127C - Advisory Commission on Military Affairs	69
Chapter 128 - Offices and Public Officers	69
Chapter 128 - Offices and Public Officers (Continuation)	70
Chapter 129 - Public Buildings and Grounds	70
Chapter 130 - Public Health [Repealed.]	70
Chapter 130A - Public Health	70
Chapter 130A - Public Health (Continuation)	71
Chapter 130A - Public Health (Continuation)	72
Chapter 130B - Hazardous Waste Management Commission [Repealed.]	72
Chapter 131 - Public Hospitals [Repealed.]	72
Chapter 131A - Health Care Facilities Finance Act	72
Chapter 131B - Licensing of Ambulatory Surgical Facilities [Repealed.]	72
Chapter 131C - Charitable Solicitation Licensure Act [Repealed.]	72
Chapter 131D - Inspection and Licensing of Facilities	72
Chapter 131E - Health Care Facilities and Services	72
Chapter 131E - Health Care Facilities and Services (Continuation)	73
Chapter 131F - Solicitation of Contributions	73
Chapter 132 - Public Records	73
Chapter 133 - Public Works	74
Chapter 134 - Youth Development [Recodified.]	74
Chapter 134A - Youth Services [Repealed.]	74
Chapter 135 - Retirement System for Teachers and State Employees; Social Security; Health Insurance Program for Children	74
Chapter 135 - Retirement System for Teachers and State Employees; Social Security; Health Insurance Program for Children	75
Chapter 136 - Transportation	75
Chapter 136 - Transportation (Continuation)	76
Chapter 137 - Rural Rehabilitation [Repealed.]	76
Chapter 138 - Salaries, Fees and Allowances	76
Chapter 138A - State Government Ethics Act	76
Chapter 139 - Soil and Water Conservation Districts	76

Chapter 140 - State Art Museum; Symphony and Art Societies	76
Chapter 140A - State Awards System	76
Chapter 141 - State Boundaries	76
Chapter 142 - State Debt	76
Chapter 143 - State Departments, Institutions, and Commissions	77
Chapter 143 - State Departments, Institutions, and Commissions (Continuation)	78
Chapter 143 - State Departments, Institutions, and Commissions (Continuation)	79
Chapter 143 - State Departments, Institutions, and Commissions (Continuation)	80
Chapter 143A - State Government Reorganization	80
Chapter 143B - Executive Organization Act of 1973	80
Chapter 143B - Executive Organization Act of 1973 (Continuation)	81
Chapter 143B - Executive Organization Act of 1973 (Continuation)	82
Chapter 143C - State Budget Act	83
Chapter 143D - The State Governmental Accountability and Internal Control Act	83
Chapter 144 - State Flag, Official Governmental Flags, Motto, and Colors	83
Chapter 145 - State Symbols and Other Official Adoptions.	83
Chapter 146 - State Lands	83
Chapter 147 - State Officers	83
Chapter 148 - State Prison System	84
Chapter 149 - State Song and Toast	84
Chapter 150 - Uniform Revocation of Licenses [Repealed.]	84
Chapter 150A - Administrative Procedure Act [Recodified.]	84
Chapter 150B - Administrative Procedure Act	84
Chapter 151 - Constables [Repealed.]	84
Chapter 152 - Coroners	84
Chapter 152A - County Medical Examiner [Repealed.]	84
Chapter 152A - County Medical Examiner [Repealed.] (Continuation)	85
Chapter 153 - Counties and County Commissioners [Repealed.]	85
Chapter 153A - Counties	85
Chapter 153B - Mountain Resources Planning Act	85
Chapter 153C - Uwharrie Regional Resources Act	85
Chapter 154 - County Surveyor [Repealed.]	85
Chapter 155 - County Treasurer [Repealed.]	85
Chapter 156 - Drainage	85
Chapter 156 – Drainage (Continuation)	86

Chapter 157 - Housing Authorities and Projects	86
Chapter 157A - Historic Properties Commissions [Transferred.]	86
Chapter 158 - Local Development	86
Chapter 159 - Local Government Finance	86
Chapter 159 - Local Government Finance (Continuation)	87
Chapter 159A - Pollution Abatement and Industrial Facilities Financing Act [Unconstitutional.]	87
Chapter 159B - Joint Municipal Electric Power and Energy Act	87
Chapter 159C - Industrial and Pollution Control Facilities Financing Act	87
Chapter 159D - The North Carolina Capital Facilities Financing Act	87
Chapter 159E - Registered Public Obligations Act	87
Chapter 159F - North Carolina Energy Development Authority [Repealed.]	87
Chapter 159G - Water Infrastructure	87
Chapter 159H - [Reserved.]	87
Chapter 159I - Solid Waste Management Loan Program and Local Government Special Obligation Bonds	87
Chapter 160 - Municipal Corporations [Repealed And Transferred.]	87
Chapter 160A - Cities and Towns	88
Chapter 160A - Cities and Towns (Continuation)	89
Chapter 160B - Consolidated City-County Act	89
Chapter 160C - Baseball Park Districts [Repealed.]	90
Chapter 161 - Register of Deeds	90
Chapter 162 - Sheriff	90
Chapter 162A - Water and Sewer Systems	90
Chapter 162B Continuity of Local Government in Emergency.	90
Chapter 163 Elections and Election Laws.	90
Chapter 163 Elections and Election Laws. (Continuation)	91
Chapter 164 Concerning the General Statutes of North Carolina.	92
Chapter 165 Veterans.	92
Chapter 166 Civil Preparedness Agencies [Repealed.]	92
Chapter 166A North Carolina Emergency Management Act.	92
Chapter 167 State Civil Air Patrol [Repealed.]	92
Chapter 168 Persons with Disabilities.	92
Chapter 168A Persons With Disabilities Protection Act.	92

Chapter 80

Trademarks, Brands, etc.

Article 1.

Trademark Registration Act.

§ 80-1. Definitions.

(a) The term "applicant" as used herein means the person filing an application for registration of a trademark under this Article, the person's legal representatives, successors or assigns.

(b) The term "mark" as used herein includes any trademark or service mark entitled to registration under this Article whether registered or not.

(c) The term "person" as used herein means any individual, firm, partnership, corporation, association, union or other organization.

(d) The term "registrant" as used herein means the person to whom the registration of a trademark under this Article is issued, the person's legal representatives, successors or assigns.

(d1) The term "Secretary" as used herein means the Secretary of State or the designee of the Secretary charged with the administration of this Article.

(e) The term "service mark" as used herein means a mark used in the sale or advertising of services to identify the services of one person and distinguish them from the services of others.

(f) The term "trademark" as used herein means any word, name, symbol, or device or any combination thereof adopted and used by a person to identify goods made, sold, or distributed by him and to distinguish them from goods made, sold, or distributed by others.

(g) The term "use" means the bona fide use of a mark in the State of North Carolina in the ordinary course of trade, and not merely the reservation of a right to a mark. For the purposes of this Article, a mark shall be deemed to be "used" in this State (i) on goods when it is placed in any manner on the goods or their containers or the displays associated therewith or on the tags or labels affixed thereto, or if the nature of the goods makes placement impractical, then on documents associated with the goods, and the goods are currently sold or otherwise distributed in the State, and (ii) on services when it is used or displayed in the sale or advertising of services and the services are currently being rendered in this State, or are being offered and are available to be rendered in this State.

(h)   A mark shall be deemed to be "abandoned" when either of the following occurs:

(1)   When its use has been discontinued with intent not to resume its use. Intent not to resume may be inferred from circumstances. Nonuse for three consecutive years shall constitute prima facie evidence of abandonment.

(2)   When any course of conduct of the owner, including acts of omission as well as commission, causes the mark to lose its significance as a mark. (1903, c. 271; Rev., s. 3012; C.S., s. 3971; 1941, c. 255, s. 1; 1967, c. 1007, s. 1; 1991, c. 626, s. 1; 1997-476, s. 1.)

§ 80-1.1. Purpose.

The purpose of this Article is to provide a system of State trademark registration and protection substantially consistent with the federal system of trademark registration and protection under the Trademark Act of 1946, 15 U.S.C. § 1051, et seq., as amended. The construction given the federal act should be examined as persuasive authority for interpreting and construing this Article. (1997-476, s. 2.)

§ 80-2. Registrability.

A mark by which the goods or services of any applicant for registration may be distinguished from the goods or services of others shall not be registered if it

(1)   Consists of or comprises immoral, deceptive or scandalous matter; or

(2) Consists of or comprises matter which may disparage or falsely suggest a connection with persons, living or dead, institutions, beliefs, or national symbols, or bring them into contempt, or disrepute; or

(3) Consists of or comprises the flag or coat of arms or other insignia of the United States, or of any state or municipality, or of any foreign nation, or any simulation thereof; or

(4) Consists of or comprises the name, signature or portrait of any living individual, except with his written consent; or

(5) Consists of a mark which (i) when applied to the goods or services of the applicant, is merely descriptive of them or merely describes one or more of the characteristics, or is deceptively misdescriptive of them, or falsely describes the nature, function, capacity, or characteristics of them, or (ii) when applied to the goods or services of the applicant, is primarily geographically descriptive or deceptively misdescriptive of them, or (iii) is primarily merely a surname; provided, however, that nothing in this subdivision (5) shall prevent the registration of a mark used in this State by the applicant which has become distinctive of the applicant's goods or services. The Secretary may accept as evidence that the mark has become distinctive, as applied to the applicant's goods or services, proof of continuous use thereof as a mark by the applicant in this State for the five years preceding the date on which the claim of distinctiveness is made; or

(6) Consists of or comprises a mark which so resembles a mark registered in this State or a mark or trade name previously used in this State by another and not abandoned, as to be likely, when applied to the goods or services of the applicant, to cause confusion or mistake or to deceive. (1903, c. 271; Rev., ss. 3012, 3017; C.S., ss. 3971, 3976; 1941, c. 255, s. 1; 1967, c. 1007, s. 1; 1991, c. 626, s. 2; 1997-476, s. 3.)

§ 80-3. Application for registration.

(a) Subject to the limitations set forth in this Article, any person who uses a mark, or any person who controls the nature and quality of the goods or services in connection with which a mark is used by another, in this State may file in the office of the Secretary in a format to be prescribed by the Secretary, an application for registration of that mark setting forth, but not limited to, the following information:

(1) The name and business address of the person applying for registration; and, if a corporation, the state of incorporation. If the application for registration relates to a mark used in connection with goods, the applicant shall list either the address of the applicant's principal place of business in North Carolina or a place of distribution and usage of the goods in this State. If the application for registration relates to a mark used in connection with services, the applicant shall list a physical location at which the services are being rendered or offered in this State;

(2) The goods or services in connection with which the mark is used and the mode or manner in which the mark is used in connection with the goods or services and the class in which the goods or services fall;

(3) The date when the mark was first used anywhere and the date when it was first used in this State by the applicant, the applicant's predecessor in business or by another under the control of the applicant; and

(4) A statement that the applicant is the owner of the mark, that the mark is in use, and that to the best of the knowledge of the person verifying the application, no other person has registered in this State, or has the right to use the mark in this State either in the identical form thereof or in such near resemblance thereto as to be likely, when applied to the goods or services of the other person, to cause confusion, or to cause mistake, or to deceive.

(b) The application shall be signed and verified by the applicant, by a partner, by a member of the firm, or an officer of the corporation or association applying for registration. In states in which a notary is not required by law to obtain a notary's stamp or seal, an original certificate of authority of the notary issued by the appropriate State agency shall be submitted with the application. If the application is signed by a person acting pursuant to a power of attorney from the applicant, an original power of attorney or a certified copy of the power of attorney shall accompany the application.

The application shall be accompanied by three specimens of the mark as currently used and by a filing fee of seventy-five dollars ($75.00), payable to the Secretary.

(c) The Secretary may require a statement as to whether an application to register the mark, or portions or a component of the mark, has been filed by the applicant or a predecessor in interest in the United States Patent and Trademark Office and, if so, the applicant shall provide any relevant information required by the Secretary, including the filing date and serial number of the application and the status of the application. If any application was finally refused registration or has otherwise not resulted in a registration, the Secretary may require the applicant to provide in the statement the reason the application was not registered. The Secretary may also require that a drawing of the mark accompany the application in a form specified by the Secretary. (1903, c. 271, s. 3; Rev., s. 3014; C.S., s. 3973; 1935, c. 60; 1941, c. 255, s. 2; 1967, c. 1007, s. 1; 1983, c. 713, s. 49; 1991, c. 626, s. 3; 1997-476, s. 4; 2002-126, s. 29A.36.)

§ 80-3.1. Examination of application.

(a) Upon filing an application for registration and payment of the application fee, the Secretary may cause the application to be examined for conformity with this Article.

(b) The applicant shall provide any additional relevant information requested by the Secretary, including a description of a design mark, and may make, or authorize the Secretary to make, any amendments to the application reasonably requested by the Secretary or deemed by the applicant to be advisable to respond to a rejection or objection.

(c) The Secretary may require the applicant to disclaim an unregisterable component of a mark otherwise registrable, and an applicant may voluntarily disclaim a component of a mark requested to be registered. No disclaimer shall prejudice or affect the applicant's or registrant's rights then existing or thereafter arising in the disclaimed matter, or the applicant's or registrant's rights of registration on another application if the disclaimed matter is distinctive of the applicant's or registrant's goods or services.

(d) The Secretary may (i) amend the application submitted by the applicant, if the applicant consents, or (ii) require a new application be submitted.

(e) If the Secretary finds that the applicant is not entitled to registration, the Secretary shall advise the applicant of the reasons the applicant is not entitled to registration. The applicant shall have a reasonable period of time, specified by the Secretary, in which to reply or to amend the application. If the applicant replies and amends the application, the Secretary shall reexamine the application. This procedure may be repeated until (i) the Secretary finally refuses registration of the mark, or (ii) the applicant fails to reply or to amend the application within the specified period. If the applicant fails to reply or to amend the application, the application shall be deemed to have been abandoned.

(f) If the Secretary finally refuses registration of the mark, the applicant may seek a writ of mandamus to compel registration. The writ may be granted, without costs to the Secretary, on proof that all the statements in the application are true and that the mark is entitled to registration.

(g) When the Secretary receives more than one application seeking registration of the same or confusingly similar marks for the same or related goods or services and processes those applications concurrently, the Secretary shall grant priority to the applications in order of filing. If a previously filed application is granted a registration, any other application shall then be rejected. A rejected applicant may bring an action for cancellation of the registration on grounds of prior or superior rights to the mark, in accordance with the provisions of this Article. (1997-476, s. 5.)

§ 80-4. Certificate of registration.

Upon compliance by the applicant with the requirements of this Article, the Secretary shall cause a certificate of registration to be issued and delivered to the applicant. The certificate of registration shall be issued under the signature of the Secretary and the seal of the State, and it shall show the name and business address and, if a corporation, the state of incorporation, of the person claiming ownership of the mark, the date claimed for the first use of the mark anywhere and the date claimed for the first use of the mark in this State, the class of goods or services and a description of the goods or services on which the mark is used, a reproduction of the mark, the registration date, the registration number and the term of the registration.

Any certificate of registration issued by the Secretary under the provisions hereof or a copy thereof duly certified by the Secretary shall be admissible in evidence as competent and sufficient proof of the registration of the mark in any action or judicial proceedings in any court of this State. (1903, c. 271, s. 4; Rev., s. 3015; C.S., s. 3974; 1967, c. 1007, s. 1; 1991, c. 626, s. 4; 1997-476, s. 6).

§ 80-5. Duration and renewal.

Registration of a mark hereunder shall be effective for a term of 10 years from the date of registration and shall be renewable for successive terms of 10 years upon application filed within six months prior to the expiration of any term. A renewal fee of thirty-five dollars ($35.00), payable to the Secretary, shall accompany the application for renewal of the registration. Within six months following the expiration of a term of five years from the date of registration, or the last renewal of registration of the mark, the applicant shall submit a specimen showing evidence of current use of the mark and a signed statement verifying the use of such mark on a form to be furnished by the Secretary of State. Use of the form furnished by the Secretary of State is mandatory. Failure to submit this verification and specimen showing evidence of current use shall be grounds for cancellation of the registration of the mark by the Secretary of State.

The Secretary of State shall notify registrants of marks hereunder of the necessity of renewal within the year next preceding the expiration of the 10 years from the date of registration, by writing to the last known address of the registrants.

The Secretary of State shall notify registrants of marks hereunder of the necessity of submitting evidence of current use of the mark after five years from the date of registration or of the last renewal of registration of the mark, by writing to the last known address of the registrants within the year preceding the due date for such submission.

Registration of marks applied for under previous acts shall be continued in force for the full 10-year term without the necessity of submitting evidence of current use of the mark during the term.

All applications for renewals under this Article, whether of registrations made under this Article or of registrations effected under any prior act, shall be filed with the Secretary in a format prescribed by the Secretary specifying the information called for by G.S. 80-3 and shall include a statement that the mark is still in use in this State, setting forth those goods or services recited in the registration in connection with which the mark is still in use. The registration shall be renewed only as to the goods and services. (1967, c. 1007, s. 1; 1991, c. 626, s. 5; 1997-476, s. 7.)

§ 80-6. Assignment.

(a) Any mark and its registration hereunder shall be assignable with the goodwill of the business in which the mark is used, or with that part of the goodwill of the business connected with the use of and symbolized by the mark. Assignment shall be by instruments in writing duly executed and may be recorded with the Secretary upon the payment of a fee of twenty-five dollars ($25.00), payable to the Secretary who, upon recording of the assignment, shall issue in the name of the assignee a new certificate for the remainder of the term of the registration or of the last renewal thereof. An assignment of any registration under this Article shall be void as against any subsequent purchaser for valuable consideration without notice, unless it is recorded with the Secretary within three months after the date thereof or prior to subsequent purchase.

(b) Any registrant or applicant effecting a change of the name of the person to whom the mark was issued or for whom an application was filed may record a certificate of change of name of the registrant or applicant with the Secretary upon payment of the recording fee required under G.S. 80-7. The Secretary may issue a certificate of registration of an assigned application in the name of the assignee. The Secretary may issue in the name of the assignee a new certificate for the remainder of the term of the registration or for the last renewal of the registration.

(c) Other instruments that relate to a mark registered or application pending pursuant to this Article, including licenses, security interests, and mortgages, may be recorded in the discretion of the Secretary, upon payment of the recording fee required under G.S. 80-7. Instruments authorized under this subsection shall be in writing and duly executed.

(d) Acknowledgment shall be prima facie evidence of the execution of an assignment or other instrument and, when recorded by the Secretary, the record shall be prima facie evidence of execution.

(e) A photocopy of any instrument referenced in subsection (a), (b), or (c) of this section shall be accepted for recording if it is certified by any party to the instrument, or the party's successor, to be a true and correct copy of the original. (Rev., s. 3016; C.S., s. 3975; 1967, c. 1007, s. 1; 1991, c. 626, s. 6; 1997-476, s. 8.)

§ 80-7. Records.

The Secretary shall keep for public examination all assignments recorded under G.S. 80-6 and a record of all marks registered or renewed under this Article. The Secretary shall collect the following fees for copying, comparing, and certifying a copy of any filed document relating to a trademark or service mark:

(1) Five dollars ($5.00) for the certificate, and

(2) One dollar ($1.00) per page for copying or comparing a copy to the original.

The Secretary shall collect a recording fee of ten dollars ($10.00) for recording name changes of corporate registrants and for recording transfers of the registration of any mark by merger or consolidation if the articles of merger or consolidation are records not on file in the Corporate Division of the Department of the Secretary of State. (1967, c. 1007, s. 1; 1991, c. 626, s. 7; 1997-476, s. 9.)

§ 80-8. Cancellation.

The Secretary shall cancel from the register, in whole or in part:

(1) Repealed by Session Laws 1991, c. 626, s. 8.

(2) Any registration concerning which the Secretary shall receive a voluntary request for cancellation thereof from the registrant or the assignee of record.

(3) All registrations granted under this Article and not renewed in accordance with the provisions hereof.

(4) Any registration concerning which a court of competent jurisdiction shall find:

a. That the registered mark has been abandoned or has become incapable of serving as a mark;

b. That the registrant is not the owner of the mark;

c. That the registration was granted improperly;

d. That the registration was obtained fraudulently;

e. That the registration is for a mark that is or has become the generic name for the goods or services for which it has been registered or for a portion of the goods or services for which it has been registered;

f. That the registration was obtained by means of materially false statements in the application for registration; or

g. That the registration is so similar to another mark used in the State as to be likely to cause confusion or mistake or to deceive if (i) the other mark was registered by another person in the United States Patent and Trademark Office prior to the date of the applicant's first use of the mark that is the subject of the application for registration, and (ii) the other mark has not been abandoned. However, if the registrant proves that the registrant is the owner of a concurrent registration of a mark in the United States Patent and Trademark Office covering an area including the entire State, the registration shall not be cancelled.

(5) Any registration when a court of competent jurisdiction shall order cancellation thereof.

(6), (7) Repealed by Session Laws 1997-476, s. 10. (1967, c. 1007, s. 1; 1991, c. 626, s. 8; 1997-476, s. 10.)

§ 80-9. Classification.

The Secretary shall establish a classification of goods and services for convenience of administration of this Article, but not to limit or extend the applicant's or registrant's rights, and a single application for registration of a mark may include any or all goods upon which, or services for which, the mark is actually being used indicating the appropriate class or classes of goods or services. When a single application includes goods or services that fall within multiple classes, the Secretary may require payment of a fee for each class. The Secretary may amend the classes herein established to conform them to the classification established for the United States Patent and Trademark Office as from time to time amended. (1967, c. 1007, s. 1; 1991, c. 626, s. 9; 1997-476, s. 11.)

§ 80-10. Fraudulent registration.

Any person who shall for himself, or on behalf of any other person, procure the filing or registration of any mark in the office of the Secretary under the provisions hereof, by knowingly making any false or fraudulent representation or declaration, verbally or in writing, or by any other fraudulent means, shall be liable to pay all damages sustained in consequence of filing or registration, to be recovered by or on behalf of the party injured thereby in any court of competent jurisdiction. (1903, c. 271, s. 5; Rev., s. 3018; C.S., s. 3977; 1967, c. 1007, s. 1; 1997-476, s. 12.)

§ 80-11. Infringement.

Subject to the provisions of G.S. 80-13, any person who shall

(1)   Use in this State without the consent of the registrant, any reproduction, counterfeit, copy, or colorable imitation of a mark registered under this Article in connection with the sale, offering for sale, or advertising of any goods or services on or in connection with which such use is likely to cause confusion or mistake or to deceive as to the source of origin of such goods or services; or

(2)   Reproduce, counterfeit, copy or colorably imitate any such mark and apply such reproduction, counterfeit, copy or colorable imitation to labels, signs, prints, packages, wrappers, receptacles, or advertisements intended to be used upon or in conjunction with the sale or other distribution in this State of such goods or services;

shall be liable to a civil action by the owner of such registered mark for any or all of the remedies provided in G.S. 80-12, except that under subdivision (2) hereof the registrant shall not be entitled to recover profits or damages or any penalty unless the acts have been committed with knowledge that such mark is intended to be used to cause confusion or mistake or to deceive. (1903, c. 271, s. 6; Rev., s. 3019; C.S., s. 3978; 1967, c. 1007, s. 1.)

§ 80-11.1. Criminal use of counterfeit trademark.

(a) For purposes of this section:

(1) "Counterfeit mark" means a mark that is used in connection with the sale or offering for sale of goods or services that are identical to or substantially indistinguishable from the goods or services with which the mark is used or registered, and the use of which is likely to cause confusion, mistake, or deception, with the use occurring without authorization of the:

a. Owner of the registered mark, and is identical to or substantially indistinguishable from a mark that is registered on the principal register of the United States Patent and Trademark Office or with the Trademark Division of the Department of the Secretary of State; or

b. Owner of the unregistered mark and is identical to or substantially indistinguishable from symbols, signs, emblems, insignias, trademarks, trade names, or words protected by section 110 of the Amateur Sports Act of 1978 (Title 36, U.S.C. § 380).

(2) "Retail sales value" means the value computed by multiplying the number of items having a counterfeit mark used thereon or in connection therewith, by the retail price at which a similar item having a mark used thereon or in connection therewith, the use of which is authorized by the owner, is offered for sale to the public.

(b) Any person who knowingly and willfully (i) uses or causes to be used a counterfeit mark on or in connection with goods or services intended for sale or (ii) has possession, custody, or control of goods having a counterfeit mark used thereon or in connection therewith, that are intended for sale, shall be punished as follows:

(1) If the goods or services having a counterfeit mark used thereon or in connection therewith, or on or in connection with which the person intends to use a counterfeit mark, have a retail sales value not exceeding three thousand dollars ($3,000), the person is guilty of a Class 2 misdemeanor;

(2) If the goods or services having a counterfeit mark used thereon or in connection therewith, or on or in connection with which the person intends to use a counterfeit mark, have a retail sales value exceeding three thousand

dollars ($3,000) but not exceeding ten thousand dollars ($10,000), the person is guilty of a Class I felony; and

(3)   If the goods or services having a counterfeit mark used thereon or in connection therewith, or on or in connection with which the person intends to use a counterfeit mark, have a retail sales value exceeding ten thousand dollars ($10,000), the person is guilty of a Class H felony.

The possession, custody, or control of more than 25 items having a counterfeit mark used thereon or in connection therewith creates a presumption that the person having possession, custody, or control of the items intended to sell those items.

(c)   Any person who knowingly (i) uses any object, tool, machine, or other device to produce or reproduce a counterfeit mark or (ii) has possession, custody, or control of any object, tool, machine, or device with intent to produce or reproduce a counterfeit mark, is guilty of a Class H felony.

(d)   Any personal property, including any item, object, tool, machine, device, or vehicle of any kind, employed as an instrumentality in the commission of, or in aiding or abetting in the commission of a violation of subsection (b) or (c) of this section, is subject to seizure and forfeiture and shall be disposed of in accordance with the provisions of Article 2 of Chapter 15 of the General Statutes.

(e)   For purposes of enforcing this section, the Department of the Secretary of State's law enforcement agents have statewide jurisdiction. These law enforcement agents may assist local law enforcement agencies in their investigations and may initiate and carry out, in coordination with local law enforcement agencies, investigations of violations of this section. These law enforcement agents have all of the powers and authority of law enforcement officers when executing arrest warrants. These agents shall be authorized to have fictitious licenses, license tags, and registrations, pursuant to G.S. 20-39(h) or G.S. 14-250, for the purpose of conducting criminal investigations.

(f)   The Secretary of State may refer any available evidence concerning violations of this section to the proper district attorney, who may, with or without such a reference, institute the appropriate criminal proceedings.

The attorneys employed by the Secretary of State shall be available to prosecute or assist in the prosecution of criminal cases when requested to do so by a district attorney and the Secretary of State approves.

(g) Pursuant to an agreement between the departments, the Secretary of State may refer any available evidence concerning violations of this section to the Secretary of Revenue for purposes of determining the obligations of the violators of this section to the State under the provisions of Chapter 105 of the General Statutes. (1995, c. 436, s. 1.)

§ 80-12. Violation a deceptive or unfair trade practice.

A violation of G.S. 80-10 or G.S. 80-11 constitutes a violation of G.S. 75-1.1. (1903, c. 271, s. 8; Rev., s. 3021; C.S., s. 3980; 1941, c. 255, s. 3; 1967, c. 1007, s. 1; 1995, c. 436, s. 2.)

§ 80-13. Common-law rights.

Nothing herein shall adversely affect the rights or the enforcement of rights in marks acquired in good faith at any time at common law. (1967, c. 1007, s. 1.)

§ 80-14. Severability of Article.

If any provision hereof, or the application of such provision to any person or circumstance is held invalid, the remainder of this Article shall not be affected thereby. (1967, c. 1007, s. 1.)

Article 2.

Timber Marks.

§ 80-15. Timber dealers may adopt.

Any person dealing in timber in any form shall be known as a timber dealer and as such may adopt a trademark, in the manner and with the effect in this Article provided. (1903, c. 261, s. 1; Rev., s. 3023; C.S., s. 3985.)

§ 80-16. How adopted, registered and published.

Every such dealer desiring to adopt a trademark may do so pursuant to the provisions of Article 1 of Chapter 80 of the General Statutes. Nothing in this section invalidates or otherwise alters the legal effect of any timber mark registered according to the law in effect at the time of registration. (1889, c. 142; 1903, c. 261, s. 2; Rev., s. 3024; C.S., s. 3986; 1999, c. 456, s. 59; 2012-18, s. 1.11.)

§ 80-17. Property in and use of trademarks.

Every trademark so adopted shall, from the date thereof, be the exclusive property of the person adopting the same. The proprietor of such trademark shall, in using the same, cause it to be plainly stamped, branded or otherwise impressed upon each piece of timber upon which the same is placed. (1889, c. 142; 1903, c. 261, ss. 3, 4; Rev., s. 3025; C.S., s. 3987.)

§ 80-18. Effect of branding timber purchased.

When timber is purchased by the proprietor of any such trademark, and the said trademark is placed thereon as hereinbefore provided, such timber shall thenceforth be deemed the property of such purchaser, without any other or further delivery thereof, and such timber shall thereafter be at the risk of the purchaser, unless otherwise provided by contract in writing between the parties. (1889, c. 142; 1903, c. 261, s. 6; Rev., s. 3026; C.S., s. 3988.)

§ 80-19. Trademark on timber evidence of ownership.

In any action, suit or contest in which the title to any timber, upon which any trademark has been placed as aforesaid, shall come in question, it shall be presumed that such timber was the property of the proprietor of such trademark, in the absence of satisfactory proof to the contrary. (1903, c. 261, s. 7; Rev., s. 3027; C.S., s. 3989.)

§ 80-20. Fraudulent use of timber trademark, misdemeanor.

If any person shall use or attempt to use any timber trademark without the written consent of the proprietor thereof, or falsely and fraudulently place any trademark on timber not the property of the owner of such trademark without his written consent, or intentionally and without lawful authority remove, deface or destroy any timber trademark or the imprint thereof on any timber or intentionally put any such timber in such a position or place so remote from the stream from which it was taken or on which it was afloat as to render it inconvenient or unnecessarily expensive to replace the same in such stream, he shall be guilty of a Class 1 misdemeanor. (1903, c. 261, ss. 3-5; Rev., s. 3854; C.S., s. 3990; 1993, c. 539, s. 584; 1994, Ex. Sess., c. 24, s. 14(c).)

§ 80-21. Larceny of branded timber.

If any person shall knowingly and unlawfully buy, sell, take and carry away, secrete, destroy or convert to his own use, any timber upon which a trademark is stamped, branded or otherwise impressed, or shall knowingly and unlawfully buy, sell, take and carry away, secrete, destroy or convert to his own use, any timber upon which a trademark has been intentionally and without lawful authority removed, defaced or destroyed, he shall be deemed guilty of larceny thereof and punished as in other cases of larceny. (1903, c. 261, s. 5; Rev., s. 3853; C.S., s. 3991.)

§ 80-22. Altering timber trademark crime.

If any person shall willfully change, alter, erase or destroy any registered timber mark or brand put or cut upon any logs, timber, lumber or boards, except by the consent of the owner thereof, with intent to steal the said logs or timber, he shall be guilty of a Class 3 misdemeanor. (1889, c. 142, s. 3; 1903, c. 41; Rev., s. 3855; C.S., s. 3992; 1943, c. 543; 1993, c. 539, s. 585; 1994, Ex. Sess., c. 24, s. 14(c).)

§ 80-23. Possession of branded logs without consent, misdemeanor.

If any person shall knowingly and willfully take up or have in his possession any log, timber, lumber or board upon which a registered timber mark or brand has been put or cut, except by the consent of the owner thereof, he shall be guilty of a Class 3 misdemeanor. (1889, c. 142, s. 4; 1903, c. 42; Rev., s. 3856; C.S., s. 3993; 1993, c. 539, s. 586; 1994, Ex. Sess., c. 24, s. 14(c).)

Article 3.

Mineral Waters and Beverages.

§§ 80-24 through 80-32: Repealed by Session Laws 1987, c. 402.

Article 4.

Farm Names.

§ 80-33: Repealed by Session Laws 2012-18, s. 1.12, effective July 1, 2012.

§ 80-34: Repealed by Session Laws 2012-18, s. 1.12, effective July 1, 2012.

§ 80-35: Repealed by Session Laws 2012-18, s. 1.12, effective July 1, 2012.

§ 80-36: Repealed by Session Laws 2012-18, s. 1.12, effective July 1, 2012.

§ 80-37: Repealed by Session Laws 2012-18, s. 1.12, effective July 1, 2012.

§ 80-38. When transfer of farm carries name.

When any owner of a farm, the name of which has been recorded in the office of the register of deeds of the county in which the farm is located according to the law in effect at the time of recording, transfers by deed or otherwise the whole of such farm, such transfer may include the registered name thereof; but if the owner shall transfer only a portion of such farm, then, in the event, the registered name thereof shall not be transferred to the purchaser unless so stated in the deed or conveyance. (1915, c. 108, s. 4; C.S., s. 4009; 2012-18, s. 1.13.)

§ 80-39. Cancellation of registry; fee.

When any owner of a farm name that has been registered in the office of the register of deeds of the county in which the farm is located desires to cancel the registered name thereof, such owner may record a duly signed and acknowledged instrument to that effect in the register of deeds real estate records. (1915, c. 108, s. 5; C.S., s. 4010; 2012-18, s. 1.14.)

Article 5.

Stamping of Gold and Silver Articles.

§ 80-40. Marking gold articles regulated.

It shall be unlawful to make for sale, or sell, or offer to sell or dispose of, or have in possession with intent to sell or dispose of, any article of merchandise made in whole or in part of gold or any alloy of gold, and having stamped, branded, engraved or imprinted thereon, or upon any tag, card or label attached thereto, or upon any box, package, cover or wrapper in which the article is enclosed, any mark indicating or designed to indicate that the gold, or alloy of gold, therein is of a greater degree of fineness than its actual fineness, unless the actual fineness, in the case of flatware and watchcases, is not less by more than three one-thousandths parts, and in the case of all other articles is not less by more than one-half karat than the fineness indicated, according to the standards and subject to the qualifications hereinafter set forth.

In any test for ascertaining the fineness of gold or alloy in the articles, according to the required standards, the part of the gold or alloy taken for the test, analysis or assay shall be a part not containing or having attached thereto any solder or alloy of inferior fineness used for brazing or uniting the parts of the articles. In addition to the foregoing tests and standards, the actual fineness of the entire quantity of gold and of its alloys contained in any article mentioned in this section (except watchcases), including all solder or alloy of inferior metal used for brazing or uniting the parts (all such gold, alloys, and solder being assayed as one piece), shall not be less by more than one karat than the fineness indicated by the mark used as above indicated. Violation of this section is a Class 1 misdemeanor. (1907, c. 331, s. 1; C.S., s. 4012; 1993, c. 539, s. 587; 1994, Ex. Sess., c. 24, s. 14(c).)

§ 80-41. Marking silver articles regulated.

It shall be unlawful to make for sale or sell or offer to sell or dispose of or have in possession with intent to sell or dispose of -

(1)   Any article of merchandise made in whole or in part of silver of any alloy of silver, and having marked, stamped, branded or engraved or imprinted thereon, or upon any tag, card or label attached thereto, or upon any box, package, cover or wrapper in which the article is enclosed, the words "sterling silver" or "sterling" or any colorable imitation thereof, unless nine hundred and twenty-five one-thousandths of the component parts of the metal appearing or purporting to be silver, of which the article is manufactured, are pure silver, subject to the qualifications hereinafter set forth: Provided, that in the case of all such articles there shall be allowed a divergence in fineness of four one-thousandths parts from the foregoing standard.

(2)   Any article of merchandise made in whole or in part of silver or of any alloy of silver, and having marked, stamped, branded, engraved or imprinted

thereon, or upon any card, tag or label attached thereto, or upon any box, package, cover or wrapper in which the article is enclosed, the words "coin" or "coin silver," or any colorable imitation thereof, unless nine hundred one-thousandths of the component parts of the metal appearing or purporting to be silver, of which the article is manufactured, are pure silver, subject to the qualifications hereinafter set forth: Provided, that in the case of all such articles there shall be allowed a divergence in fineness of four one-thousandths parts from the foregoing standards.

(3)   Any article of merchandise made in whole or in part of silver or of any alloy of silver, and having stamped, branded, engraved or imprinted thereon, or upon any tag, card or label attached thereto, or upon any box, package, cover or wrapper in which the article is enclosed, any mark or word (other than the word "sterling" or the word "coin") indicating, or designed to indicate, that the silver or alloy of silver in the article is of a greater degree of fineness than its actual fineness, unless the actual fineness is not less by more than four one-thousandths parts than the actual fineness indicated by the use of such mark or word, subject to the qualifications hereinafter set forth.

In any test for ascertaining the fineness of the articles mentioned in this section, according to the foregoing standards, the part taken for test, analysis or assays shall be a part not containing or having attached thereto any solder or alloy of inferior metal used for brazing or uniting the parts of such article. In addition to the foregoing test and standards, the actual fineness of the entire quantity of metal purporting to be silver contained in any article mentioned in this section, including all solder or alloy of inferior fineness used for brazing or uniting the parts (all such silver, alloy or solder being assayed as one piece), shall not be less by more than ten one-thousandths parts than the fineness indicated according to the foregoing standards, by the mark employed as above indicated. Violation of this section is a Class 1 misdemeanor. (1907, c. 331, s. 2; C.S., s. 4013; 1993, c. 539, s. 588; 1994, Ex. Sess., c. 24, s. 14(c).)

§ 80-42. Marking articles of gold plate regulated.

It shall be unlawful to make for sale, or sell, or offer to sell or dispose of, or have in possession with intent to sell or dispose of, any article of merchandise made in whole or in part of inferior metal, having deposited or plated thereon or brazed or otherwise affixed thereto a plate, plating, covering or sheet of gold, or of any alloy of gold, which article is known in the market as "rolled gold plate," "gold plate," "gold-filled," or "gold electroplate," or by any similar designation, and having stamped, branded, engraved or imprinted thereon, or upon any tag, card or label attached thereto, or upon any box, package, cover or wrapper in which the article is enclosed, any word or mark usually employed to indicate the fineness of gold, unless such word be accompanied by other words plainly indicating that such article or some part thereof is made of rolled gold plate, or gold plate, or gold electroplate, or is gold-filled, as the case may be. Violation of this section is a Class 1 misdemeanor. (1907, c. 331, s. 3; C.S., s. 4014; 1993, c. 539, s. 589; 1994, Ex. Sess., c. 24, s. 14(c).)

§ 80-43. Marking articles of silver plate regulated.

It shall be unlawful to make for sale, or sell, or offer to sell or dispose of, or have in possession with intent to sell or dispose of, any article of merchandise made in whole or in part of inferior metal, having deposited or plated thereon or brazed or otherwise affixed thereto, a plate, plating, covering or sheet of silver or of any alloy of silver, which article is known in the market as "silver plate" or "silver electroplate," or by any similar designation, and having stamped, branded, engraved or imprinted thereon, or upon any tag, card or label attached thereto, or upon any box, package, cover or wrapper in which the article is enclosed, the word "sterling" or the word "coin," either alone or in conjunction with any other words or marks. Violation of this section is a Class 1 misdemeanor. (1907, c. 331, s. 4; C.S., s. 4015; 1993, c. 539, s. 590; 1994, Ex. Sess., c. 24, s. 14 (c)

§ 80-44. Violation of Article misdemeanor.

Every person, firm, corporation or association guilty of a violation of any one of the preceding sections of this Article, and every officer, manager, director or managing agent of any such person, firm, corporation or association directly participating in such violation or consenting thereto, shall be guilty of a Class 1 misdemeanor: Provided, that if the person charged with violation of this Article shall prove that the article concerning which the charge was made was manufactured prior to June 13, 1907, then the charge shall be dismissed. (1907, c. 331, s. 5; C.S., s. 4016; 1993, c. 539, s. 591; 1994, Ex. Sess., c. 24, s. 14(c).)

Article 6.

Cattle Brands.

§ 80-45. Owners of stock to register brand or marks.

Every person who has any horses, cattle, hogs or sheep may have an earmark or brand different from the earmark or brand of all other persons, which he shall record with the clerk of the board of commissioners of the county where his horses, cattle, hogs or sheep are; and he may brand all horses 18 months old and upwards with the said brand, and earmark all his hogs and sheep six months old and upwards with the said earmark; and earmark or brand all his cattle 12 months old and upwards; and if any dispute shall arise about any earmark or brand, the same shall be decided by the record thereof. (R.C., c. 17, s. 1; Code, s. 2317; Rev., s. 3028; C.S., s. 4017.)

Article 7.

Recording of Cattle Brands and Marks with Commissioner of Agriculture.

§§ 80-46 through 80-56: Repealed by Session Laws 1975, c. 261, s. 1.

Article 8.

Registration and Protection of Livestock Brands.

§ 80-57. Purpose.

The purpose of this Article is to discourage livestock theft by allowing for the voluntary individual registration of brand marks for certain livestock. (1975, c. 261, s. 1.)

§ 80-58. Definitions.

(a) "Board". - The term "Board" means the North Carolina Board of Agriculture.

(b) "Brand". - The term "brand" means an identification mark permanently affixed into the hide of livestock by a hot iron or an extremely cold brand known as a "freeze brand."

(c) "Commissioner". - The term "Commissioner" means the Commissioner of Agriculture of the State of North Carolina.

(d) "Livestock". - The term "livestock" means cattle, horses, ponies, mules, and asses.

(e) "Person". - The term "person" means an individual, firm, company, association, partnership or corporation. (1935, c. 232, s. 1; 1975, c. 261, s. 1.)

§ 80-59. Responsibility and authority of Commissioner of Agriculture; application for registration; transfer of ownership of brand.

The Commissioner shall record livestock brands and maintain a record of such brands pursuant to this Article. Such records shall be public and shall be prima facie evidence of ownership of livestock which is properly branded under this Article. The Commissioner shall authorize such agents within the North Carolina Department of Agriculture and Consumer Services as he deems necessary to implement this Article.

Any person desiring the exclusive use of a brand shall make application to the Commissioner on forms prescribed by the Board. The transfer of ownership of a brand registration may be done only at the written request of the brand registrant of record. The Commissioner shall receive a fee of ten dollars ($10.00) for recording such transfer. (1935, c. 232, ss. 3-5; 1975, c. 261, s. 1; 1997-261, s. 109.)

§ 80-60. No brands duplicated.

No brand shall be registered that is a reasonable facsimile of another registered brand or that will likely be confused with another brand registered under this Article. (1975, c. 261, s. 1.)

§ 80-61. Rules and regulations.

The Board shall have authority to promulgate reasonable rules and regulations for implementation of this Article which shall include, but not be limited to, the location of and the size of brand marks. (1975, c. 261, s. 1.)

§ 80-62. Fees for recording.

The Commissioner is authorized to collect a fee of twenty-five dollars ($25.00) for the recording of each new brand, or for rerecording of each brand, and shall issue one certified copy of each brand recording to the holder of said brand. Duplicate certificates of registration may be issued by the Commissioner upon payment of a fee of two dollars ($2.00). Revenues collected pursuant to this Article shall be deposited with the State Treasurer to the account of the North Carolina Department of Agriculture and Consumer Services. (1935, c. 232, ss. 5, 6; 1975, c. 261, s. 1; 1997-261, s. 109.)

§ 80-63. Records to be kept of sales and slaughter.

Persons or agents selling or bartering or exchanging branded livestock in the State of North Carolina shall provide the purchaser or new owner with a bill of sale showing a reasonable facsimile of the brand on any and all livestock having a brand as defined in this Article. Such bills of sale shall be prima facie evidence of transfer of ownership of branded livestock. Slaughter facilities in the State of North Carolina shall affix to their normal records of receipt of livestock a reasonable facsimile of the brand on any branded livestock received by them. Such records shall be maintained for at least 12 months. (1935, c. 232, ss. 8, 9; 1975, c. 261, s. 1.)

§ 80-64. Defacing of brands prohibited.

No person may change, conceal, deface, disfigure or obliterate any brand previously branded, impressed, or marked on any livestock, or put his or any other brand upon or over any part of any brand previously branded or marked upon any livestock, and no person shall make or use any counterfeit of any brand of any other person. (1935, c. 232, s. 10; 1975, c. 261, s. 1.)

§ 80-65. Rerecording.

Every brand recorded under this Article, in order to remain effective, must be rerecorded with the Commissioner during the tenth year from its next previous recordation. Each person having a brand registered in the State of North Carolina shall be notified in writing by the Commissioner that said brand must be rerecorded to prohibit its disenrollment from the record of such brand maintained by the Commissioner. (1975, c. 261, s. 1.)

§ 80-66. Violation a misdemeanor.

Any person who violates any provision of this Article or any rule or regulation of the Board promulgated hereunder shall be guilty of a Class 2 misdemeanor. (1935, c. 232, s. 11; 1975, c. 261, s. 1; 1993, c. 539, s. 592; 1994, Ex. Sess., c. 24, s. 14(c).)

Chapter 81.

Weights and Measures.

§§ 81-1 through 81-82: Recodified as §§ 81A-1 to 81A-88.

Chapter 81A.

Weights and Measures Act of 1975.

Article 1.

Administration of Chapter.

§ 81A-1. Weights and measures program provided for.

In order to protect the purchasers or sellers of any commodity, and to provide uniform standards of weight and uniform standards of measure throughout the State, which must be in conformity with the standards of weight and the standards of measure established by Congress, the Commissioner is hereby authorized to establish and maintain a weights and measures program as is hereinafter provided. (1927, c. 261, s. 1; 1945, c. 280, s. 1; 1975, c. 544.)

§ 81A-2. Administration of these Articles.

The provisions of this Chapter shall be administered by the Commissioner or his authorized agent. For the purpose of administering and giving effect to the provisions of this Chapter, the provisions of Handbook 44 as adopted by the National Conference on Weights and Measures, are hereby adopted except insofar as modified or rejected by the North Carolina Board of Agriculture. The North Carolina Board of Agriculture is empowered to make such further rules and regulations as may be necessary to make effective the purposes and provisions of this Chapter. Except as otherwise provided in G.S. 81A-30.1, all fees or moneys received by the Commissioner pursuant to this Chapter shall be placed in the Department of Agriculture and Consumer Services fund for the purpose of enforcing this Chapter. (1927, c. 261, s. 2; 1931, c. 150; 1943, c. 762, s. 1; 1949, c. 984; 1975, c. 544; 1997-261, s. 109; 1998-215, s. 4(b).)

§ 81A-3. Systems of weights and measures.

The system of weights and measures in customary use in the United States and the metric system of weights and measures are jointly recognized, and either one or both of these systems shall be used for all commercial purposes in the State. The definitions of basic units of weight and measure, the tables of weight and measure, and weights and measures equivalents as published by the National Bureau of Standards are recognized and shall govern weighing and measuring equipment and transactions in the State. (1975, c. 544.)

§ 81A-4. Board of Agriculture authorized to establish standards of weights and measures for commodities having none.

The Board of Agriculture is authorized and directed and empowered to establish standards of weights and measures for any commodity if no standard has been established by Congress or by the laws of the State of North Carolina; provided, however, that when a standard is established by Congress, or by the laws of the State of North Carolina, such standard shall supersede the standard or standards established by the Board of Agriculture. (1945, c. 280, s. 1; 1949, c. 984; 1975, c. 544.)

§ 81A-5. Employment of Director of Weights and Measures and authorized agents.

The Commissioner may employ a Director of Weights and Measures and such other employees as may be necessary in carrying out the provisions of this Chapter and he may fix and regulate their duties. All authority vested in the Commissioner by virtue of the provisions of this Chapter may with like force and effect, be executed by such authorized agents of the Commissioner as defined in this Chapter. (1927, c. 261, ss. 3, 4; 1949, c. 984; 1975, c. 544.)

§ 81A-6. Salaries and expenses.

The Commissioner shall request sufficient funds for the proper administration of the duties prescribed in this Chapter. (1927, c. 261, s. 5; 1931, c. 150; 1949, c. 984; 1975, c. 544.)

§ 81A-7. Local inspection of weights and measures.

When any city or county appoints a local inspector of weights and measures, the appointment and regulation of his work must be pursuant to the rules and regulations of the Department of Agriculture and Consumer Services and his work shall be subject to the supervision of the Commissioner or his authorized agent. (1927, c. 261, s. 6; 1949, c. 984; 1975, c. 544; 1997-261, s. 109.)

§ 81A-8. Standards of weights and measures.

Weights and measures that are traceable to the U.S. Prototype Standards supplied by the United States, or approved as being satisfactory by the National Institute of Standards and Technology, shall be the State primary standards of weights and measures, and shall be maintained in such calibration as prescribed by the National Institute of Standards and Technology. All secondary standards may be prescribed by the Commissioner and shall be verified upon their initial receipt and as often thereafter as deemed necessary by the Commissioner or his authorized agent. Complete record of the standards belonging to the State shall be maintained by the Commissioner. (1927, c. 261, s. 9; 1943, c. 543; 1949, c. 984; 1975, c. 544; 1991, c. 636, s. 22.)

§ 81A-9. Definitions.

The following words and phrases as used in this Chapter, unless a different meaning is plainly required by the context, shall have the following meanings:

(1) Adjustment. - "Adjustment" is an act involving the tightening or loosening, or lengthening or shortening, or movement, of any part of a weighing or measuring device, or the coordination of mechanical action of parts or electronic components with or upon each other, so as to make the weighing or measuring device give correct indications of applied weight or measure values within legal tolerance, and the correctness of indications shall be determined by test provided for under definition of the term "service" as defined in this Chapter.

(2) Authorized Agent. - An "authorized agent" is any employee of the North Carolina Department of Agriculture and Consumer Services designated by the Commissioner to enforce any provisions of this Chapter and who is designated by an official identification card issued by the Commissioner.

(3) Barrel. - The term "barrel," when used in connection with beer, ale, porter, and other similar fermented liquor is a unit of 31 liquid gallons; fractional parts of a barrel shall be understood to mean like fractional parts of 31 gallons.

(4) Bulk Sale. - The term "bulk sale" is the sale of commodities when the quantity is determined at the time of sale.

(5) Bushel. - The term "bushel" when used in connection with dry measure and standard containers is a unit of 2150.42 cubic inches, of which the dry quart and dry pint, respectively, are the one-thirty-second and one-sixty-fourth parts.

(6) Commissioner of Agriculture. - "Commissioner" is the Commissioner of Agriculture of the State of North Carolina.

(7) Condemned Equipment. - "Condemned equipment" is equipment that is permanently out of service.

(8) Cord. - "Cord" when used in connection with purchases of wood is a quantity of wood consisting of any number of sticks, bolts or pieces laid parallel and together so as to form a rick or stack occupying a space four feet wide, four feet high and eight feet long, or such other dimensions that will when multiplied together equal 128 cubic feet by volume, construed as being seventy percent (70%) solid and thirty percent (30%) air space or 90 solid cubic feet.

(9) Correct. - "Correct" is conformance to all applicable requirements of this Chapter.

(10) Flour. - "Flour" is any finely ground product of wheat, or other grain, corn, peas, beans, seed or other substance, with or without added ingredients, intended for use as food for man.

(11) Gallon. - "Gallon" when used in connection with liquid measure is a unit of 231 cubic inches, of which the liquid quart, liquid pint and gill are, respectively, the quarter, the one-eighth and the one-thirty-second parts.

(12) Installation. - "Installation" is an act involving the erection, or building, or assembling of parts, or the placing or setting up of a weighing or measuring device so as to give correct indications of applied weight or measure values within legal tolerance when used for the purpose intended, and the correctness of indications shall be determined by test provided for under definition of the term "service" as defined in this Chapter.

(13) Maintenance. - "Maintenance" is an act pursuant to the retention of a weighing or measuring device in such working condition as to give correct applied weight or measure value indications within legal tolerance when used as intended, which may involve either or both adjustment or repair before or after inaccuracy develops in fact, and the correctness of indications shall be

determined by test provided for under the term "service" as defined in this Chapter.

(14) Meal. - "Meal" is any product of grain, corn, peas, beans, seed or other substance coarsely ground, with or without added ingredients, either bolted, or unbolted, including grits and hominy, intended for use as food for man.

(15) Package. - "Package" is any commodity put up or packaged in any manner in advance of sale in units suitable for either wholesale or retail sale.

(16) Person. - "Person" is both plural and singular, as the case demands, and includes individuals, partnerships, corporations, companies, firms, societies, and associations.

(17) Pound. - "Pound," used in connection with weight is the avoirdupois pound as declared by act of the United States Congress, except in those cases where it is common practice to use the "troy" pound or "apothecaries" pound, and the "ounce" is one-sixteenth part of an avoirdupois pound.

(18) Primary Standards. - "Primary standards" are the physical standards of the State which serve as the legal reference from which all other standards, weights and measures are derived.

(19) Rejected Equipment. - "Rejected equipment" is equipment that is incorrect, which is considered susceptible of proper repair.

(20) Repair. - "Repair" is an act involving the replacement or mending of a broken or nonadjustable part or parts and the restoration of a weighing or measuring device to such working condition as to give correct indications of applied weight or measure values within legal tolerance when used for the purpose intended, and the correctness of indications shall be determined by test provided for under the term "service" as defined in this Chapter.

(21) Sale or Sell. - "Sale" or "sell" is the ordinary meaning of said words and includes barter and exchange.

(22) Scale Technician. - A "scale technician" is any person who, for hire or award, renders service involving adjustment, installation, repair, or maintenance of a scale or weighing device, either used or intended to be used in determining weight value, or values, by either physical act, instruction, or supervision.

(23) Secondary Standards. - "Secondary standards" are the physical standards which are traceable to the primary standards through comparisons, using acceptable laboratory procedures, and used in the enforcement of weights and measures laws and regulations.

(24) Service. - "Service" is activity involving adjustment, installation, repair, or maintenance or a combination of two or more of these activities with respect to a weighing or measuring device.

(25) Ton. - "Ton" is a unit of 2,000 pounds, avoirdupois weight.

(26) Weight. - "Weight" when used in connection with any commodity is net weight; provided, however, where the label declares that the product is sold by drained weight, weight means net drained weight.

(27) Weight(s) and (or) Measure(s). - "Weight(s) and (or) measure(s)" are all weights and measures of every kind, instruments, and devices for weighing and measuring, and any appliance and accessories associated with any or all such instruments and devices. (1927, c. 261, ss. 20, 21; 1941, c. 237, s. 2; 1945, c. 280, s. 1; 1947, c. 380; 1975, c. 544; 1991, c. 636, s. 23; 1997-261, s. 7.)

§ 81A-10. Reimbursement of expenses.

When any manufacturer requests prototype approval of any commercial weighing or measuring device, said manufacturer shall reimburse the Department of Agriculture and Consumer Services for expenses incurred in the prototype examination of the device before final prototype approval is granted. Travel expenses shall be at the rates established by G.S. 138-6 or any law enacted in substitution therefor. (1981, c. 495, s. 1; 1997-261, s. 109.)

§ 81A-11: Repealed by Session Laws 2005-276, s. 42.1(h), effective September 1, 2005.

§ 81A-12. Fee schedule.

The following fees apply to all weights that are tested and certified to meet tolerances less stringent than the American Society for Testing and Materials (ASTM) Standard E617 Class 4. This includes the National Institutes of Standards and Technology (NIST) Class F tolerance. If the weight error exceeds three-fourths of the applicable tolerance, adjustment may be required at an additional fee equal to the normal fee. No extra fee shall be charged for the normal adjustment of a weight cart. Even if weights are rejected or condemned, fees shall be assessed for the test performed.

Even if weights are rejected or condemned, fees shall be assessed for the test performed.

Customary	Fee/Unit	Metric	Fee/Unit
0-10 lb	$ 5.00	0-5 kg	$ 5.00
11-100 lb	$ 10.00	6-50 kg	$ 10.00
101-1000 lb	$ 20.00	51-500 kg	$ 20.00
1001-2500 lb	$ 30.00	501-1000 kg	$ 30.00
2501-6000 lb	$ 50.00	1001-2500 kg	$ 50.00
Weight Carts up to 6000 lb	$ 125.00 (includes adjustment)		

(b) The following fees apply to all weights that are tested and certified to meet ASTM Standard E617 Class 4 or the International Organization of Legal Metrology (IOLM) R111 Class F2 tolerances. If the weight error exceeds three-fourths of the applicable tolerance, adjustment may be required at an additional fee equal to the normal fee. Even if weights are rejected or condemned, fees shall be assessed for the test performed.

Customary	Fee/Unit	Metric	Fee/Unit
0-10 lb	$ 10.00	0-5 kg	$ 10.00
11-100 lb	$ 20.00	6-50 kg	$ 20.00
101-1000 lb	$ 40.00	51-500 kg	$ 40.00
1001-2500 lb	$ 60.00	501-1000 kg	$ 60.00
2501-6000 lb	$ 100.00	1001-2500 kg	$ 100.00

(c) The following fees apply to all weights that are calibrated. Calibration means determining actual mass and conventional mass values with an assigned uncertainty specific to the test. If necessary and considered feasible by the metrologist, adjustments to ASTM Class 1, 2, or 3 tolerances or IOLM Class E2, F1, or F2 tolerances may be made for an additional fee of two times the normal fee. Adjustments to weights of this group shall require a minimum of 10 days for weights to return to environmental equilibrium before a final calibration value can be assigned. Even if weights are rejected or condemned, fees shall be assessed for the test performed.

Customary	Fee/Unit	Metric	Fee/Unit
0-20 lb	$ 20.00	0-10 kg	$ 20.00
21-50 lb	$ 40.00	11-30 kg	$ 40.00
51-1000 lb	$ 70.00	31-500 kg	$ 70.00

1001-2500 lb	$ 130.00	501-1000 kg	$ 130.00
2501-6000 lb	$ 200.00	1001-2500 kg	$ 200.00

(d)   The following fees apply to all weights that are calibrated using NIST weighing designs. These weights are tested in groups (typically either a 1, 2, 3, 5 series or a 1, 2, 2, 5 series) and are subject to the minimum per series fee shown. The best uncertainty possible from the North Carolina Standards Laboratory shall be assigned to the mass values of the weights. If necessary and considered feasible by the metrologist, adjustments to ASTM Class 0, 1, 2, or 3 tolerances or IOLM Class E1, E2, F1, or F2 tolerances may be made for an additional fee of two times the normal fee. Adjustments to weights of this group shall require a minimum of 10 days for weights to return to environmental equilibrium before a final calibration value can be assigned.

Weight Range	Fee/Unit or Series
0-1 kg per series	$30.00 each, with a minimum charge of $90.00 (3 weights)
2-30 kg per series	$50.00 each, with a minimum charge of $150.00 (3 weights)
0-2 lb per series	$30.00 each, with a minimum charge of $90.00 (3 weights)
3-50 lb per series	$50.00 each, with a minimum charge of $150.00 (3 weights)

(e)   The following fees apply to volumetric standard calibration.

Provers or Test Measures Tested By the Volume Transfer Method

Customary	Fee/Test Point	Metric	Fee/Test Point
0-5 gal	$30.00	0-20 liters	$30.00

| Over 5 gal | Add $0.40 per each | Over 20 liters | Add $0.10 per each |
| | additional gallon | | additional liter |

Volumetric Flasks, Graduates, Provers, Slicker Plate Standards, or Test Measures Tested By the Gravimetric Calibration Method

Customary Fee/Test Point	Fee/Test Point	Metric	Fee/Test Point
0-100 gal set-up fee	$50.00	0-500 liters set-up fee	$50.00
Calibration Fee	Add $2.00 per gallon	Calibration Fee	Add $0.50 per liter

Small Volume Provers (SVPs) Tested By the Gravimetric Calibration Method

Customary Fee/Test Point	Fee/Test Point	Metric	Fee/Test Point
0-100 gal set-up fee	$100.00	0-500 liters set-up fee	$100.00
Calibration Fee	Add $2.00 per gallon	Calibration Fee	Add $0.50 per liter

(f) The following fees apply to tape measures and rigid rules.

Set-Up Fee	$40.00 per instrument
Calibration Fee interval	$10.00 per calibration

(g) The following fees apply to liquid-in-glass and electronic thermometers.

Set-Up Fee	$40.00 per instrument
Calibration Fee point	$20.00 per calibration
Resistance Thermometry Coefficient	
Calculation and Report	$100.00 per instrument

(h) Any special tests or weight cleaning shall be billed at the rate of seventy dollars ($70.00) per hour prorated to the nearest tenth of an hour, with a minimum charge of thirty-five dollars ($35.00).

(i) A minimum charge of twenty-five dollars ($25.00) per invoice shall apply.

(j) If travel is required in connection with the performance of any of these services, the Department shall be reimbursed at the rates provided in G.S. 138-6.

(k) The Department may refuse to accept for testing any weight or measure the Department deems unsuited for its intended use.

(l) The fee for tests performed on weights or measures that will be used primarily outside of the State of North Carolina shall be twice the amounts set forth in this section. (2005-276, s. 42.1(i).)

§ 81A-13. Reserved for future codification purposes.

§ 81A-14. Reserved for future codification purposes.

Article 2.

Powers and Duties of Commissioner.

§ 81A-15. General duties.

The Commissioner shall:

(1) Have and keep general supervision of commercial weighing and measuring devices offered for sale, sold or used in the State.

(2) Upon written request from any person or educational institution in the State test or cause to be tested, or calibrate, weights, measures and weighing and measuring devices used as standards in the State.

(3) Enforce all the provisions of this Chapter.

(4) Conduct investigations to insure compliance with this Chapter.

(5) Inspect and test weights and measures kept, offered, or exposed for sale.

(6) Inspect, and test to ascertain if they are correct, weights and measures commercially used (i) in determining the weight, measure, or count of commodities or things sold, or offered or exposed for sale, on the basis of weight, measure or count or (ii) in computing the basic charge or payment for services rendered on the basis of weight, measure or count.

(7) Approve for use, and may mark, such weights and measures and weighing and measuring devices as he finds to be correct, and shall reject and mark as rejected such weights and measures as he finds incorrect. Weights and measures and weighing and measuring devices that have been rejected may be seized if not corrected within 10 days, or if used or disposed of in a manner not specifically authorized. Weights and measures found to be incorrect that are not capable of being made correct shall be condemned and may be seized by the Commissioner without any court order or other legal process.

(8) Weigh, measure, or inspect packaged commodities kept, offered, or exposed for sale, sold or in the process of delivery, to determine whether they contain the amounts represented and whether they are kept, offered, or exposed for sale in accordance with this Chapter or regulations promulgated

pursuant thereto. In carrying out the provisions of this section, recognized sampling procedures shall be used.

(9)   Allow reasonable variations from the stated quantity of contents, which shall include those caused by loss or gain of moisture during the course of good distribution practice or by unavoidable deviations in good manufacturing practice only after the commodity has entered intrastate commerce.

(10)   Delegate to authorized agents any of these responsibilities for the proper administration of this Chapter. (1927, c. 261, s. 10; 1949, c. 984; 1975, c. 544; 1991, c. 636, s. 24.)

§ 81A-16. Police powers.

When necessary for the enforcement of this Chapter or regulations promulgated pursuant thereto the Commissioner or his authorized agent is:

(1)   Authorized to enter any commercial premises during normal business hours, except that in the event such premises are not open to the public, he shall first present his credentials and obtain consent before making entry thereto, unless a search warrant has previously been obtained.

(2)   Empowered to issue stop-use, hold, and removal orders with respect to any weights and measures commercially used, and stop-sale, hold, and removal orders with respect to any packaged commodities or bulk commodities kept, offered, or exposed for sale.

(3)   Empowered to seize, for use as evidence, without warrant or other legal writ, any incorrect or unapproved weight, measure, package, or commodity found to be used, retained, offered, or exposed for sale or sold in violation of the provisions of this Chapter or regulations promulgated pursuant thereto.

(4)   Empowered to stop any commercial vehicle wherever found in the State and, after presentment of his credentials, inspect the contents, require that the person in charge of that vehicle produce any documents in his possession concerning the contents, and require him to proceed with the vehicle to some specified place for inspection.

(5)   Authorized to arrest, without warrant, any violator of this Chapter. Such authorized agent shall proceed forthwith with such person before a magistrate or other person authorized to issue arrest warrants. (1927, c. 261, ss. 11-13; 1975, c. 544.)

§§ 81A-17 through 81A-21. Reserved for future codification purposes.

Article 3.

Violations.

§ 81A-22. Misrepresentation of quantity.

No person shall sell, offer or expose for sale less than the quantity he represents. No buyer shall take more than the quantity he represents when he furnishes the weight or measure by means of which the quantity of any commodity, thing or service is determined. (1927, c. 261, s. 19; 1945, c. 280, s. 1; 1949, c. 984; 1975, c. 544.)

§ 81A-23. Misrepresentation of pricing.

No person shall misrepresent the price of any commodity or service sold, offered, exposed, or advertised for sale by weight, measure, or count, nor represent the price in any manner calculated or tending to mislead or in any way deceive a person. (1975, c. 544.)

§ 81A-24. Commodities to be sold by weight, measure or numerical count.

It shall be unlawful to sell, except for immediate consumption by the purchaser, on the premises of the seller, liquid commodities in any other manner than by weight or liquid measure, or commodities not liquid in any other manner than by measure of time, by length, by volume, by weight or by numerical count. When a commodity is sold by numerical count in excess of one unit, the units which constitute said numerical count shall be uniform in size and/or weight, and be so exposed as to be readily observed by the purchaser. (1945, c. 280, s. 1; 1949, c. 973; 1975, c. 544.)

§ 81A-25. Unlawful for package to mislead purchaser.

It shall be unlawful to keep for the purpose of sale, offer or expose for sale, or sell, any commodity in package form when said package is so made, or formed, or filled, or wrapped, or exposed, or marked, or labeled as to mislead or deceive the purchaser as to the quantity of its contents. (1945, c. 280, s. 1; 1975, c. 544.)

§ 81A-26. Sale from bulk.

(a) Whenever the quantity is determined by the seller, bulk sales in excess of twenty dollars ($20.00) and all bulk deliveries of heating fuel shall be accompanied by a delivery ticket containing the following information:

(1) The name and address of the vendor and the name of the purchaser,

(2) The date delivered,

(3) The quantity delivered and the quantity upon which the price is based, if this differs from the delivered quantity,

(4) The identity of the commodity in the most descriptive terms commercially practicable, including any quality representation made in connection with the sale,

(5) The count of individually wrapped packages, if more than one, and

(6) For heating fuels which are liquids and gases, the price per gallon and any other charges associated with the delivery. This subdivision applies only to residential, retail deliveries.

(b) Any invoice corresponding to the delivery ticket required under the preceding subsection (a) shall contain the information set forth in the preceding subdivisions (a)(1) through (6), and shall also state the amount of sales tax, if any, and the grand total. This subsection does not apply to any subsequent billing when the seller has previously complied with the requirements of subsections (a) and (b) of this section.

(c) Whenever a seller quotes a price or other terms and conditions to a potential purchaser under this section, if those terms and conditions include a low, introductory price, other reduced charges, or other special conditions not representative of the prices or terms and conditions that apply to existing customers of the same type or class, the seller shall clearly and conspicuously disclose: (i) those facts, (ii) the price and terms and conditions that would on that date apply to existing customers of the same type or class as the potential purchaser, and (iii) the amount of time that the introductory or unrepresentative price or terms and conditions will remain in effect. (1975, c. 544; 1991, c. 642, s. 1; 1997-456, s. 11.)

§ 81A-27. Information required on packages.

Except as otherwise provided in this Chapter or by regulations promulgated pursuant thereto, any package kept for the purpose of sale or offered or exposed for sale shall bear on the outside of the package a definite, plain, and conspicuous declaration of:

(1) The identity of the commodity in the package, unless the same can easily be identified through the wrapper or container,

(2) The quantity of contents in terms of weight, measure, or count, and

(3) The name and place of business of the manufacturer, packer, or distributor, in the case of any package kept, offered, or exposed for sale, or sold in any place other than on the premises where packed. (1927, c. 261, s. 16; 1945, c. 280, s. 1; 1975, c. 544.)

§ 81A-28. Declarations of unit price on random packages.

In addition to the declarations required by G.S. 81A-27, any package being one of a lot containing random weights of the same commodity and bearing the total selling price of the package shall bear on the outside of the package a plain and conspicuous declaration of the price per single unit of weight at the time it is offered for retail sale. (1975, c. 544.)

§ 81A-29. Offenses and penalties.

Any person who violates any provision of this section or any provision of this Chapter or regulations promulgated pursuant thereto for which a specific penalty has not been prescribed shall be guilty of a Class 2 misdemeanor upon a first conviction. Upon a subsequent conviction thereof, said person shall be guilty of a Class 1 misdemeanor. No person shall:

(1)   Use or have in possession for use in commerce any incorrect weight or measure.

(2)   Remove any tag, seal, or mark from any weight or measure without specific written authorization from the Commissioner or his authorized agent.

(3)   Hinder or obstruct any weights-and-measures official in the performance of his duties.

(4)   Impersonate in any way any employee of the North Carolina Department of Agriculture and Consumer Services designated by the Commissioner to enforce any part of this Chapter.

(5)   Use in retail trade, except in the preparation of packages put up in advance of sale, a weighing or measuring device which is not so positioned so that its indications may be accurately read and the weighing or measuring operation observed from some position which may be reasonably assumed by a customer.

(6)   Manufacture, use or possess a counterfeit seal, tag, mark, certificate, label or decal representing, imitating or copying the same issued by the Commissioner under this Chapter. (1927, c. 261, ss. 14, 15, 19; 1945, c. 280, s. 1; 1949, c. 984; 1975, c. 544; 1981, c. 607, s. 1; 1993, c. 539, s. 593; 1994, Ex. Sess., c. 24, s. 14(c); 1997-261, s. 8.)

§ 81A-30. Injunction.

The Commissioner or his authorized agent is authorized to apply to any court of competent jurisdiction for a temporary restraining order or a preliminary or permanent injunction restraining any person from violating any provision of this Chapter. (1975, c. 544.)

§ 81A-30.1. Civil penalties.

A civil penalty of not more than five thousand dollars ($5,000) for each violation may be assessed by the Commissioner against any person who willfully violates this Chapter. In determining the amount of the penalty, the Commissioner shall consider the degree and extent of harm caused by the violation. No civil penalty shall be assessed under this section unless the person has been given an opportunity for a hearing pursuant to the Administrative Procedure Act. If not paid within 30 days after the effective date of a final decision by the Commissioner, the penalty may be collected by any lawful manner for the collection of a debt.

The clear proceeds of civil penalties assessed pursuant to this section shall be remitted to the Civil Penalty and Forfeiture Fund in accordance with G.S. 115C-457.2. (1991, c. 642, s. 2; 1998-215, s. 4(a).)

§ 81A-31. Presumptive evidence.

Whenever there shall exist a weight or measure or weighing or measuring device in or about any place in which or from which buying or selling is commonly carried on, there shall be a rebuttable presumption that such weight or measure or weighing or measuring device is regularly used for the business purposes of that place. (1975, c. 544.)

§§ 81A-32 through 81A-36. Reserved for future codification purposes.

Article 4.

Uniform Weights and Measures.

§§ 81A-37 through 81A-40. Repealed by Session Laws 1981, c. 607, s. 2.

§ 81A-41. Repealed by Session Laws 1999-44, s. 1.

§ 81A-42. Standard weights and measures.

Whenever any commodity named in this section shall be quoted or sold by the bushel, the bushel shall be the number of pounds stated in this section and whenever quoted or sold in subdivisions of the bushel, the number of pounds shall be the fractional part of the number of pounds as set forth herein for the bushel, and when sold by the barrel shall consist of the number of pounds constituting 3.281 bushels.

Commodity	Lbs. per bu.	Commodity	Lbs. per bu.
Alfalfa seed...............	60 44	Hemp	
Apples, dried............ Hominy.....................	24 62		
Apple seed............... Horseradish..............	40 50		
Barley....................... plaster......................	48 100	Land	
Beans, castor........... unslaked...................	46 80	Lime,	

58

Beans, dry lima............	60	Lime, slaked............	40
Beans, green in-pod lima............	30	Meal, corn, whether bolted or unbolted............	48
Beans, soy............	60		
Beef, net (per bbl.)............	200	Melon, canteloupe............	50
Beets............	50	Millet............	50
Blackberries............	48	Mustard............	58
Blackberries, dried............	28	Nuts, chestnuts............	50
Bran............	20	Nuts, hickory, without hulls............	50
Broomcorn............	44		
Buckwheat............	50	Nuts, walnut, without hulls............	50
Cabbage............	50		
Canary seed............	60	Oats, seed............	32
Carrots............	50	Onions, button sets............	32
Cement............	80	Onions, top buttons............	28

Charcoal.. 22
matured.. 57

Cherries, with stems................................ 56
seed.. 33

Cherries, without stems........................... 64
Parsnips... 50

Clover seed, red and white..................... 60
matured.. 50

Clover, Burr... 8
dried.. 25

Clover, German...................................... 60
seed.. 50

Clover, Japan, Lespedeza....................... 25
Spanish.. 30

Coal, stone... 80
Peanuts... 22

Coke... 40
matured.. 56

Corn, shelled... 56
dried.. 26

Corn, Kaffir.. 50
field.. 60

Corn, pop... 70
field.. 30

Cotton seed.. 30
Pieplant.. 50

Cotton seed, Sea Island......................... 44
Plums... 64

Onions,

Osage orange

Peaches,

Peaches,

Peach

Peanuts,

Pears,

Pears,

Peas, dried

Peas, green in hull

Cucumbers.. 48	Pork net (per bbl.)................................... 200
Fish.. 100	Potatoes, Irish... 56
Flax seed.. 56	Potatoes, sweet green.............................. 56
Grapes, with stems................................. 48	Potatoes, sweet, dry weight..................... 47
Grapes, without stems............................ 60	Quinces, matured.................................... 48
Gooseberries.. 48	Raspberries.. 48
Grass seed, Bermuda.............................. 14	Rice, rough... 44
Grass seed, blue..................................... 14	Rye seed.. 56
Grass seed, Hungarian............................ 48	Sage.. 4
Grass seed, Johnson............................... 25	Salads, mustard, spinach, turnips, and
Grass seed, Italian rye............................ 20	kale.. 10
Grass seed, orchard................................ 14	Salt... 50
Grass seed, tall meadow and fescue........ 24	Sorghum molasses (per gal.)................... 12

Grass seed, all meadow...............................	Sorghum
seed... 50	
and fescue except tall............................... 14	
Strawberries.. 48	
Grass seed, perennial rye......................... 14	Sunflower
seed... 24	
Grass seed, timothy................................... 45	
Teosinte.. 59	
Grass [seed], redtop.................................. 14	
Tomatoes... 56	
Grass seed, velvet....................................... 7	
Turnips.. 50	
Hair, plaster... 8	
Wheat.. 60	

It shall be unlawful to purchase or sell, or barter or exchange, any article named in this section on any other basis than as stated herein; provided, however, that any such articles may be sold by weight. (Code, ss. 3849, 3850; 1885, c. 26; 1905, c. 126; Rev., s. 3066; 1909, c. 555, s. 1; c. 835; 1915, c. 230, s. 1; 1917, c. 34; Ex. Sess. 1921, c. 87; 1931, c. 76; 1933, c. 523, s. 3; 1937, c. 354; 1949, c. 984; 1975, c. 544.)

§ 81A-43. Repealed by Session Laws 1981, c. 607, s. 2.

§ 81A-44: Repealed by Session Laws 1999-44, s. 2.

§§ 81A-45 through 81A-49. Reserved for future codification purposes.

Article 5.

Public Weighmasters.

§ 81A-50. Repealed by Session Laws 1981, c. 607, s. 2.

§ 81A-50.1. Purpose.

This Article licenses and regulates public weighmasters in order to ensure accurate quantities of products upon sale to purchasers. (1981, c. 607, s. 3.)

§ 81A-51. Definitions.

For purposes of this Article, the following words, terms and phrases are defined as follows:

(1) "Board" means North Carolina Board of Agriculture.

(2) "Commissioner" means the North Carolina Commissioner of Agriculture or his designated agent.

(3) "Department" means the North Carolina Department of Agriculture and Consumer Services.

(4) "Product" means any product, commodity or article.

(5) "Public weighmaster" means any person who shall weigh, measure or count, or who shall ascertain from a weighing, measuring or recording device for any other person and declare the weight to be the accurate weight of the product upon which the purchase, sale or exchange is based, and receive compensation for the act.

(6) "Weigh" means weigh, measure, count, read or record.

(7) "Weight" means weight, measure, count, reading or recording. (1939, c. 285, s. 1; 1945, c. 1067; 1971, c. 1085, s. 1; 1975, c. 544; 1981, c. 607, s. 4; 1997-261, s. 9.)

§ 81A-52. License.

All public weighmasters shall be licensed. Any person not less than 18 years of age who wishes to be a public weighmaster shall apply to the Department on a form provided by the Department. A person operating as a public weighmaster outside of this State shall include with the person's application for licensure in this State a copy of the most recent weighing device inspection report performed by the person's local or state weights and measures officials within the 12-month period immediately preceding the date of application. The Board may adopt rules for determining the qualifications of the applicant for a license. Public weighmasters shall be licensed for a period of one year beginning the first day of July and ending on the thirtieth day of June, and a fee of nineteen dollars ($19.00) shall be paid for each person licensed at the time of the filing of the application. (1939, c. 285, s. 2; 1949, c. 983, s. 1; 1975, c. 544; 1981, c. 607, s. 4; 1989, c. 544, s. 20; 2005-276, s. 42.1(f); 2009-87, s. 1.)

§ 81A-53. Certificates of weight.

All public weighmasters shall issue certificates of weight, measure, count, reading or recording on forms approved by the Commissioner and shall enforce the provisions of this Chapter and all rules and regulations promulgated thereunder without compensation from the State. Each certificate issued shall indicate the date on which a product is weighed, counted, read or recorded. A certificate issued by a public weighmaster shall be considered the accurate weight of a product at the time the product is put into the natural channels of trade, with the qualification that reasonable variations or tolerances shall be permitted as established by rules and regulations enacted pursuant to this Chapter. If any person questions the accuracy of the weight of any product for which a certificate has been issued, a complaint shall be made to the public weighmaster who issued the certificate or to the Commissioner before the product is moved from the city, town or community where the certificate was issued. The product shall be reweighed by the public weighmaster issuing the certificate or by the Commissioner, if the product is kept in accordance with G.S. 81A-58. If, upon reweighing, a difference in excess of the tolerance allowed by the Chapter is found in the original weight, the cost of reweighing shall be borne by the public weighmaster responsible for issuing the faulty certificate. Otherwise, the cost shall be borne by the complainant. (1939, c. 285, s. 3; 1975, c. 544; 1981, c. 607, s. 4.)

§ 81A-54. Official seal of the public weighmaster.

It shall be the duty of every public weighmaster to obtain from the Department an official seal for the sum of six dollars ($6.00), inscribed with the following words: "North Carolina Public Weighmaster" and any other design or legend the Commissioner considers necessary. The seal shall be stamped or impressed on every certificate issued pursuant to this Article. The weighers of tobacco in leaf tobacco warehouses may use, instead of the seal, their signatures in ink or other indelible substance posted in a conspicuous and accessible place in the warehouse. All seals remain the property of the State and shall be returned to the Commissioner upon termination of duties as a public weighmaster. (1939, c. 285, s. 4; 1941, c. 317, s. 1; 1975, c. 544; 1981, c. 607, s. 4; 1989, c. 544, s. 21.)

§ 81A-55. Violations by public weighmasters; by others; penalties.

(a)   Any public weighmaster who refuses to issue a certificate as prescribed by this Article, or who issues a certificate giving a false weight, or who misrepresents the weight to any person, or who otherwise violates any provisions of this Article or the rules and regulations pursuant to this Article, may have his license revoked, suspended or terminated by the Commissioner.

(b)   The following acts by other persons are also violations of this Article:

(1)   Requesting a public weighmaster to weigh a product inaccurately;

(2)   Requesting an inaccurate certificate prescribed by this Article;

(3)   Impersonating a public weighmaster;

(4)   Erasing, changing or altering any certificate issued by a public weighmaster;

(5)   Increasing or decreasing the weight of a product for the purpose of deception; or

(6)   Violating any other provision of this Article. (1939, c. 285, s. 5; 1975, c. 544; 1981, c. 607, s. 4.)

§§ 81A-56 through 81A-57. Repealed by Session Laws 1981, c. 607, s. 2.

§ 81A-58. Duty of custodian of product.

If any product is to be offered for sale, or is sold, and is weighed or measured or counted by any public weighmaster and a certificate is issued prior to sale or acceptance of the product by the purchaser, or if any product is offered for sale, sold or delivered pending the weighing, measuring or counting of the product by any public weighmaster and the issuance of a certificate, the person who is in custody of the product shall keep, protect and prevent any increase or decrease in weight in the time intervening between the weighing and the issuance of the certificate and the sale, and the time intervening between the sale and the presentation of the product to the weighmaster for weighing, measuring or counting and the issuance of a certificate. Any loss sustained in the weight of the product while in custody shall be borne by the custodian. (1939, c. 285, s. 8; 1975, c. 544; 1981, c. 607, s. 5.)

§ 81A-59. Weighing tobacco.

All leaf tobacco offered for sale in a leaf tobacco warehouse in North Carolina shall remain in the custody of the warehouse operator from and after the time it is weighed by the public weighmaster until it is sold or the bid is rejected by the owner. (1945, c. 1067; 1975, c. 544; 1981, c. 607, s. 5.)

§ 81A-60. Repealed by Session Laws 1981, c. 607, s. 2.

§ 81A-61. Approval of devices used.

When making a weight determination, a public weighmaster shall use a weighing device that is of a type suitable for the weighing of the product to be weighed and that has been tested and approved for use by the Commissioner or by the public weighmaster's local or state weights and measures officials within the 12-month period immediately preceding the date of the weighing. (1939, c. 285, s. 10; 1975, c. 544; 1981, c. 607, s. 6; 2009-87, s. 2.)

§§ 81A-62 through 81A-64. Repealed by Session Laws 1981, c. 607, s. 2.

§§ 81A-65 through 81A-69. Reserved for future codification purposes.

Article 6.

Scale Technician.

§ 81A-70. Purpose of Article.

The purpose of this Article shall be to protect the owners and users of scales and weighing devices in their needs for scale repair and service, and to provide for scale technician registration. (1941, c. 237, s. 1; 1947, c. 380; 1975, c. 544; 1983, c. 111, s. 1.)

§ 81A-71. Prerequisites for scale technician.

It shall be unlawful for any scale technician to render service as a scale technician until after he or she has complied with the following requirements:

(1) Obtained from the Department of Agriculture and Consumer Services a copy of this Article, a copy of regulations pertinent to said Article, and an application form for registration.

(2) to (4) Repealed by Session Laws 1983, c. 111, s. 2.

(5) Obtained a registration card or certificate from the Commissioner or his authorized agent and a model form of service certificate.

(6) Obtained from the Department an annual certification of the standards of weight which will be used by the scale technician.

The provisions of this Article shall not apply to a full-time employee who renders service only on a scale or weighing device, or on scales or weighing devices, owned solely by his or her employer unless additional pay or compensation is received for such service. (1941, c. 237, s. 3; 1947, c. 380; 1975, c. 544; 1983, c. 111, s. 2; 1997-261, s. 10.)

§ 81A-72. Registration; certificate of registration; annual renewal.

The Commissioner or his authorized agent shall register any person who has complied with the requirements of this Article by making a record of receipt of application, and the issuing of a certificate or card of registration to applicant, whereupon the applicant becomes a registered scale technician and shall be known thereafter as such. Such registration shall be in effect from date of registration until July 1 next and shall be renewed on the first day of July of each year thereafter. A fee of twenty dollars ($20.00) shall accompany each application for registration and each annual registration renewal. (1941, c. 237, ss. 4, 5; 1943, c. 543; 1947, c. 380; 1975, c. 544; 1983, c. 111, s. 3; 2005-276, s. 42.1(g).)

§ 81A-73. Service certificate.

Whenever any service is rendered on any scale or weighing device used or intended to be used in this State by a scale technician, a certificate shall be issued by such scale technician who rendered said service, which shall be known as a "service certificate." The size and form of said service certificate shall be determined by the Commissioner or his authorized agent. Inclusive of other pertinent information or statements, the said certificate shall bear a statement expressed in ink or other indelible substance naming the kind of service rendered, whether adjustment, installation, repair, or maintenance, and stating that a service test as defined under the term "service" has been made, and that the service rendered is guaranteed to be as represented. The service certificate shall be made out in triplicate, with original going to the owner of such scale of weighing device or his agent, and a duplicate shall be sent to the Commissioner or his authorized agent and the triplicate copy shall be retained by the scale technician issuing such certificate. (1947, c. 380; 1975, c. 544; 1983, c. 111, s. 4.)

§ 81A-74: Repealed by Session Laws 1983, c. 111, s. 5.

§ 81A-75. Scale removal.

When a scale or weighing device is removed from the premises where located by a scale technician, the scale technician or his servant or agent shall issue a receipt for said scale or weighing device, on which shall be written in ink or other indelible substance the name and address of the owner, the name and address of receiving agent, date of receipt, anticipated date of return, name or make of scale, and such other information pertinent to its identification. The form of receipt shall be approved by the Commissioner or his authorized agent. (1947, c. 380; 1975, c. 544.)

§ 81A-76. Control of condemned or rejected scale.

It shall be unlawful for any owner of a scale or weighing device which has been condemned or rejected by the Commissioner or his authorized agent to either use or dispose of same in any manner other than at the direction of the Commissioner or his authorized agent; provided, however, said rejected scale or weighing device may be removed from the premises temporarily for repairs or service only. (1947, c. 380; 1975, c. 544.)

§ 81A-77. Secondhand scale.

It shall be unlawful for any person to sell, or offer for sale, or put into use, a secondhand or rebuilt or reconditioned scale or weighing device unless said scale shall have been tested and approved by the Commissioner or his authorized agent, or shall be accompanied by a service certificate as provided for in this Article. Said service certificate shall be retained by the purchaser or user of said scale until an inspector of weights and measures has tested and approved such secondhand scale. The said certificate shall serve as proof of the accuracy of scale at the time scale was purchased or put into service. A secondhand or rebuilt or reconditioned scale or weighing device as referred to in this section shall be considered as being a scale or weighing device in the channels of trade which does not belong to the previous user. (1947, c. 380; 1975, c. 544.)

§ 81A-78. Scale location.

It shall be unlawful for any scale or weighing device to be installed, set up, put into service, or used on a foundation or support that aids in giving false indication of weight values applied to platter, platform, or other load receiving element. (1947, c. 380; 1975, c. 544.)

§ 81A-79. Exemption.

The provisions of this Article shall not prohibit the user of a scale or weighing device from employing some person other than a scale technician to render service as defined by this Article upon his or her scale or weighing device, nor apply to the person so employed, who does not solicit such employment, provided that said user shall not be relieved of his or her responsibility or liability concerning the accuracy of the scale or weighing device after service has been rendered. (1947, c. 380; 1975, c. 544.)

§ 81A-80. Suspension or revocation of registration; penalty.

(a) The Commissioner may suspend or revoke the registration of any scale technician who violates any provisions of this Article or regulations adopted thereunder or who shall fail to issue a service certificate or who shall issue a service certificate bearing false statements regarding service rendered.

(b) Any person who violates any provision of this Article shall be guilty of a Class 2 misdemeanor. (1941, c. 237, s. 7; 1947, c. 380; 1949, c. 983, s. 2; 1975, c. 544; 1983, c. 111, s. 6; 1993, c. 539, s. 594; 1994, Ex. Sess., c. 24, s. 14(c).)

§§ 81A-81 through 81A-85. Reserved for future codification purposes.

Article 7.

General Provisions.

§ 81A-86. Regulations to be unaffected by repeal of prior enabling statute.

The adoption of this Chapter or any of its provisions shall not affect any regulations promulgated pursuant to the authority of any earlier enabling statute unless inconsistent with this Chapter or modified or revoked. (1975, c. 544.)

§ 81A-87. Severability provision.

If any provision of this Chapter is declared unconstitutional, or the applicability thereof to any person or circumstance is held invalid, the constitutionality of the remainder of the Chapter and the applicability thereof to other persons and circumstances shall not be affected thereby. (1975, c. 544.)

§ 81A-88. Repeal of conflicting laws.

All laws and parts of laws contrary to or inconsistent with the provisions of this Chapter are repealed except as to offenses committed, liabilities incurred, and claims made thereunder prior to July 1, 1976. (1975, c. 544.)

Chapter 82.

Wrecks.

§§ 82-1 through 82-18. Repealed by Session Laws 1971, c. 882, s. 5.

Chapter 83.

Architects.

§§ 83-1 through 83-15. Recodified as §§ 83A-1 to 83A-17.

Chapter 83A.

Architects.

§ 83A-1. Definitions.

When used in this Chapter, unless the context otherwise requires:

(1) "Architect" means a person who is duly licensed to practice architecture.

(2) "Board" means the North Carolina Board of Architecture.

(3) "Corporate certificate" means a certificate of corporate registration issued by the Board recognizing the corporation named in the certificate as meeting the requirements for the corporate practice of architecture.

(4) "Corporate practice of architecture" means "practice" as defined in G.S. 83A-1(7) by a corporation which is organized or domesticated in this State, and which holds a current "corporate certificate" from this Board.

(5) "Good moral character" means such character as tends to assure the faithful discharge of the fiduciary duties of an architect to his client. Evidence of lack of such character shall include the willful commission of an offense justifying discipline under this Chapter, the practice of architecture in violation of this Chapter, or of the laws of another jurisdiction, or the conviction of a felony.

(6) "License" means a certificate of registration issued by the Board recognizing the individual named in the certificate as meeting the requirements for registration under this Chapter.

(7) "Practice of architecture" means performing or offering to perform or holding oneself out as legally qualified to perform professional services in connection with the design, construction, enlargement or alteration of buildings, including consultations, investigations, evaluations, preliminary studies, the preparation of plans, specifications and contract documents, administration of

construction contracts and related services or combination of services in connection with the design and construction of buildings, regardless of whether these services are performed in person or as the directing head of an office or organization. (1915, c. 270, s. 9; C.S., s. 4985; 1941, c. 369, s. 3; 1951, c. 1130, s. 1; 1957, c. 794, ss. 1, 2; 1979, c. 871, s. 1.)

§ 83A-2. North Carolina Board of Architecture; creation; appointment, terms and oath of members; vacancies; officers; bond of treasurer; notice of meetings; quorum.

(a)   The North Carolina Board of Architecture shall have the power and responsibility to administer the provisions of this Chapter in compliance with the Administrative Procedure Act.

(b)   The Board shall consist of seven members appointed by the Governor. Five of the members of the Board shall be licensed architects appointed for five year terms; the terms shall be staggered so that the term of one architect member expires each year. No architect member shall be eligible to serve more than two consecutive terms; if a vacancy occurs during a term, the Governor shall appoint a person to fill the vacancy for the remainder of the unexpired term. Two of the members of the Board shall be persons who are not licensed architects and who represent the interest of the public at large; the Governor shall appoint these members not later than July 1, 1979. The public members shall have full voting powers and shall serve at the pleasure of the Governor. Each Board member shall file with the Secretary of State an oath faithfully to perform duties as a member of the Board, and to uphold the Constitution of North Carolina and the Constitution of the United States.

(c)   Officers of the Board shall include a president, vice-president, secretary and treasurer elected at the annual meeting for terms of one year. The treasurer shall give bond in such sum as the Board shall determine, with such security as shall be approved by the Board, said bond to be conditioned for the faithful performance of the duties of his office and for the faithful accounting of all moneys and other property as shall come into his hands. Notice of the annual meeting, and the time and place of the annual meeting shall be given each member by letter at least 10 days prior to such meeting and public notice of annual meetings shall be published at least once each week for two weeks preceding such meetings in one or more newspapers of general circulation in this State. A majority of the members of the Board shall constitute a quorum.

(1915, c. 270, ss. 1, 2; C.S., ss. 4986-4988, 4990; 1957, c. 794, ss. 3, 4, 6; 1979, c. 871, s. 1.)

§ 83A-3. Expenses of Board members; Board finances.

(a)   Each member of the Board shall be entitled to receive travel and expense reimbursement as authorized by G.S. 93B-5 for similar boards.

(b)   All funds received by the Board under the provisions of this Chapter shall be deposited by the treasurer or such other officer or staff employee as the Board may designate in such depository and under such security as the Board may direct. All expenses incurred by the Board shall be paid out of funds derived from examination, licensing, renewal or other fees herein provided and shall be paid by the treasurer upon vouchers drawn by the secretary and approved by the president. The Board shall have the power to determine necessary expenses, and to fix the compensation for board employees and for professional services. The State of North Carolina shall not be liable for the compensation of any Board members or officers. Payment of expenses and salaries pursuant to administration of this Chapter may not exceed available funds of the Board. All Board receipts and disbursements shall be subject to audit and accounting procedures established by the State for similar boards.

(c)   The Board shall have the power to acquire, hold, rent, encumber, alienate, and otherwise deal with real property in the same manner as a private person or corporation, subject only to approval of the Governor and the Council of State. Collateral pledged by the Board for an encumbrance shall be limited to the assets, income, and revenues of the Board. (1915, c. 270, s. 6; C.S., s. 4994; 1957, c. 794, s. 9; 1979, c. 871, s. 1; 2013-410, s. 31.)

§ 83A-4. Fees.

All fees and charges by the Board shall be established by Board rule subject to the provisions of the Administrative Procedure Act.

Fees set by the Board shall not exceed the following amounts:

Initial Application

	Individual	
	Residents	$50.00
	Nonresidents	$50.00
	Corporate	$75.00
Reexamination		$25.00
Annual License Renewal		
	Individual	$75.00
	Corporate	$100.00
Late Renewal Penalty		
	Up-to-30 days	$50.00
	30 days to 1 year	$50.00
Reciprocal Registration		$150.00

The above fees are provided in addition to any other fees prescribed by law. Reasonable fees for examination materials, certificates, rosters and other published materials shall be established by the Board, but the Board shall not collect any fees not authorized by this Chapter. (1915, c. 270, ss. 3, 6; 1919, c. 336, ss. 1, 2; C.S., ss. 4992, 4994, 4995; 1951, c. 1130, s. 2; 1957, c. 794, ss. 7, 9, 10; 1971, c. 1231, s. 1; 1979, c. 871, s. 1; 1985, c. 364.)

§ 83A-5. Board records; rosters; seal.

(a) The Board shall maintain records of board meetings, of applications for individual or corporate registration and the action taken thereon, of the results of examinations, of all disciplinary proceedings, and of such other information as deemed necessary by the Board or required by the Administrative Procedure Act or other provisions of the General Statutes.

(b) A complete roster showing the name and last known address of all resident and nonresident architects and architectural firms holding current licenses from the Board shall be published by the Board at least once each year, and shall include each registrant's authorization or registration number. Copies of the roster shall be filed with the Secretary of State and the Attorney General, and other applicable State or local agencies, and upon request, may be distributed or sold to the public.

(c) The Board shall adopt a seal containing the name of the Board for use on its official records and reports. (1915, c. 270, ss. 1, 5; C.S., ss. 4989, 4991; 1957, c. 794, s. 5; 1979, c. 871, s. 1.)

§ 83A-6. Board rules; bylaws; standards of professional conduct.

(a) The Board shall have the power to adopt bylaws, rules, and standards of professional conduct to carry out the purposes of this Chapter, including, but not limited to:

(1) The adoption of bylaws governing its meetings and proceedings;

(2) The establishment of qualification requirements for admission to examinations, and for individual or corporate licensure as provided in G.S. 83A-7 and 83A-8;

(3) The establishment of the types and contents of examinations, their conduct, and the minimum scores or other criteria for passing such examinations;

(4) The adoption of mandatory standards of professional conduct concerning misrepresentations, conflicts of interest, incompetence, disability, violations of law, dishonest conduct, or other unprofessional conduct for those persons or corporations regulated by this Chapter, which standards shall be enforceable under the disciplinary procedures of the Board;

(5) The establishment or approval of requirements for renewal of licenses designed to promote the continued professional development and competence

of licensees. Such requirements shall be designed solely to improve the professional knowledge and skills of a licensee directly related to the current and emerging bodies of knowledge and skills of the licensee's profession.

When necessary to protect the public health, safety, or welfare, the Board shall require such evidence as it deems necessary to establish the continuing competency of architects as a condition of renewal of licenses.

(b)   The Board shall not adopt any rule or regulation which prohibits advertising.

(c)   The adoption, amendment or revocation of rules, regulations, and standards of professional conduct, and the publication and distribution of the same shall be subject to the provisions of the Administrative Procedure Act. (1979, c. 871, s. 1.)

§ 83A-7. Qualifications and examination requirements.

(a)   Licensing by Examination. - Any individual who is at least 18 years of age and of good moral character may make written application for examination by completion of a form prescribed by the Board accompanied by the required application fee. Subject to qualification requirements of this section, the applicant shall be entitled to an examination to determine his qualifications for licensure.

(1)   The qualification requirements for registration as a duly licensed architect shall be:

a.   Professional education and at least three years practical training and experience as specified by rules of the Board.

b.   The successful completion of a licensure examination in architecture as specified by the rules of the Board.

(2)   The Board shall adopt rules to set requirements for professional education, practical training and experience, and examination which must be met by applicants for licensure and which may be based on the published guidelines of nationally recognized councils or agencies for the accreditation, examination, and licensing for the architectural profession.

(b) Licensing by Reciprocity. - Any individual holding a current license for the practice of architecture from another state or territory, and holding a certificate of qualification issued by the National Council of Architectural Registration Boards, may upon application and within the discretion of the Board be licensed without written examination. The Board may waive the requirement for National Council registration if the qualifications, examination and licensing requirements of the state in which the applicant is licensed are substantially equivalent to those of this State and the applicant otherwise meets the requirements of this Chapter. (1915, c. 270, s. 3; 1919, c. 336, s. 1; C.S., s. 4992; 1957, c. 794, s. 7; 1971, c. 1231, s. 1; 1979, c. 871, s. 1; 1983, c. 47; 1989, c. 62.)

§ 83A-8. Qualification for corporate practice.

(a) Any corporation desiring to practice architecture in this State shall file corporate application on forms provided by the Board, accompanied by the required application fee. To be eligible for a corporate certificate, the corporation must meet all requirements of the Professional Corporation Act.

(b) Architectural corporations of other states may be granted corporate certificates for practice in this State upon filing application with the Board and satisfying the Board that they meet the requirements of subsection (a) above. Such corporations shall designate the individual or individuals licensed to practice architecture in this State who shall be in responsible charge of all architectural work offered or performed by such corporation in this State. Such corporations shall notify the Board of changes in such designation.

(c) All corporations holding corporate certificates from the Board shall be subject to the applicable rules and regulations adopted by the Board, and to all the disciplinary powers applicable to individual licensees who are officers or employees of the corporation. Corporations may perform no acts or things forbidden to officers or employees as licensees. (1979, c. 871, s. 1.)

§ 83A-9. Partnership practice.

This Chapter neither prevents practice of architecture by a partnership nor requires partnership seals or certificates of practice provided that the members of the partnership are duly licensed to practice architecture, and, provided that the partnership files with the Board and keeps current a list of the partners, their license identifications, and the types of services offered by the partnership. (1979, c. 871, s. 1.)

§ 83A-10. Professional seals.

Every licensed architect shall have a seal of a design authorized by the Board, and shall imprint all drawings and sets of specifications prepared for use in this State with an impression of such seal. Licensed architectural corporations shall employ corporate professional seals, of a design approved by the Board, for use in identifying plans, specifications and other professional documents issued by the corporation, but use of such corporate seals shall be in addition to and not in substitution for the requirement that the individual seal of the author of such plans and professional documents be affixed. (1915, c. 270, s. 7; C.S., s. 4997; 1979, c. 871, s. 1.)

§ 83A-11. Expirations and renewals.

Certificates must be renewed on or before the first day of July in each year. No less than 30 days prior to the renewal date, a renewal application shall be mailed to each individual and corporate licensee. The completed application together with the required renewal fee shall be returned to the Board on or before the renewal date. When the Board is satisfied as to the continuing competency of an architect, it shall issue a renewal of the certificate. Upon failure to renew within 30 days after the date set for expiration, the license shall be automatically revoked but such license may be renewed at any time within one year following the expiration date upon proof of continuing competency and payment of the renewal fee plus a late renewal fee. After one year from the date of revocation, reinstatement may be made by the Board, or in its discretion, the application may be treated as new subject to reexamination and qualification requirements as in the case of new applications. (1919, c. 336, s. 2; C.S., s. 4995; 1951, c. 1130, s. 2; 1957, c. 794, s. 10; 1979, c. 871, s. 1.)

§ 83A-12. Prohibited practice.

The purpose of the Chapter is to safeguard life, health and property. It shall be unlawful for any individual, firm or corporation to practice or offer to practice architecture in this State as defined in this Chapter, or to use the title "Architect" or any form thereof, except as provided in Chapter 89A for Landscape Architects, or to display or use any words, letters, figures, titles, sign, card, advertisement, or other device to indicate that such individual or firm practices or offers to practice architecture as herein defined or is an architect or architectural firm qualified to perform architectural work, unless such person holds a current individual or corporate certificate of admission to practice architecture under the provisions of this Chapter. (1915, c. 270, s. 4; C.S., s. 4996; 1941, c. 369, ss. 1, 2; 1951, c. 1130, s. 3; 1957, c. 794, s. 11; 1965, c. 1100; 1969, c. 718, s. 21; 1973, c. 1414, s. 1; 1979, c. 871, s. 1.)

§ 83A-13. Exemptions.

(a)   Nothing in this Chapter shall be construed to prevent the practice of general contracting under the provisions of Article 1 of Chapter 87, or the practice by any person who is qualified under law as a "registered professional engineer" of such architectural work as is incidental to engineering projects or utilities, or the practice of any other profession under the applicable licensure provisions of the General Statutes.

(b)   Nothing in this Chapter shall be construed to prevent a duly licensed general contractor, professional engineer or architect, acting individually or in combination thereof, from participating in a "Design/Build" undertaking including the preparation of plans and/or specifications and entering individual or collective agreements with the owner in order to meet the owner's requirements for pre-determined costs and unified control in the design and construction of a project, and for the method of compensation for the design and construction services rendered; provided, however, that nothing herein shall be construed so as to allow the performance of any such services or any division thereof by one who is not duly licensed to perform such service or services in accordance with applicable licensure provisions of the General Statutes; provided further, that full disclosure is made in writing to the owner as to the duties and responsibilities of each of the participating parties in such agreements; and, provided further, nothing in this Chapter shall prevent the administration by any of the said licensees of construction contracts and related services or combination of services in connection with the construction of buildings.

(c) Nothing in this Chapter shall be construed to require an architectural license for the preparation, sale, or furnishing of plans, specifications and related data, or for the supervision of construction pursuant thereto, where the building, buildings, or project involved is in one of the following categories:

(1) A family residence, up to eight units attached with grade level exit, which is not a part of or physically connected with any other buildings or residential units;

(2) A building upon any farm for the use of any farmer, unless the building is of such nature and intended for such use as to substantially involve the health or safety of the public;

(3) An institutional or commercial building if it does not have a total value exceeding ninety thousand dollars ($90,000);

(4) An institutional or commercial building if the total building area does not exceed 2,500 square feet in gross floor area;

(5) Alteration, remodeling, or renovation of an existing building that is exempt under this section, or alteration, remodeling, or renovation of an existing building or building site that does not alter or affect the structural system of the building; change the building's access or exit pattern; or change the live or dead load on the building's structural system. This subdivision shall not limit or change any other exemptions to this Chapter or to the practice of engineering under Chapter 89C of the General Statutes.

(6) The preparation and use of details and shop drawings, assembly or erection drawings, or graphic descriptions utilized to detail or illustrate a portion of the work required to construct the project in accordance with the plans and specifications prepared or to be prepared under the requirements or exemptions of this Chapter.

(d) Nothing in this Chapter shall be construed to prevent any individual from making plans or data for buildings for himself.

(e) Plans and specifications prepared by persons or corporations under these exemptions shall bear the signature and address of such person or corporate officer. (1979, c. 871, s. 1; 1997-457, s. 1.)

§ 83A-13.1. Architect who volunteers during an emergency or disaster; qualified immunity.

(a) A professional architect who voluntarily, without compensation, provides structural, electrical, mechanical, or other architectural services at the scene of a declared disaster or emergency, declared under federal law or in accordance with the provisions of Article 1A of Chapter 166A of the General Statutes, at the request of a public official, law enforcement official, public safety official, or building inspection official, acting in an official capacity, shall not be liable for any personal injury, wrongful death, property damage, or other loss caused by the professional architect's acts or omissions in the performance of the architectural services.

(b) The immunity provided in subsection (a) of this section applies only to an architectural service:

(1) For any structure, building, piping, or other architectural system, either publicly or privately owned.

(2) That occurs within 45 days after the declaration of the emergency or disaster, unless the 45-day immunity period is extended by an executive order issued by the Governor under the Governor's emergency executive powers.

(c) The immunity provided in subsection (a) of this section does not apply if it is determined that the personal injury, wrongful death, property damage, or other loss was caused by the gross negligence, wanton conduct, or intentional wrongdoing of the professional architect or arose out of the operation of a motor vehicle.

(d) As used in this section:

(1) "Building inspection official" means any appointed or elected federal, State, or local official with overall executive responsibility to coordinate building inspection in the jurisdiction in which the emergency or disaster is declared.

(2) "Law enforcement official" means any appointed or elected federal, State, or local official with overall executive responsibility to coordinate law enforcement in the jurisdiction in which the emergency or disaster is declared.

(3) "Public official" means any federal, State, or locally elected official with overall executive responsibility in the jurisdiction in which the emergency or disaster is declared.

(4) "Public safety official" means any appointed or elected federal, State, or local official with overall executive responsibility to coordinate public safety in the jurisdiction in which the emergency or disaster is declared. (1995, c. 416, s. 2; 2012-12, s. 2(p).)

§ 83A-14. Disciplinary action and procedure.

Any person may file with the Board a charge of unprofessional conduct, negligence, incompetence, dishonest practice, or other misconduct or of any violation of this Chapter or of a Board rule adopted and published by the Board. Upon receipt of such charge, or upon its own initiative, the Board may give notice of an administrative hearing under the Administrative Procedure Act, or may dismiss the charge as unfounded or trivial, upon a statement of the reasons therefor which shall be mailed to the architect and the person who filed the charge by registered or certified mail. (1979, c. 871, s. 1.)

§ 83A-15. Denial, suspension or revocation of license.

(a) The Board shall have the power to suspend or revoke a license or certificate of registration, to deny a license or certificate of registration, or to reprimand or levy a civil penalty not in excess of five hundred dollars ($500.00) per violation against any registrant who is found guilty of:

(1) Dishonest conduct, including but not limited to:

a. The commission of any fraud, deceit or misrepresentation in any professional relationship with clients or other persons; or with reference to obtaining or maintaining license, or with reference to qualifications, experience and past or present service; or

b. Using or permitting an individual professional seal to be used by or for others, or otherwise representing registrant as the author of drawings or specifications other than those prepared personally by or under direct supervision of registrant.

(2) Incompetence, including but not limited to:

a. Gross negligence, recklessness, or excessive errors or omissions or building failures in registrant's record of professional practice; or

b. Mental or physical disability or addiction to alcohol or drugs so as to endanger health, safety and interest of the public by impairing skill and care in professional services.

(3) Unprofessional conduct, including but not limited to:

a. Practicing or offering to practice architecture without a current license from this Board;

b. Knowingly aiding or abetting others to evade or violate the provisions of this Chapter, or the health and safety laws of this or other states;

c. Knowingly undertaking any activity or having any significant financial or other interest, or accepting any compensation or reward except from registrant's clients, any of which would reasonably appear to compromise registrant's professional judgment in serving the best interest of clients or public;

d. Willfully violating this Chapter or any rule or standard of conduct published by the Board, or pleading guilty or nolo contendere to a felony or any crime involving moral turpitude.

(b) Actions to recover civil penalties against any registrant may be commenced by the Board pursuant to Chapter 150B of the General Statutes. In determining the amount of any civil penalty, the Board shall consider the degree and extent of harm caused by the violation. The clear proceeds of any civil penalty collected hereunder shall be remitted to the Civil Penalty and Forfeiture Fund in accordance with G.S. 115C-457.2. (1915, c. 270, s. 5; 1919, c. 336, s. 3; C.S., s. 4993; 1953, c. 1041, s. 1; 1957, c. 794, s. 8; 1973, c. 1331, s. 3; 1979, c. 871, s. 1; 1989, c. 81; 1998-215, s. 128.)

§ 83A-16. Violations of Chapter; penalties.

(a) Any individual or corporation not registered under this Chapter, who shall wrongfully use the title "Architect" or represent himself or herself to the public as an architect, or practice architecture as herein defined, or seek to avoid the provisions of this Chapter by the use of any other designation than "Architect": (i) shall be guilty of a Class 2 misdemeanor; and (ii) be subject to a civil penalty not to exceed five hundred dollars ($500.00) per day of such violation. Each day of such unlawful practice shall constitute a distinct and separate violation. The clear proceeds of any civil penalty collected hereunder shall be remitted to the Civil Penalty and Forfeiture Fund in accordance with G.S. 115C-457.2.

(b) Actions and prosecutions under this section shall be commenced in the county in which the defendant resides, or has his principal place of business, or in the case of an out-of-state corporation, is conducting business.

(c) Actions to recover civil penalties shall be initiated by the Attorney General. (1915, c. 270, s. 4; C.S., s. 4996; 1941, c. 369, ss. 1, 2; 1951, c. 1130, s. 3; 1957, c. 794, s. 11; 1965, c. 1100; 1969, c. 718, s. 21; 1973, c. 1414, s. 1; 1979, c. 871, s. 1; 1993, c. 539, s. 595; 1994, Ex. Sess., c. 24, s. 14(c); 1998-215, s. 129.)

§ 83A-17. Power of Board to seek injunction.

The Board may appear in its own name and apply to courts having jurisdiction for injunctions to prevent violations of this Chapter or of rules issued pursuant thereto, and such courts are empowered to grant such injunctions regardless of whether criminal prosecution or other action has been or may be instituted as a result of such violation. A single act of unauthorized or illegal practice shall be sufficient, if shown, to invoke the injunctive relief of this section or criminal penalties under G.S. 83A-16. (1979, c. 871, s. 1.)

Chapter 84.

Attorneys-at-Law.

Article 1.

Qualifications of Attorney; Unauthorized Practice of Law.

§ 84-1. Oaths taken in open court.

Attorneys before they shall be admitted to practice law shall, in open court before a justice or judge of the General Court of Justice, personally appear and take the oath prescribed for attorneys by G.S. 11-11, and also the oaths of allegiance to the State, and to support the Constitution of the United States, prescribed for all public officers by Article VI, Sec. 7 of the North Carolina Constitution and G.S. 11-7, and the same shall be entered on the records of the court; and, upon such qualification had, and oath taken may act as attorneys during their good behavior. (1777, c. 115, s. 8; R.C., c. 9, s. 3; Code, s. 19; Rev., s. 209; C.S., s. 197; 1969, c. 44, s. 58; 1973, c. 108, s. 35; 1995, c. 431, s. 1.)

§ 84-2. Persons disqualified.

No justice, judge, magistrate, full-time district attorney, full-time assistant district attorney, public defender, assistant public defender, clerk, deputy or assistant clerk of the General Court of Justice, register of deeds, deputy or assistant register of deeds, sheriff or deputy sheriff shall engage in the private practice of law. Persons violating this provision shall be guilty of a Class 3 misdemeanor and only fined not less than two hundred dollars ($200.00). (C.C.P., s. 424; 1870-1, c. 90; 1871-2, c. 120; 1880, c. 43; 1883, c. 406; Code, ss. 27, 28, 110; Rev., ss. 210, 3641; 1919, c. 205; C.S., s. 198; 1933, c. 15; 1941, c. 177; 1943, c. 543; 1965, c. 418, s. 1; 1969, c. 44, s. 59; 1973, c. 47, s. 2; c. 108, s. 36; 1981, c. 788, s. 1; 1993, c. 539, s. 596; 1994, Ex. Sess., c. 24, s. 14(c); 1995, c. 431, s. 2; 2007-484, s. 28(a).)

§ 84-2.1. "Practice law" defined.

The phrase "practice law" as used in this Chapter is defined to be performing any legal service for any other person, firm or corporation, with or without compensation, specifically including the preparation or aiding in the preparation of deeds, mortgages, wills, trust instruments, inventories, accounts or reports of guardians, trustees, administrators or executors, or preparing or aiding in the preparation of any petitions or orders in any probate or court proceeding;

abstracting or passing upon titles, the preparation and filing of petitions for use in any court, including administrative tribunals and other judicial or quasi-judicial bodies, or assisting by advice, counsel, or otherwise in any legal work; and to advise or give opinion upon the legal rights of any person, firm or corporation: Provided, that the above reference to particular acts which are specifically included within the definition of the phrase "practice law" shall not be construed to limit the foregoing general definition of the term, but shall be construed to include the foregoing particular acts, as well as all other acts within the general definition. The phrase "practice law" does not encompass the drafting or writing of memoranda of understanding or other mediation summaries by mediators at community mediation centers authorized by G.S. 7A-38.5 or by mediators of employment-related matters for The University of North Carolina or a constituent institution, or for an agency, commission, or board of the State of North Carolina. (C.C.P., s. 424; 1870-1, c. 90; 1871-2, c. 120; 1880, c. 43; 1883, c. 406; Code, ss. 27, 28, 110; Rev., ss. 210, 3641; 1919, c. 205; C.S., s. 198; 1933, c. 15; 1941, c. 177; 1943, c. 543; 1945, c. 468; 1995, c. 431, s. 3; 1999-354, s. 2; 2004-154, s. 2; 2013-410, s. 32.)

§ 84-3. Repealed by Session Laws 1973, c. 108, s. 37.

§ 84-4. Persons other than members of State Bar prohibited from practicing law.

Except as otherwise permitted by law, it shall be unlawful for any person or association of persons, except active members of the Bar of the State of North Carolina admitted and licensed to practice as attorneys-at-law, to appear as attorney or counselor at law in any action or proceeding before any judicial body, including the North Carolina Industrial Commission, or the Utilities Commission; to maintain, conduct, or defend the same, except in his own behalf as a party thereto; or, by word, sign, letter, or advertisement, to hold out himself, or themselves, as competent or qualified to give legal advice or counsel, or to prepare legal documents, or as being engaged in advising or counseling in law or acting as attorney or counselor-at-law, or in furnishing the services of a lawyer or lawyers; and it shall be unlawful for any person or association of persons except active members of the Bar, for or without a fee or consideration, to give legal advice or counsel, perform for or furnish to another legal services, or to prepare directly or through another for another person, firm or corporation, any will or testamentary disposition, or instrument of trust, or to organize corporations or prepare for another person, firm or corporation, any other legal document. Provided, that nothing herein shall prohibit any person from drawing a will for another in an emergency wherein the imminence of death leaves insufficient time to have the same drawn and its execution supervised by a licensed attorney-at-law. The provisions of this section shall be in addition to and not in lieu of any other provisions of this Chapter. Provided, however, this section shall not apply to corporations authorized to practice law under the provisions of Chapter 55B of the General Statutes of North Carolina. (1931, c. 157, s. 1; 1937, c. 155, s. 1; 1955, c. 526, s. 1; 1969, c. 718, s. 19; 1981, c. 762, s. 3; 1995, c. 431, s. 4.)

§ 84-4.1. Limited practice of out-of-state attorneys.

Any attorney domiciled in another state, and regularly admitted to practice in the courts of record of and in good standing in that state, having been retained as attorney for a party to any civil or criminal legal proceeding pending in the General Court of Justice of North Carolina, the North Carolina Utilities Commission, the North Carolina Industrial Commission, the Office of Administrative Hearings of North Carolina, or any administrative agency, may, on motion, be admitted to practice in that forum for the sole purpose of appearing for a client in the proceeding. The motion required under this section shall be signed by the attorney and shall contain or be accompanied by:

(1)   The attorney's full name, post-office address, bar membership number, and status as a practicing attorney in another state.

(2)   A statement, signed by the client, setting forth the client's address and declaring that the client has retained the attorney to represent the client in the proceeding.

(3)   A statement that unless permitted to withdraw sooner by order of the court, the attorney will continue to represent the client in the proceeding until its final determination, and that with reference to all matters incident to the proceeding, the attorney agrees to be subject to the orders and amenable to the disciplinary action and the civil jurisdiction of the General Court of Justice and the North Carolina State Bar in all respects as if the attorney were a regularly admitted and licensed member of the Bar of North Carolina in good standing.

(4)   A statement that the state in which the attorney is regularly admitted to practice grants like privileges to members of the Bar of North Carolina in good standing.

(5)   A statement to the effect that the attorney has associated and is personally appearing in the proceeding, with an attorney who is a resident of this State, has agreed to be responsible for filing a registration statement with the North Carolina State Bar, and is duly and legally admitted to practice in the General Court of Justice of North Carolina, upon whom service may be had in all matters connected with the legal proceedings, or any disciplinary matter, with the same effect as if personally made on the foreign attorney within this State.

(6)   A statement accurately disclosing a record of all that attorney's disciplinary history. Discipline shall include (i) public discipline by any court or lawyer regulatory organization, and (ii) revocation of any pro hac vice admission.

(7)   A fee in the amount of two hundred twenty-five dollars ($225.00), of which two hundred dollars ($200.00) shall be remitted to the State Treasurer for support of the General Court of Justice and twenty-five dollars ($25.00) shall be transmitted to the North Carolina State Bar to regulate the practice of out-of-state attorneys as provided in this section.

Compliance with the foregoing requirements does not deprive the court of the discretionary power to allow or reject the application. (1967, c. 1199, s. 1; 1971, c. 550, s. 1; 1975, c. 582, ss. 1, 2; 1977, c. 430; 1985 (Reg. Sess., 1986), c. 1022, s. 8; 1991, c. 210, s. 2; 1995, c. 431, s. 5; 2003-116, s. 1; 2004-186, s. 4.2; 2005-396, s. 1; 2007-200, s. 4; 2007-323, s. 30.8(k).)

§ 84-4.2. Summary revocation of permission granted out-of-state attorneys to practice.

Permission granted under G.S. 84-4.1 may be summarily revoked by the General Court of Justice or any agency, including the North Carolina Utilities Commission, on its own motion and in its discretion. (1967, c. 1199, s. 2; 1971, c. 550, s. 2; 1995, c. 431, s. 6.)

§ 84-5. Prohibition as to practice of law by corporation.

(a) It shall be unlawful for any corporation to practice law or appear as an attorney for any person in any court in this State, or before any judicial body or the North Carolina Industrial Commission, Utilities Commission, or the Department of Commerce, Division of Employment Security, or hold itself out to the public or advertise as being entitled to practice law; and no corporation shall organize corporations, or draw agreements, or other legal documents, or draw wills, or practice law, or give legal advice, or hold itself out in any manner as being entitled to do any of the foregoing acts, by or through any person orally or by advertisement, letter or circular. The provisions of this section shall be in addition to and not in lieu of any other provisions of Chapter 84. Provided, that nothing in this section shall be construed to prohibit a banking corporation authorized and licensed to act in a fiduciary capacity from performing any clerical, accounting, financial or business acts required of it in the performance of its duties as a fiduciary or from performing ministerial and clerical acts in the preparation and filing of such tax returns as are so required, or from discussing the business and financial aspects of fiduciary relationships. Provided, however, this section shall not apply to corporations authorized to practice law under the provisions of Chapter 55B of the General Statutes of North Carolina.

To further clarify the foregoing provisions of this section as they apply to corporations which are authorized and licensed to act in a fiduciary capacity:

(1) A corporation authorized and licensed to act in a fiduciary capacity shall not:

a. Draw wills or trust instruments; provided that this shall not be construed to prohibit an employee of such corporation from conferring and cooperating with an attorney who is not a salaried employee of the corporation, at the request of such attorney, in connection with the attorney's performance of services for a client who desires to appoint the corporation executor or trustee or otherwise to utilize the fiduciary services of the corporation.

b. Give legal advice or legal counsel, orally or written, to any customer or prospective customer or to any person who is considering renunciation of the right to qualify as executor or administrator or who proposes to resign as guardian or trustee, or to any other person, firm or corporation.

c. Advertise to perform any of the acts prohibited herein; solicit to perform any of the acts prohibited herein; or offer to perform any of the acts prohibited herein.

(2) Except as provided in subsection (b) of this section, when any of the following acts are to be performed in connection with the fiduciary activities of such a corporation, said acts shall be performed for the corporation by a duly licensed attorney, not a salaried employee of the corporation, retained to perform legal services required in connection with the particular estate, trust or other fiduciary matter:

a. Offering wills for probate.

b. Preparing and publishing notice of administration to creditors.

c. Handling formal court proceedings.

d. Drafting legal papers or giving legal advice to spouses concerning rights to an elective share under Article 1A of Chapter 30 of the General Statutes.

e. Resolving questions of domicile and residence of a decedent.

f. Handling proceedings involving year's allowances of widows and children.

g. Drafting deeds, notes, deeds of trust, leases, options and other contracts.

h. Drafting instruments releasing deeds of trust.

i. Drafting assignments of rent.

j. Drafting any formal legal document to be used in the discharge of the corporate fiduciary's duty.

k. In matters involving estate and inheritance taxes, gift taxes, and federal and State income taxes:

1. Preparing and filing protests or claims for refund, except requests for a refund based on mathematical or clerical errors in tax returns filed by it as a fiduciary.

2. Conferring with tax authorities regarding protests or claims for refund, except those based on mathematical or clerical errors in tax returns filed by it as a fiduciary.

3. Handling petitions to the tax court.

l. Performing legal services in insolvency proceedings or before a referee in bankruptcy or in court.

m. In connection with the administration of an estate or trust:

1. Making application for letters testamentary or letters of administration.

2. Abstracting or passing upon title to property.

3. Handling litigation relating to claims by or against the estate or trust.

4. Handling foreclosure proceedings of deeds of trust or other security instruments which are in default.

(3) When any of the following acts are to be performed in connection with the fiduciary activities of such a corporation, the corporation shall comply with the following:

a. The initial opening and inventorying of safe deposit boxes in connection with the administration of an estate for which the corporation is executor or administrator shall be handled by, or with the advice of, an attorney, not a salaried employee of the corporation, retained by the corporation to perform legal services required in connection with that particular estate.

b. The furnishing of a beneficiary with applicable portions of a testator's will relating to such beneficiary shall, if accompanied by any legal advice or opinion, be handled by, or with the advice of, an attorney, not a salaried employee of the corporation, retained by the corporation to perform legal services required in connection with that particular estate or matter.

c. In matters involving estate and inheritance taxes and federal and State income taxes, the corporation shall not execute waivers of statutes of limitations without the advice of an attorney, not a salaried employee of the corporation, retained by the corporation to perform legal services in connection with that particular estate or matter.

d. An attorney, not a salaried employee of the corporation, retained by the corporation to perform legal services required in connection with an estate or trust shall be furnished copies of inventories and accounts proposed for filing with any court and proposed federal estate and North Carolina inheritance tax returns and, on request, copies of proposed income and intangibles tax returns, and shall be afforded an opportunity to advise and counsel the corporate fiduciary concerning them prior to filing.

(b) Nothing in this section shall prohibit an attorney retained by a corporation, whether or not the attorney is also a salaried employee of the corporation, from representing the corporation or an affiliate, or from representing an officer, director, or employee of the corporation or an affiliate in any matter arising in connection with the course and scope of the employment of the officer, director, or employee. Notwithstanding the provisions of this subsection, the attorney providing such representation shall be governed by and subject to all of the Rules of Professional Conduct of the North Carolina State Bar to the same extent as all other attorneys licensed by this State. (1931, c. 157, s. 2; 1937, c. 155, s. 2; 1955, c. 526, s. 2; 1969, c. 718, s. 20; 1971, c. 747; 1997-203, s. 1; 2000-178, s. 8; 2011-401, s. 3.5.)

§ 84-5.1. Rendering of legal services by certain nonprofit corporations.

(a) Subject to the rules and regulations of the North Carolina State Bar, as approved by the Supreme Court of North Carolina, a nonprofit corporation, tax exempt under 26 U.S.C. § 501(c)(3), organized or authorized under Chapter 55A of the General Statutes of North Carolina and operating as a public interest law firm as defined by the applicable Internal Revenue Service guidelines or for the primary purpose of rendering indigent legal services, may render such services provided by attorneys duly licensed to practice law in North Carolina, for the purposes for which the nonprofit corporation was organized. The nonprofit corporation must have a governing structure that does not permit an individual or group of individuals other than an attorney duly licensed to practice law in North Carolina to control the manner or course of the legal services rendered and must continually satisfy the criteria established by the Internal Revenue Service for 26 U.S.C. § 501(c)(3) status, whether or not any action has been taken to revoke that status.

(b) In no instance may legal services rendered by a nonprofit corporation under subsection (a) of this section be conditioned upon the purchase or payment for any product, good, or service other than the legal service rendered. (1977, c. 841, s. 1; 2009-231, s. 1.)

§ 84-6. Exacting fee for conducting foreclosures prohibited to all except licensed attorneys.

It shall be unlawful to exact, charge, or receive any attorney's fee for the foreclosure of any mortgage under power of sale, unless the foreclosure is conducted by licensed attorney-at-law of North Carolina, and unless the full amount charged as attorney's fee is actually paid to and received and retained by such attorney, without being directly or indirectly shared with or rebated to anyone else, and it shall be unlawful for any such attorney to make any showing that he has received such a fee unless he has received the same, or to share with or rebate to any other person, firm, or corporation such fee or any part thereof received by him; but such attorney may divide such fee with another licensed attorney-at-law maintaining his own place of business and not an officer or employee of the foreclosing party, if such attorney has assisted in performing the services for which the fee is paid, or resides in a place other than that where the foreclosure proceedings are conducted, and has forwarded the case to the attorney conducting such foreclosure. (1931, c. 157, s. 3.)

§ 84-7. District attorneys, upon application, to bring injunction or criminal proceedings.

The district attorney of any of the superior courts shall, upon the application of any member of the Bar, or of any bar association, of the State of North Carolina, bring such action in the name of the State as may be proper to enjoin any such person, corporation, or association of persons who it is alleged are violating the provisions of G.S. 84-4 to 84-8, and it shall be the duty of the district attorneys of this State to indict any person, corporation, or association of persons upon the receipt of information of the violation of the provisions of G.S. 84-4 to 84-8. (1931, c. 157, s. 4; 1973, c. 47, s. 2.)

§ 84-7.1. Legal clinics of law schools and certain law students and lawyers excepted.

The provisions of G.S. 84-4 through G.S. 84-6 shall not apply to any of the following:

(1) Any law school conducting a legal clinic and receiving as its clientage only those persons unable financially to compensate for legal advice or services rendered and any law student permitted by the North Carolina State Bar to act as a legal intern in such a legal clinic.

(2) Any law student permitted by the North Carolina State Bar to act as a legal intern for a federal, State, or local government agency.

(3) Any lawyer licensed by another state and permitted by the North Carolina State Bar to represent indigent clients on a pro bono basis under the supervision of active members employed by nonprofit corporations qualified to render legal services pursuant to G.S. 84-5.1. This provision does not apply to a lawyer whose license has been suspended or revoked in any state. (2011-336, s. 5.)

§ 84-8. Punishment for violations.

(a) Any person, corporation, or association of persons violating any of the provisions of G.S. 84-4 through G.S. 84-6 or G.S. 84-9 shall be guilty of a Class 1 misdemeanor.

(b) No person shall be entitled to collect any fee for services performed in violation of G.S. 84-4 through G.S. 84-6, G.S. 84-9, or G.S. 84-10.1. (1931, c. 157, s. 5; c. 347; 1993, c. 539, s. 597; 1994, Ex. Sess., c. 24, s. 14(c); 2007-200, s. 3; 2011-336, s. 4.)

§ 84-9. Unlawful for anyone except attorney to appear for creditor in insolvency and certain other proceedings.

It shall be unlawful for any corporation, or any firm or other association of persons other than a law firm, or for any individual other than an attorney duly licensed to practice law, to appear for another in any bankruptcy or insolvency proceeding, or in any action or proceeding for or growing out of the appointment of a receiver, or in any matter involving an assignment for the benefit of creditors, or to present or vote any claim of another, whether under an assignment or transfer of such claim or in any other manner, in any of the actions, proceedings or matters hereinabove set out. (1931, c. 208, s. 2.)

§ 84-10: Repealed by Session Laws 2011-336, s. 6, effective December 1, 2011, and applicable to offenses committed on or after December 1, 2011.

§ 84-10.1. Private cause of action for the unauthorized practice of law.

If any person knowingly violates any of the provisions of G.S. 84-4 through G.S. 84-6 or G.S. 84-9, fraudulently holds himself or herself out as a North Carolina certified paralegal by use of the designations set forth in G.S. 84-37(a), or knowingly aids and abets another person to commit the unauthorized practice of law, in addition to any other liability imposed pursuant to this Chapter or any other applicable law, any person who is damaged by the unlawful acts set out in this section shall be entitled to maintain a private cause of action to recover damages and reasonable attorneys' fees. (2011-336, s. 7.)

Article 2.

Relation to Client.

§ 84-11. Authority filed or produced if requested.

Every attorney who claims to enter an appearance for any person shall, upon being required so to do, produce and file in the clerk's office of the court in which he claims to enter an appearance, a power or authority to that effect signed by the persons or some one of them for whom he is about to enter an appearance, or by some person duly authorized in that behalf, otherwise he shall not be allowed so to do: Provided, that when any attorney claims to enter an appearance by virtue of a letter to him directed (whether such letter purport a general or particular employment), and it is necessary for him to retain the letter in his own possession, he shall, on the production of said letter setting forth such employment, be allowed to enter his appearance, and the clerk shall make a note to that effect upon the docket. (R.C., c. 31, s. 57; Code, s. 29; Rev., s. 213; C.S., s. 200.)

§ 84-12. Failure to file complaint, attorney liable for costs.

When a plaintiff is compelled to pay the costs of his suit in consequence of a failure on the part of his attorney to file his complaint in proper time, he may sue such attorney for all the costs by him so paid, and the receipt of the clerk may be given in evidence in support of such claim. (1786, c. 253, s. 6; R.C., c. 9, s. 5; Code, s. 22; Rev., s. 214; C.S., s. 201.)

§ 84-13. Fraudulent practice, attorney liable in double damages.

If any attorney commits any fraudulent practice, he shall be liable in an action to the party injured, and on the verdict passing against him, judgment shall be given for the plaintiff to recover double damages. (1743, c. 37; R.C., c. 9, s. 6; Code, s. 23; Rev., s. 215; C. S., s. 202.)

Article 3.

Arguments.

§ 84-14: Recodified as § 7A-97 by Session Laws 1995, c. 431, s. 7.

Article 4.

North Carolina State Bar.

§ 84-15. Creation of North Carolina State Bar as an agency of the State.

There is hereby created as an agency of the State of North Carolina, for the purposes and with the powers hereinafter set forth, the North Carolina State Bar. (1933, c. 210, s. 1.)

§ 84-16. Membership and privileges.

The membership of the North Carolina State Bar shall consist of two classes, active and inactive.

The active members shall be all persons who have obtained a license or certificate, entitling them to practice law in the State of North Carolina, who have paid the membership dues specified, and who have satisfied all other obligations of membership. No person other than a member of the North Carolina State Bar shall practice in any court of the State except foreign attorneys as provided by statute and natural persons representing themselves.

Inactive members shall be:

(1)   All persons who have obtained a license to practice law in the State but who have been found by the Council to be not engaged in the practice of law and not holding themselves out as practicing attorneys and not occupying any public or private positions in which they may be called upon to give legal advice or counsel or to examine the law or to pass upon, adjudicate, or offer an opinion concerning the legal effect of any act, document, or law.

(2)   Persons allowed by the Council solely to represent indigent clients on a pro bono basis under the supervision of an active member employed by a nonprofit corporation qualified to render legal services pursuant to G.S. 84-5.1.

All active members shall be required to pay annual membership fees, and shall have the right to vote in elections held by the district bar in the judicial district in which the member resides. If a member desires to vote with the bar of some district in which the member practices, other than that in which the member resides, the member may do so by filing with the Secretary of the North Carolina State Bar a statement in writing that the member desires to vote in the other district; provided, however, that in no case shall the member be entitled to vote in more than one district. (1933, c. 210, s. 2; 1939, c. 21, s. 1; 1941, c. 344, ss. 1, 2, 3; 1969, c. 44, s. 60; c. 1190, s. 52; 1973, c. 1152, s. 1; 1981, c. 788, s. 2; 1983, c. 589, s. 1; 1985, c. 621; 1995, c. 431, s. 8; 2007-200, s. 1.)

§ 84-17. Government.

The government of the North Carolina State Bar is vested in a council of the North Carolina State Bar referred to in this Chapter as the "Council." The Council shall be composed of a variable number of councilors equal to the number of judicial districts plus 16, the officers of the North Carolina State Bar, who shall be councilors during their respective terms of office, and each retiring president of the North Carolina State Bar who shall be a councilor for one year from the date of expiration of his term as president. Notwithstanding any other provisions of the law, the North Carolina State Bar may borrow money and may acquire, hold, rent, encumber, alienate, lease, and otherwise deal with real or personal property in the same manner as any private person or corporation, subject only to the approval of the Governor and the Council of State as to the borrowing of money and the acquisition, rental, encumbering, leasing and sale of real property. The Council shall be competent to exercise the entire powers of the North Carolina State Bar in respect of the interpretation and administration of this Article, the borrowing of money, the acquisition, lease, sale, or mortgage of property, real or personal, the seeking of amendments to this Chapter, and all other matters. There shall be one councilor from each judicial district and 16 additional councilors. The additional councilors shall be allocated and reallocated by the North Carolina State Bar every six years based on the number of active members of each judicial district bar according to the records of the North Carolina State Bar and in accordance with a formula to be adopted by the North Carolina State Bar, to insure an allocation based on lawyer population of each judicial district bar as it relates to the total number of active members of the State Bar.

A councilor whose seat has been eliminated due to a reallocation shall continue to serve on the Council until expiration of the remainder of the current term. A councilor whose judicial district is altered by the General Assembly during the councilor's term shall continue to serve on the Council until the expiration of the term and shall represent the district wherein the councilor resides or with which the councilor has elected to be affiliated. If before the alteration of the judicial district of the councilor the judicial district included both the place of residence and the place of practice of the councilor, and if after the alteration of the judicial district the councilor's place of residence and place of practice are located in different districts, the councilor must, not later than 10 days from the effective date of the alteration of the district, notify the Secretary of the North Carolina State Bar of an election to affiliate with and represent either the councilor's district of residence or district of practice.

In addition to the councilors, there shall be three public members not licensed to practice law in this or any other state who shall be appointed by the Governor. The public members may vote and participate in all matters before the Council to the same extent as councilors elected or appointed from the various judicial districts. (1933, c. 210, s. 3; 1937, c. 51, s. 1; 1955, c. 651, s. 1; 1961, c. 641; 1973, c. 1152, s. 2; 1977, c. 841, s. 2; 1979, c. 570, ss. 1, 2; 1981, c. 788, s. 3; 1985, c. 60, s. 1; 1987, c. 316, s. 1; 1995, c. 431, s. 9; 2007-200, s. 2; 2009-82, s. 1.)

§ 84-18. Terms, election and appointment of councilors.

(a) Except as set out in this section, the terms of councilors are fixed at three years commencing on the first day of January in the year following their election. A year shall be the calendar year. No councilor may serve more than three successive three-year terms but a councilor may serve an unlimited number of three successive three-year terms provided a three-year period of nonservice intervenes in each instance. Any councilor serving a partial term of 18 months or more is considered to have served a full term and shall be eligible to be elected to only two successive three-year terms in addition to the partial term. Any councilor serving a partial term of less than 18 months is eligible to be elected to three successive three-year terms in addition to the partial term. This paragraph shall not apply to officers of the State Bar.

The secretary of a judicial district bar shall notify the secretary-treasurer of the State Bar in writing of any additions to or deletions from the delegation of councilors representing the district within 90 days of the effective date of the change. No new councilor shall assume a seat until official notice of the election has been given to the secretary-treasurer of the State Bar.

Any active member of the North Carolina State Bar is eligible to serve as a councilor from the judicial district in which the member is eligible to vote.

(b) The Council may promulgate rules to govern the election and appointment of councilors. The election and appointment of councilors shall be as follows:

Each judicial district bar shall elect one eligible North Carolina State Bar member for each Council vacancy in the district. Any vacancy occurring after the election, whether caused by resignation, death, reconfiguration of the district by the General Assembly, or otherwise shall be filled by the judicial district bar in which the vacancy occurs. The appointment shall be for the unexpired portion of the term and shall be certified to the Council by the judicial district bar. Any appointed councilor shall be subject to the terms set forth in subsection (a) of G.S. 84-18.

(c) Public members shall serve three-year terms. No public member shall serve more than two complete consecutive terms. The Secretary of the North Carolina State Bar shall promptly inform the Governor when any seat occupied by a public member becomes vacant. The successor shall serve the remainder of the term. Any public member serving a partial term of 18 months or more is considered to have served a full term and is eligible to be elected to only one additional three-year term in addition to the partial term. Any public member serving a partial term of less than 18 months is eligible to be elected to two successive three-year terms in addition to the partial term. (1933, c. 210, s. 4; 1953, c. 1310, s. 1; 1979, c. 570, s. 3; 1981, c. 788, s. 4; 1985, c. 60, ss. 2, 3; 1987, c. 316, s. 2; 1995, c. 431, s. 10.)

§ 84-18.1. Membership and fees of district bars.

(a) The district bar shall be a subdivision of the North Carolina State Bar subject to the general supervisory authority of the Council and may adopt rules, regulations and bylaws that are not inconsistent with this Article. A copy of any rules, regulations and bylaws that are adopted, along with any subsequent amendments, shall be transmitted to the Secretary-Treasurer of the North Carolina State Bar.

(b) Any district bar may from time to time by a majority vote of the members present at a duly called meeting prescribe an annual membership fee to be paid by its active members as a service charge to promote and maintain its administration, activities and programs. The fee shall be in addition to, but shall not exceed, the amount of the membership fee prescribed by G.S. 84-34 for active members of the North Carolina State Bar. The district bar may also charge a late fee, which shall not exceed fifteen dollars ($15.00), for the failure to pay judicial district bar dues on time. The district bar shall mail a written notice to every active member of the district bar at least 30 days before any meeting at which an election is held to impose or increase mandatory district bar dues. Every active member of a district bar which has prescribed an annual membership fee shall keep its secretary-treasurer notified of his correct mailing address and shall pay the prescribed fee at the time and place set forth in the demand for payment mailed to him by its secretary-treasurer. The name of each active member of a district bar who is more than 12 full calendar months in arrears in the payment of any fee shall be furnished by the secretary-treasurer of the district bar to the Council. In the exercise of its powers as set forth in G.S. 84-23, the Council shall thereupon take disciplinary or other action with reference to the delinquent as it considers necessary and proper. (1969, c. 241; 1983, c. 390, s. 1; 1995, c. 431, s. 11; 2005-396, s. 2.)

§ 84-19. Judicial districts definition.

For purposes of this Article, the term "judicial district" refers to prosecutorial districts established by the General Assembly and includes the High Point Superior Court District as described under G.S. 7A-41(b)(13). The term "district bar" means the bar of a judicial district as defined by this section. (1933, c. 210, s. 5; 1955, c. 651, s. 2; 1979, c. 570, s. 4; 1987, c. 316, s. 3; 1995, c. 431, s. 12; 2011-28, s. 1.)

§ 84-20. Compensation of councilors.

The members of the Council and members of committees when actually engaged in the performance of their duties, including committees sitting upon disbarment proceedings, shall receive as compensation for the time spent in attending meetings an amount to be determined by the Council, subject to approval of the North Carolina Supreme Court, and shall receive actual expenses of travel and subsistence while engaged in their duties provided that for transportation by use of private automobile the expense of travel shall not exceed the business standard mileage rate set by the Internal Revenue Service per mile of travel. The Council shall determine per diem and mileage to be paid. The allowance fixed by the Council shall be paid by the secretary-treasurer of the North Carolina State Bar upon presentation of appropriate documentation by each member. (1933, c. 210, s. 6; 1935, c. 34; 1953, c. 1310, s. 2; 1971, c. 13, s. 1; 1995, c. 431, s. 13; 2006-66, s. 22.23; 2006-221, s. 24.)

§ 84-21. Organization of Council; publication of rules, regulations and bylaws.

(a) The Council shall adopt the rules pursuant to G.S. 45A-9.

(b) The rules and regulations adopted by the Council under this Article may be amended by the Council from time to time in any manner not inconsistent with this Article. Copies of all rules and regulations and of all amendments adopted by the Council shall be certified to the Chief Justice of the Supreme Court of North Carolina, entered by the North Carolina Supreme Court upon its minutes, and published in the next ensuing number of the North Carolina Reports and in the North Carolina Administrative Code: Provided, that the court may decline to have so entered upon its minutes any rules, regulations and amendments which in the opinion of the Chief Justice are inconsistent with this Article. (1933, c. 210, s. 7; 1991, c. 418, s. 7; 1995, c. 431, s. 14; 2011-336, s. 8.)

§ 84-22. Officers and committees of the North Carolina State Bar.

The officers of the North Carolina State Bar and the Council shall consist of a president, president-elect, vice-president and an immediate past president, who shall be deemed members of the Council in all respects. The president, president-elect and vice-president need not be members of the Council at the time of their election. There shall be a secretary-treasurer who shall also have the title of executive director, but who shall not be a member of the Council. All officers shall be elected annually by the Council at an election to take place at the annual meeting of the North Carolina State Bar. The regular term of all officers is one year. The Council is the judge of the election and qualifications of its members.

In addition to the committees and commissions as may be specifically established or authorized by law, the North Carolina State Bar may have committees, standing or special, as from time to time the Council deems appropriate for the proper discharge of the duties and functions of the North Carolina State Bar. The Council shall determine the number of members, composition, method of appointment or election, functions, powers and duties, structure, authority to act, and other matters relating to each committee. Any committee may, at the discretion of the appointing or electing authority, be composed of Council members or members of the North Carolina State Bar who are not members of the Council, or of lay persons, or of any combination. (1933,

c. 210, s. 8; 1941, c. 344, ss. 4, 5; 1973, c. 1152, s. 3; 1979, c. 570, s. 5; 1995, c. 431, s. 15.)

§ 84-23. Powers of Council.

(a)   The Council is vested, as an agency of the State, with the authority to regulate the professional conduct of licensed lawyers and State Bar certified paralegals. Among other powers, the Council shall administer this Article; take actions that are necessary to ensure the competence of lawyers and State Bar certified paralegals; formulate and adopt rules of professional ethics and conduct; investigate and prosecute matters of professional misconduct; grant or deny petitions for reinstatement; resolve questions pertaining to membership status; arbitrate disputes concerning legal fees; certify legal specialists and paralegals and charge fees to applicants and participants necessary to administer these certification programs; determine whether a member is disabled; maintain an annual registry of interstate and international law firms doing business in this State; and formulate and adopt procedures for accomplishing these purposes. The Council may do all things necessary in the furtherance of the purposes of this Article that are not otherwise prohibited by law.

(b)   The Council or any committee of the Council, including the Client Security Fund and the Disciplinary Hearing Commission or any committee of the Commission, may subpoena financial records of any licensed lawyers, lawyers whose licenses have been suspended, or disbarred lawyers, relating to any account into which client or fiduciary funds have been deposited.

(c)   The Council may publish an official journal concerning matters of interest to the legal profession.

(d)   The Council may acquire, hold, rent, encumber, alienate, lease, and otherwise deal with real or personal property in the same manner as any private person or corporation, subject only to the approval of the Governor and the Council of State as to the acquisition, rental, encumbering, leasing and sale of real property. The Council may borrow money upon its bonds, notes, debentures, or other evidences of indebtedness sold through public or private sale pursuant to a loan agreement or a trust agreement or indenture with a trustee, with such borrowing either unsecured or secured by a mortgage on the Council's interest in real or personal property, and engage and contract with attorneys, underwriters, financial advisors, and other parties as necessary for such borrowing, with such borrowing and security subject to the approval of the Governor and the Council of State. The Council may utilize the services of the Purchase and Contract Division of the Department of Administration to procure personal property, in accordance with the provisions of Article 3 of Chapter 143 of the General Statutes. However, the Council shall: (i) submit all proposed contracts for supplies, materials, printing, equipment, and contractual services that exceed one million dollars ($1,000,000) authorized by this subsection to the Attorney General or the Attorney General's designee for review as provided in G.S. 114-8.3; and (ii) include in all contracts to be awarded by the Council under this subsection a standard clause which provides that the State Auditor and internal auditors of the Council may audit the records of the contractor during and after the term of the contract to verify accounts and data affecting fees and performance. The Council shall not award a cost plus percentage of cost agreement or contract for any purpose. (1933, c. 210, s. 9; 1935, c. 74, s. 1; 1937, c. 51, s. 2; 1975, c. 582, s. 3; 1977, c. 841, s. 2; 1995, c. 431, s. 16; 2003-116, s. 2; 2004-174, s. 1; 2005-396, s. 4; 2009-82, s. 2; 2010-194, s. 12; 2011-326, s. 15(l).)

§ 84-23.1. Prepaid legal services.

(a) This section is in addition to and not a limitation of the powers and responsibilities of the council set out in G.S. 84-23. To the extent that this section deals with the same powers and responsibilities it shall be taken to be in amplification of those powers and not in derogation thereof.

(b) Repealed by Session Laws 1991, c. 210, s. 1.

(b1) All organizations offering prepaid legal services plans shall register those plans with the North Carolina State Bar Council on forms provided by the Council. Each plan shall be registered prior to its implementation or operation in this State and shall renew its registration with the State Bar annually.

(b2) Every plan shall pay an administrative fee to the Council for the initial registration and an annual renewal fee in amounts determined by the Council.

(c) Repealed by Session Laws 1991, c. 210, s. 1.

(d) Notwithstanding registration of the plan with the North Carolina State Bar Council pursuant to subsection (b1), any plan for prepaid legal services is subject to regulation under Chapter 58 of the General Statutes if offered by a company engaged in the insurance business or if the plan itself constitutes the offering of insurance.

(e) Repealed by Session Laws 1991, c. 210, s. 1. (1975, c. 707, s. 1; 1991, c. 210, s. 1; 2005-396, ss. 5, 6.)

§ 84-24. Admission to practice.

For the purpose of examining applicants and providing rules and regulations for admission to the Bar including the issuance of license therefor, there is hereby created the Board of Law Examiners, which shall consist of 11 members of the Bar, elected by the Council, who need not be members of the Council. No teacher in any law school, however, shall be eligible. The members of the Board of Law Examiners elected from the Bar shall each hold office for a term of three years.

The Board of Law Examiners shall elect a member of the Board as chair thereof, and the Board may employ an executive secretary and provide such assistance as may be required to enable the Board to perform its duties promptly and properly. The chair and any employees shall serve for a period of time determined by the Board.

The examination shall be held in the manner and at the times as the Board of Law Examiners may determine.

The Board of Law Examiners shall have full power and authority to make or cause to be made such examinations and investigations as may be deemed by it necessary to satisfy it that the applicants for admission to the Bar possess the qualifications of character and general fitness requisite for an attorney and counselor-at-law and to this end the Board of Law Examiners shall have the power of subpoena and to summons and examine witnesses under oath and to compel their attendance and the production of books, papers and other documents and writings deemed by it to be necessary or material to the inquiry and shall also have authority to employ and provide assistance as may be required to enable it to perform its duties promptly and properly. Records, papers, and other documents containing information collected and compiled by the Board or its members or employees as a result of investigations, inquiries, or interviews conducted in connection with examinations or licensing matters, are not public records within the meaning of Chapter 132 of the General Statutes.

All applicants for admission to the Bar shall be fingerprinted to determine whether the applicant has a record of criminal conviction in this State or in any other state or jurisdiction. The information obtained as a result of the fingerprinting of an applicant shall be limited to the official use of the Board of Law Examiners in determining the character and general fitness of the applicant.

The Department of Justice may provide a criminal record check to the Board of Law Examiners for a person who has applied for a license through the Board. The Board shall provide to the Department of Justice, along with the request, the fingerprints of the applicant, any additional information required by the Department of Justice, and a form signed by the applicant consenting to the check of the criminal record and to the use of the fingerprints and other identifying information required by the State or national repositories. The applicant's fingerprints shall be forwarded to the State Bureau of Investigation for a search of the State's criminal history record file, and the State Bureau of Investigation shall forward a set of the fingerprints to the Federal Bureau of Investigation for a national criminal history check. The Board shall keep all information pursuant to this subsection privileged, in accordance with applicable State law and federal guidelines, and the information shall be confidential and shall not be a public record under Chapter 132 of the General Statutes.

The Department of Justice may charge each applicant a fee for conducting the checks of criminal history records authorized by this section.

The Board of Law Examiners, subject to the approval of the Council, shall by majority vote, from time to time, make, alter, and amend such rules and regulations for admission to the Bar as in their judgment shall promote the welfare of the State and the profession: Provided, that any change in the educational requirements for admission to the Bar shall not become effective within two years from the date of the adoption of the change.

All rules and regulations, and modifications, alterations and amendments thereof, shall be recorded and promulgated as provided in G.S. 84-21 in relation to the certificate of organization and the rules and regulations of the Council.

Whenever the Council shall order the restoration of license to any person as authorized by G.S. 84-32, it shall be the duty of the Board of Law Examiners to issue a written license to the person, noting thereon that the license is issued in compliance with an order of the Council, whether the license to practice law was issued by the Board of Law Examiners or the Supreme Court in the first instance.

Appeals from the Board shall be had in accordance with rules or procedures as may be approved by the Supreme Court as may be submitted under G.S. 84-21 or as may be promulgated by the Supreme Court. (1933, c. 210, s. 10; c. 331; 1935, cc. 33, 61; 1941, c. 344, s. 6; 1947, c. 77; 1951, c. 991, s. 1; 1953, c. 1012; 1965, cc. 65, 725; 1973, c. 13; 1977, c. 841, s. 2; 1983, c. 177; 1991, c. 210, s. 4; 1995, c. 431, s. 17; 2002-147, s. 5.)

§ 84-25. Fees of applicants.

All applicants before the Board of Law Examiners shall pay such fees as prescribed under the rules of said Board as may be promulgated under G.S. 84-21 and 84-24. (1935, c. 33, s. 1; 1955, c. 651, s. 3.)

§ 84-26. Expenses of Board of Law Examiners.

Notwithstanding G.S. 93B-5(b), each member of the Board of Law Examiners shall receive the member's actual expenses of travel and subsistence while engaged in duties assigned to the member; provided, however, that for transportation by the use of private automobile the expense of that transportation shall be the same as paid other boards and commissions by the State. (1935, c. 33, s. 2; 1937, c. 35; 1953, c. 1310, s. 3; 1971, c. 13, s. 2; 1973, c. 1368; 2013-9, s. 1.)

§ 84-27. Repealed by Session Laws 1945, c. 782.

§ 84-28. Discipline and disbarment.

(a) Any attorney admitted to practice law in this State is subject to the disciplinary jurisdiction of the Council under such rules and procedures as the Council shall adopt as provided in G.S. 84-23.

(b) The following acts or omissions by a member of the North Carolina State Bar or any attorney admitted for limited practice under G.S. 84-4.1, individually or in concert with any other person or persons, shall constitute misconduct and shall be grounds for discipline whether the act or omission occurred in the course of an attorney-client relationship or otherwise:

(1) Conviction of, or a tender and acceptance of a plea of guilty or no contest to, a criminal offense showing professional unfitness;

(2) The violation of the Rules of Professional Conduct adopted and promulgated by the Council in effect at the time of the act;

(3) Knowing misrepresentation of any facts or circumstances surrounding any complaint, allegation or charge of misconduct; failure to answer any formal inquiry or complaint issued by or in the name of the North Carolina State Bar in any disciplinary matter; or contempt of the Council or any committee of the North Carolina State Bar.

(c) Misconduct by any attorney shall be grounds for:

(1) Disbarment;

(2) Suspension for a period up to but not exceeding five years, any portion of which may be stayed upon reasonable conditions to which the offending attorney consents;

(3) Censure - A censure is a written form of discipline more serious than a reprimand issued in cases in which an attorney has violated one or more provisions of the Rules of Professional Conduct and has caused significant harm or potential significant harm to a client, the administration of justice, the profession or members of the public, but the protection of the public does not require suspension of the attorney's license;

(4) Reprimand - A reprimand is a written form of discipline more serious than an admonition issued in cases in which an attorney has violated one or more provisions of the Rules of Professional Conduct, but the protection of the

public does not require a censure. A reprimand is generally reserved for cases in which the attorney's conduct has caused harm or potential harm to a client, the administration of justice, the profession, or members of the public; or

(5)   Admonition - An admonition is a written form of discipline imposed in cases in which an attorney has committed a minor violation of the Rules of Professional Conduct.

Any order disbarring or suspending an attorney may impose reasonable conditions precedent to reinstatement. No attorney who has been disbarred by the Disciplinary Hearing Commission, the Council, or by order of any court of this State may seek reinstatement to the practice of law prior to five years from the effective date of the order of disbarment. Any order of the Disciplinary Hearing Commission or the Grievance Committee imposing an admonition, reprimand, censure, or stayed suspension may also require the attorney to complete a reasonable amount of continuing legal education in addition to the minimum amount required by the North Carolina Supreme Court.

(d)   Any attorney admitted to practice law in this State, who is convicted of or has tendered and has had accepted, a plea of guilty or no contest to, a criminal offense showing professional unfitness, may be disciplined based upon the conviction, without awaiting the outcome of any appeals of the conviction. An order of discipline based solely upon a conviction of a criminal offense showing professional unfitness shall be vacated immediately upon receipt by the Secretary of the North Carolina State Bar of a certified copy of a judgment or order reversing the conviction. The fact that the attorney's criminal conviction has been overturned on appeal shall not prevent the North Carolina State Bar from conducting a disciplinary proceeding against the attorney based upon the same underlying facts or events that were the subject of the criminal proceeding.

(d1)   An attorney who is disciplined as provided in subsection (d) of this section may petition the court in the trial division in the judicial district where the conviction occurred for an order staying the disciplinary action pending the outcome of any appeals of the conviction. The court may grant or deny the stay in its discretion upon such terms as it deems proper. A stay of the disciplinary action by the court shall not prevent the North Carolina State Bar from going forward with a disciplinary proceeding against the attorney based upon the same underlying facts or events that were the subject of the criminal proceeding.

(e) Any attorney admitted to practice law in this State who is disciplined in another jurisdiction shall be subject to the same discipline in this State: Provided, that the discipline imposed in the other jurisdiction does not exceed that provided for in subsection (c) above and that the attorney was not deprived of due process in the other jurisdiction.

(f) Upon application by the North Carolina State Bar, misconduct by an attorney admitted to practice in this State may be restrained or enjoined where the necessity for prompt action exists regardless of whether a disciplinary proceeding in the matter of the conduct is pending. The application shall be filed in the Superior Court of Wake County and shall be governed by the procedure set forth in G.S. 1A-1, Rule 65.

(g) Any member of the North Carolina State Bar may be transferred to disability inactive status for mental incompetence, physical disability, or substance abuse interfering with the attorney's ability to competently engage in the practice of law under the rules and procedures the Council adopts pursuant to G.S. 84-23.

(h) There shall be an appeal of right by either party from any final order of the Disciplinary Hearing Commission to the North Carolina Court of Appeals. Review by the appellate division shall be upon matters of law or legal inference. The procedures governing any appeal shall be as provided by statute or court rule for appeals in civil cases. A final order which imposes disbarment or suspension for 18 months or more shall not be stayed except upon application, under the rules of the Court of Appeals, for a writ of supersedeas. A final order imposing suspension for less than 18 months or any other discipline except disbarment shall be stayed pending determination of any appeal of right.

(i) The North Carolina State Bar may invoke the process of the General Court of Justice to enforce the powers of the Council or any committee to which the Council delegates its authority.

(j) The North Carolina State Bar may apply to appropriate courts for orders necessary to protect the interests of clients of missing, suspended, disbarred, disabled, or deceased attorneys.

The senior regular resident judge of the superior court of any district wherein a member of the North Carolina State Bar resides or maintains an office shall have the authority and power to enter orders necessary to protect the interests of the clients, including the authority to order the payment of compensation by the member or the estate of a deceased or disabled member to any attorney appointed to administer or conserve the law practice of the member. Compensation awarded to a member serving under this section awarded from the estate of a deceased member shall be considered an administrative expense of the estate for purposes of determining priority of payment. (1933, c. 210, s. 11; 1937, c. 51, s. 3; 1959, c. 1282, ss. 1, 2; 1961, c. 1075; 1969, c. 44, s. 61; 1975, c. 582, s. 5; 1979, c. 570, ss. 6, 7; 1983, c. 390, ss. 2, 3; 1985, c. 167; 1987, c. 316, s. 4; 1989, c. 172, s. 2; 1991, c. 210, s. 5; 1995, c. 431, s. 18; 2005-237, s. 1.)

§ 84-28.1. Disciplinary hearing commission.

(a) There shall be a disciplinary hearing commission of the North Carolina State Bar which shall consist of 20 members. Twelve of these members shall be members of the North Carolina State Bar, and shall be appointed by the Council. The other eight shall be citizens of North Carolina not licensed to practice law in this or any other state, four of whom shall be appointed by the Governor, two by the General Assembly upon the recommendation of the President Pro Tempore of the Senate in accordance with G.S. 120-121, and two by the General Assembly upon the recommendation of the Speaker of the House of Representatives in accordance with G.S. 120-121. The Council shall designate one of its appointees as chair and another as vice-chair. The chair shall have actively practiced law in the courts of the State for at least 10 years. Except as set out herein, the terms of members of the commission are set at three years commencing on the first day of July of the year of their appointment. The Council, the Governor, and the General Assembly respectively, shall appoint members to fill unexpired terms when vacancies are created by resignation, disqualification, disability or death, except that vacancies in appointments made by the General Assembly may also be filled as provided by G.S. 120-122. No member may serve more than a total of seven years or a one-year term and two consecutive three-year terms: Provided, that any member or former member who is designated chair may serve one additional three-year term in that capacity. No member of the Council may be appointed to the commission.

(b) The disciplinary hearing commission of the North Carolina State Bar, or any committee of the disciplinary hearing commission, may hold hearings in discipline, incapacity and disability matters, make findings of fact and conclusions of law after these hearings, enter orders necessary to carry out the duties delegated to it by the Council, and tax the costs to an attorney who is disciplined or is found to be incapacitated or disabled.

(b1) The disciplinary hearing commission of the North Carolina State Bar, or any committee thereof, acting through its chairman, shall have the power to hold persons, firms or corporations in contempt as provided in Chapter 5A.

(c) Members of the disciplinary hearing commission shall receive the same per diem and travel expenses as are authorized for members of State commissions under G.S. 138-5. (1975, c. 582, s. 6; 1979, c. 570, s. 8; 1983, c. 390, s. 4; 1995, c. 431, s. 19; c. 490, s. 51; 2003-116, s. 3; 2005-396, s. 3.)

§ 84-28.2. Persons immune from suit.

Persons shall be immune from suit for all statements made without malice, and intended for transmittal to the North Carolina State Bar or any board, committee, officer, agent or employee thereof, or given in any investigation or proceedings, pertaining to alleged misconduct or disability or to reinstatement of an attorney. The protection of this immunity does not exist, however, as to statements made to others not intended for this use. (1975, c. 582, s. 4; 1995, c. 431, s. 20.)

§ 84-29. Evidence and witnesses.

In any investigation of charges of professional misconduct or disability or in petitions for reinstatement, the Council and any committee thereof, and the disciplinary hearing commission, and any committee thereof, may administer oaths and affirmations and shall have the power to subpoena and examine witnesses under oath, and to compel their attendance, and the production of books, papers and other documents or writings deemed by it necessary or material to the inquiry. Each subpoena shall be issued under the hand of the secretary-treasurer or the president of the Council or the chair of the committee appointed to hear the charges, and shall have the force and effect of a summons or subpoena issued by a court of record, and any witness or other person who shall refuse or neglect to appear in obedience thereto, or to testify or produce the books, papers, or other documents or writings required, shall be liable to punishment for contempt either by the Council or its committee or a hearing committee of the disciplinary hearing commission through its chair pursuant to the procedures set out in Chapter 5A of the General Statutes, but with the right to appeal therefrom. Depositions may be taken in any investigations of professional misconduct as in civil proceedings, but the Council or the committee hearing the case may, in its discretion, whenever it believes that the ends of substantial justice so require, direct that any witness within the State be brought before it. Witnesses giving testimony under a subpoena before the Council or any committee thereof, or the disciplinary hearing commission or any committee thereof, or by deposition, shall be entitled to the same fees as in civil actions.

In cases heard before the Council or any committee thereof or the disciplinary hearing commission or any committee thereof, if the party shall be convicted of the charges, the party shall be taxed with the cost of the hearings: Provided, however, that the bill of costs shall not include any compensation to the members of the Council or committee before whom the hearings are conducted. (1933, c. 210, s. 12; 1959, c. 1282, s. 2; 1975, c. 582, s. 7; 1983, c. 390, s. 6; 1995, c. 431, s. 21.)

§ 84-30. Rights of accused person.

Any person who shall stand charged with an offense cognizable by the council or any committee thereof or the disciplinary hearing commission or any committee thereof shall have the right to invoke and have exercised in his favor the powers of the council or any committee, in respect of compulsory process for witnesses and for the production of books, papers, and other writings and documents, and shall also have the right to be represented by counsel. (1933, c. 210, s. 13; 1959, c. 1282, s. 2; 1975, c. 582, s. 8.)

§ 84-31. Counsel; investigators; powers; compensation.

The Council may appoint a member of the North Carolina State Bar to represent the North Carolina State Bar in any proceedings in which it has an interest including reinstatement and the prosecution of charges of misconduct or disability in the hearings that are held, including appeals, and may authorize counsel to employ assistant counsel, investigators, and administrative assistants in such numbers as it deems necessary. Counsel and investigators engaged in discipline, reinstatement, and disability matters shall have the authority throughout the State to serve subpoenas or other process issued by the Council or any committee thereof or the disciplinary hearing commission or any committee thereof, in the same manner and with the same effect as an officer authorized to serve process of the General Court of Justice. The Council may allow counsel, assistant counsel, investigators and administrative assistants such compensation as it deems proper. (1933, c. 210, s. 14; 1969, c. 44, s. 62; 1975, c. 582, s. 9; 1995, c. 431, s. 22.)

§ 84-32. Records and judgments and their effect; restoration of licenses.

(a) In cases heard by the disciplinary hearing commission or any committee thereof, the proceedings shall be recorded by a certified court reporter and an official copy of all exhibits introduced into evidence shall be made and preserved in the office of the secretary-treasurer. Final judgments of suspension or disbarment shall be entered upon the judgment docket of the superior court in the district wherein the respondent resides or practices law, and also upon the minutes of the Supreme Court of North Carolina; and the judgment shall be effective throughout the State.

(b) Whenever any attorney desires to voluntarily surrender his license, the attorney must tender the license and a written resignation to the Council. The Council, in its discretion, may accept or reject the tender. If the tender is accepted, the Council shall enter an order of disbarment. A copy of any order of disbarment shall be filed with the clerk of the superior court of the county where the respondent resides, maintains an office, or practices law and also upon the minutes of the Supreme Court of North Carolina. The judgment shall be effective throughout the State.

(c) Whenever any attorney has been deprived of the attorney's license by suspension or disbarment, the Council or the disciplinary hearing commission or the secretary-treasurer may, in accordance with rules and regulations prescribed by the Council, restore the license upon due notice being given and satisfactory evidence produced of proper reformation of the suspended or disbarred attorney and of satisfaction of any conditions precedent to restoration.

(d) The Council has jurisdiction to determine any petition seeking the reinstatement of the license of any attorney disbarred or suspended by any court in its inherent power when requested by the court. The proceeding shall be governed by the rules and regulations adopted by the Council. The disbarred or suspended attorney shall satisfy all conditions precedent to reinstatement generally imposed upon attorneys disbarred or suspended by the disciplinary hearing commission or the Council, as well as any conditions imposed by the court. Under no circumstances shall an attorney disbarred by a court or by the North Carolina State Bar be reinstated prior to five years from the effective date of the order of disbarment. (1933, c. 210, s. 15; 1935, c. 74, s. 2; 1953, c. 1310, s. 4; 1959, c. 1282, s. 2; 1975, c. 582, s. 10; 1983, c. 390, s. 5; 1995, c. 431, s. 23.)

§ 84-32.1. Confidentiality of records.

(a) All documents, papers, letters, recordings, electronic records, or other documentary materials, regardless of physical form or characteristic, in the possession of the State Bar or its staff, employees, legal counsel, councilors, and Grievance Committee advisory members concerning any investigation, inquiry, complaint, disability, or disciplinary matter in connection with the State Bar Grievance Committee, the State Bar's Trust Accounting Supervisory Program, or any audit of an attorney trust account shall not be considered public records within the meaning of Chapter 132 of the General Statutes.

(b) All documents, papers, letters, recordings, electronic records, or other documentary materials containing or reflecting the deliberations of the Disciplinary Hearing Commission in disciplinary or disability matters shall not be considered public records within the meaning of Chapter 132 of the General Statutes.

(c) Notwithstanding any other provision of this section, any record, paper, or other document containing information collected and compiled by or on behalf of the State Bar that is admitted as evidence in any hearing before the Disciplinary Hearing Commission, or any court or tribunal, shall be a public record within the meaning of Chapter 132 of the General Statutes unless it is admitted into evidence under seal by order of the Disciplinary Hearing Commission, or the court or tribunal in which the proceeding is held.

(d) All documents, papers, letters, recordings, electronic records, or other documentary materials in the possession of the State Bar or its staff, employees, legal counsel, and Lawyer Assistance Program volunteers, relating in any way to a member's participation or prospective participation in the Lawyer Assistance Program, including, but not limited to, any medical, counseling, substance abuse, or mental health records, shall not be considered public records within the meaning of Chapter 132 of the General Statutes. Neither the State Bar nor any person acting under the authority of the State Bar or of the Lawyer Assistance Program shall be required to produce or testify regarding the contents or existence of such documents. (2011-267, s. 5.)

§ 84-33. Annual and special meetings.

The Council shall hold an annual meeting and other meetings necessary to conduct the business of the North Carolina State Bar. (1933, c. 210, s. 16; 1969, c. 104; 1995, c. 431, s. 24.)

§ 84-34. Membership fees and list of members.

Every active member of the North Carolina State Bar shall, prior to the first day of July of each year, pay to the secretary-treasurer an annual membership fee in an amount determined by the Council but not to exceed three hundred dollars ($300.00), and every member shall notify the secretary-treasurer of the member's correct mailing address. Any member who fails to pay the required dues by the last day of June of each year shall be subject to a late fee in an amount determined by the Council but not to exceed thirty dollars ($30.00). All dues for prior years shall be as were set forth in the General Statutes then in effect. The membership fee shall be regarded as a service charge for the maintenance of the several services authorized by this Article, and shall be in addition to all fees required in connection with admissions to practice, and in addition to all license taxes required by law. The fee shall not be prorated: Provided, that no fee shall be required of an attorney licensed after this Article shall have gone into effect until the first day of January of the calendar year following that in which the attorney was licensed; but this proviso shall not apply to attorneys from other states admitted on certificate. The fees shall be disbursed by the secretary-treasurer on the order of the Council. The secretary-treasurer shall annually, at a time and in a law magazine or daily newspaper to be prescribed by the Council, publish an account of the financial transactions of the Council in a form to be prescribed by it. The secretary-treasurer shall compile and keep currently correct from the names and mailing addresses forwarded to the secretary-treasurer and from any other available sources of information a list of members of the North Carolina State Bar and furnish to the clerk of the superior court in each county, not later than the first day of October in each year, a list showing the name and address of each attorney for that county who has not complied with the provisions of this Article. The name of each of the active members who are in arrears in the payment of membership fees shall be furnished to the presiding judge at the next term of the superior court after the first day of October of each year, by the clerk of the superior court of each county wherein the member or members reside, and the court shall thereupon take action that is necessary and proper. The names and addresses of attorneys so certified shall be kept available to the public. The Secretary of Revenue is hereby directed to supply the secretary-treasurer, from records of license tax payments, with any information for which the secretary-treasurer may call in order to enable the secretary-treasurer to comply with this requirement.

The list submitted to several clerks of the superior court shall also be submitted to the Council at its October meeting of each year and it shall take the action thereon that is necessary and proper. (1933, c. 210, s. 17; 1939, c. 21, ss. 2, 3; 1953, c. 1310, s. 5; 1955, c. 651, s. 4; 1961, c. 760; 1971, c. 18; 1973, c. 476, s. 193; c. 1152, s. 4; 1977, c. 841, s. 2; 1981, c. 788, s. 5; 1989, c. 172, s. 1; 1995, c. 431, s. 25; 2005-237, s. 2; 2005-276, s. 23A.1(a); 2013-360, s. 21.1(b); 2013-381, s. 38.1(d).)

§ 84-34.1. Deposits of the North Carolina State Bar.

Deposits of the North Carolina State Bar, its boards, agencies, and committees shall be secured as provided in G.S. 159-31(b). (1991, c. 210, s. 3.)

§ 84-34.2. Specific statutory authority for certain fees.

In addition to fees the Council is elsewhere authorized to charge and collect, the Council may charge and collect the following fees in amounts determined by the Council:

(1) A reinstatement fee for any attorney seeking reinstatement from inactive status, administrative suspension, or suspension for failure to comply with the annual continuing legal education requirements.

(2) A registration fee and annual renewal fee for an interstate or international law firm.

(3) An attendance fee for continuing legal education programs that may include a fee to support the Chief Justice's Commission on Professionalism.

(4) A late fee for failing to file timely the continuing legal education annual report form, for failure to pay attendance fees, or failure to complete the annual continuing legal education requirements.

(5) An administrative fee for any attorney against whom discipline has been imposed. (2005-396, s. 7.)

§ 84-35. Saving as to North Carolina Bar Association.

Nothing in this Article contained shall be construed as affecting in any way the North Carolina Bar Association, or any local bar association. (1933, c. 210, s. 18.)

§ 84-36. Inherent powers of courts unaffected.

Nothing contained in this Article shall be construed as disabling or abridging the inherent powers of the court to deal with its attorneys. (1937, c. 51, s. 4.)

§ 84-36.1. Clerks of court to certify orders.

The clerk of any court of this State in which a member of the North Carolina State Bar is convicted of any criminal offense, disciplined, found to be in contempt of the court or adjudged incompetent shall transmit a certified copy of the order or judgment to the secretary-treasurer of the North Carolina State Bar within 10 days of the entry of such judgment or order. (1975, c. 582, s. 11.)

§ 84-37. State Bar may investigate and enjoin unauthorized activities.

(a) The Council or any committee appointed by it for that purpose may inquire into and investigate any charges or complaints of (i) unauthorized or unlawful practice of law or (ii) the use of the designations, "North Carolina Certified Paralegal," "North Carolina State Bar Certified Paralegal," or "Paralegal Certified by the North Carolina State Bar Board of Paralegal Certification," by individuals who have not been certified in accordance with the rules adopted by the North Carolina State Bar. The Council may bring or cause to be brought and maintained in the name of the North Carolina State Bar an action or actions, upon information or upon the complaint of any person or entity against any person or entity that engages in rendering any legal service, holds himself or herself out as a North Carolina certified paralegal by use of the designations set forth in this subsection, or makes it a practice or business to render legal services that are unauthorized or prohibited by law. No bond for cost shall be required in the proceeding.

(b) In an action brought under this section, the final judgment if in favor of the plaintiff shall perpetually restrain the defendant or defendants from the commission or continuance of the unauthorized or unlawful act or acts. A temporary injunction to restrain the commission or continuance of the act or acts may be granted upon proof or by affidavit, that the defendant or defendants have violated any of the laws applicable to unauthorized or unlawful practice of law or the unauthorized use of the designations set forth in subsection (a) of this section or any other designation implying certification by the State Bar. The provisions of law relating generally to injunctions as provisional remedies in actions shall apply to a temporary injunction and the proceedings for temporary injunctions.

(c) The venue for actions brought under this section shall be the superior court of any county in which the relevant acts are alleged to have been committed or in which there appear reasonable grounds that they will be committed in the county where the defendants in the action reside, or in Wake County.

(d) The plaintiff in the action shall be entitled to examine the adverse party and witnesses before filing complaint and before trial in the same manner as provided by law for examining parties.

(e) This section shall not repeal or limit any remedy now provided in cases of unauthorized or unlawful practice of law. Nothing contained in this section shall be construed as disabling or abridging the inherent powers of the court in these matters.

(f) The Council or its duly appointed committee may issue advisory opinions in response to inquiries from members or the public regarding whether contemplated conduct would constitute the unauthorized practice of law. (1939, c. 281; 1979, c. 570, s. 9; 1995, c. 431, s. 26; 2004-174, s. 2.)

§ 84-38. Solicitation of retainer or contract for legal services prohibited; division of fees.

It shall be unlawful for any person, firm, corporation, or association or his or their agent, agents, or employees, acting on his or their behalf, to solicit or procure through solicitation either directly or indirectly, any legal business, whether to be performed in this State or elsewhere, or to solicit or procure through solicitation either directly or indirectly, a retainer or contract, written or oral, or any agreement authorizing an attorney or any other person, firm, corporation, or association to perform or render any legal services, whether to be performed in this State or elsewhere.

It shall be unlawful for any person, firm, corporation, or association to divide with or receive from any attorney-at-law, or group of attorneys-at-law, whether practicing in this State or elsewhere, either before or after action is brought, any portion of any fee or compensation charged or received by such attorney-at-law, or any valuable consideration or reward, as an inducement for placing or in consideration of being placed in the hands of such attorney or attorneys-at-law, or in the hands of another person, firm, corporation or association, a claim or demand of any kind, for the purpose of collecting such claim or instituting an action thereon or of representing claimant in the pursuit of any civil remedy for the recovery thereof, or for the settlement or compromise thereof, whether such compromise, settlement, recovery, suit, claim, collection or demand shall be in this State or elsewhere. This paragraph shall not apply to agreements between attorneys to divide compensation received in cases or matters legitimately, lawfully and properly received by them.

Any person, firm, corporation or association of persons violating the provisions of this section shall be guilty of a Class 1 misdemeanor.

The council of the North Carolina State Bar is hereby authorized and empowered to investigate and bring action against persons charged with violations of this section and the provisions as set forth in G.S. 84-37 shall apply. Nothing contained herein shall be construed to supersede the authority of district attorneys to seek injunctive relief or institute criminal proceedings in the same manner as provided for in G.S. 84-7. Nothing herein shall be construed as abridging the inherent powers of the courts to deal with such matters. (1947, c. 573; 1973, c. 47, s. 2; 1993, c. 539, s. 599; 1994, Ex. Sess., c. 24, s. 14(c).)

Chapter 84A.

Foreign Legal Consultants.

§ 84A-1. License to practice as a foreign legal consultant.

(a) The North Carolina Supreme Court may issue a license to practice in the form of a certificate of registration as a foreign legal consultant to any applicant who satisfies all of the following requirements:

(1) Has been admitted to practice as an attorney, or the equivalent thereof, in a foreign country for at least five years as of the date of application for a certificate of registration;

(2) Possesses the character, ethical, and moral qualifications required of a member of the North Carolina State Bar;

(3) Intends to practice in the State as a foreign legal consultant and intends to maintain an office in the State for this practice;

(4) Is at least 21 years of age;

(5) Has been actively and substantially engaged in the practice of law or a profession or occupation that requires admission to the practice of law, or the equivalent thereof, in the foreign country in which the applicant holds a license for at least five of the seven years immediately preceding the date of application for a certificate of registration and is in good standing as an attorney, or the equivalent thereof, in that country; and

(6) Obtains a certificate of registration as a foreign legal consultant pursuant to G.S. 84A-3.

(b) An applicant is not required to take an examination to be licensed under this Chapter.

(c) As used in this section, "foreign country" means any country other than the United States of America. "Foreign country" includes Puerto Rico, Guam, the Virgin Islands, and the possessions of the United States. (1995, c. 427, s. 1.)

§ 84A-2. Application for a certificate of registration.

(a) Any person desiring to obtain a certificate of registration as a foreign legal consultant shall file an application, in duplicate, with the North Carolina State Bar on a form prescribed by the North Carolina State Bar. The application shall be made under oath, and shall contain information relating to the applicant's age, residence, address, citizenship, occupation, general education, legal education, moral character, and any other matters requested by the North Carolina State Bar.

(b) An applicant shall submit two 2-inch by 3-inch photographs of the applicant showing a front view of the applicant's head and shoulders.

(c) The applicant shall submit an application fee required by the North Carolina State Bar with the application. An application fee imposed under this subsection may not exceed two hundred dollars ($200.00). Applications that are received without fees or applications that are not substantially complete shall be promptly returned to the applicant, with a notice stating the reasons for returning the application unprocessed and stating any additional fees that the State Bar determines are required as a condition of reapplication.

(d) The application shall be accompanied by all of the following documents, and, if any documents are not in English, accompanied by duly authenticated English translations of:

(1) A certificate from the authority that has final jurisdiction regarding matters of professional discipline in the foreign country or jurisdiction in which the applicant was admitted to practice law, or the equivalent thereof. This certificate must be signed by a responsible official or one of the members of the

executive body of the authority, imprinted with the official seal of the authority, if any, and must certify:

a. The authority's jurisdiction in such matters;

b. The applicant's admission to practice law, or the equivalent thereof, in the foreign country, the date of admission, and the applicant's standing as an attorney or the equivalent thereof; and

c. Whether any charge or complaint ever has been filed with the authority against the applicant, and, if so, the substance of and adjudication or resolution of each charge or complaint.

(2) A letter of recommendation from one of the members of the executive body of this authority or from one of the judges of the highest law court or court of general original jurisdiction of the foreign country, certifying the applicant's professional qualifications, and a certificate from the clerk of this authority or the clerk of the highest law court or court of general original jurisdiction, attesting to the genuineness of the applicant's signature.

(3) A letter of recommendation from at least two attorneys, or the equivalent thereof, admitted in and practicing law in the foreign country, stating the length of time, when, and under what circumstances they have known the applicant and their appraisal of the applicant's moral character.

(4) Any other relevant documents or information as may be required by the North Carolina State Bar.

(e) In addition to the documents set forth in subsection (d) of this section, the North Carolina State Bar may require other evidence as to the applicant's education, professional qualification, character, fitness, and moral qualification.

(f) Records, papers, and other documents containing information collected or compiled by the North Carolina State Bar or any of its members or employees as a result of any investigation, application, inquiry or interview conducted in connection with an application for a certificate of registration are not public records within the meaning of Chapter 132 of the General Statutes.

(g) Reciprocity between North Carolina and the foreign country in which the applicant is licensed is required for the applicant to be licensed as a foreign legal consultant under this Chapter. (1995, c. 427, s. 1.)

§ 84A-3. Issuance of a certificate of registration; waiver.

(a) The North Carolina State Bar shall review the statements and the supporting documents contained in an application submitted pursuant to G.S. 84A-2 and shall report the results of their review, with recommendations, to the North Carolina Supreme Court.

(b) The North Carolina Supreme Court may issue to an applicant a certificate of registration as a foreign legal consultant.

(c) The North Carolina Supreme Court shall not grant a certificate of registration as a foreign legal consultant unless it is satisfied that the applicant possesses good moral character.

(d) Upon a showing that strict compliance with all of the provisions of G.S. 84A-2 would cause the applicant unnecessary hardship or upon a showing of professional qualifications to practice as a foreign legal consultant satisfactory to the North Carolina Supreme Court, the North Carolina Supreme Court may issue a certificate of registration under this Chapter to an applicant who did not satisfy the provisions of G.S. 84A-2. (1995, c. 427, s. 1.)

§ 84A-4. Scope of practice.

(a) Subject to the limitations set forth in subsections (b) and (c) of this section, a person licensed as a foreign legal consultant under this Chapter may provide legal services in the State and be compensated for those legal services.

(b) A person licensed as a foreign legal consultant shall not engage in any of the following:

(1) Appear on behalf of another person or entity as the attorney for that person or entity in any legal proceeding or before any judicial officer or State or municipal agency or tribunal.

(2) Sign or file in the capacity of an attorney any pleadings, motions, or other documents in any legal proceeding or before any judicial officer or State or municipal agencies, or tribunal.

(3) Prepare any deed, deed of trust, mortgage, option, lease, assignment, agreement or contract of sale, or any other instrument that may affect title to real estate located in the United States.

(4) Prepare any will or trust instrument affecting the disposition of any property located in the United States and owned by a resident of the United States.

(5) Prepare any instrument relating to the administration of a decedent's estate in the United States.

(6) Prepare any instrument affecting the marital relationship, rights, or duties of a resident of the United States or affecting the custody or care of the children of such a resident.

(7) Render professional legal advice regarding State law, the laws of any other state, the laws of the District of Columbia, the laws of the United States or the laws of any foreign country other than the country in which the foreign legal consultant is admitted to practice as an attorney or the equivalent thereof.

(8) In any way represent that the foreign legal consultant is licensed as an attorney in the State or in any other jurisdiction unless he or she is licensed in that jurisdiction.

(9) Use any title other than "foreign legal consultant"; provided, however, that the foreign legal consultant's authorized title and firm name in the foreign country in which he or she is admitted to practice as an attorney or the equivalent thereof, may be used, if the title, firm name, and the name of the foreign country are stated together with the title "foreign legal consultant". Nothing may be added to the title to create the impression that the foreign legal consultant holds a license to practice law in North Carolina.

(10) Be hired by a firm as a partner, member, or in any capacity other than as a foreign legal consultant whose services shall be overseen by an attorney licensed to practice law in North Carolina.

(c) If a particular matter requires legal advice from a person admitted to practice law as an attorney in a jurisdiction other than the one in which the foreign legal consultant is admitted to practice law, or its equivalent thereof, then the foreign legal consultant shall consult an attorney, or the equivalent thereof, in that other jurisdiction, obtain written legal advice on the particular matter, and transmit the written legal advice to the client. (1995, c. 427, s. 1.)

§ 84A-5. Duties of a foreign legal consultant.

A foreign legal consultant shall:

(1)   Be subject to rules adopted by the North Carolina Supreme Court and the North Carolina State Bar and be subject to professional discipline in the same manner as is prescribed for disciplinary proceedings against attorneys;

(2)   Be subject to a proceeding brought by the North Carolina State Bar in superior court pursuant to G.S. 84-28(j) to protect the interests of clients of disabled, incapacitated, or deceased foreign legal consultants;

(3)   Provide the Clerk of the North Carolina Supreme Court with evidence of professional liability insurance, in an amount as prescribed by the Supreme Court to assure the foreign legal consultant's proper professional conduct and responsibility;

(4)   Subject his or her trust accounts to audit in the same manner as is prescribed for attorneys licensed to practice law in North Carolina;

(5)   Execute and file with the Clerk of the North Carolina Supreme Court, in a form and manner as prescribed by the Clerk:

a.   An oath attesting that the foreign legal consultant will abide by the Rules of Professional Conduct of the North Carolina State Bar and those rules and directives of the North Carolina Supreme Court that are applicable to foreign legal consultants;

b.   A document setting forth the foreign legal consultant's address in the State and designating the Clerk of the North Carolina Supreme Court as agent upon whom process may be served, with the same effect as if served personally upon the foreign legal consultant in any judicial, quasi-judicial, or administrative proceeding brought against the foreign legal consultant arising out of or based upon any legal services rendered or offered to be rendered by the foreign legal consultant within the State or to residents of the State; and

c. The foreign legal consultant's commitment to notify the Clerk of the North Carolina Supreme Court of any resignation or revocation of the foreign legal consultant's admission to practice law, or the equivalent thereof, in the foreign country in which he or she is admitted to practice as an attorney, or the equivalent thereof, and of any censure, suspension, reprimand, or expulsion with respect to that admission, or of any change of address within the State.

(6) Pay an annual administration fee to the North Carolina State Bar equal in amount to the annual membership fee charged to active members of the North Carolina State Bar. Such fee shall be due on January 1 and delinquent on July 1 for each year or portion of a year in which the foreign legal consultant holds a certificate of registration. No portion of the annual administrative fee shall be waived or prorated. The State Bar's rules and regulations regarding enforcement and collection of annual membership fees shall apply to the enforcement of the obligation to pay the administrative fee. (1995, c. 427, s. 1.)

§ 84A-6. Service of process on foreign legal consultant.

Service of process on the Clerk of the North Carolina Supreme Court, pursuant to this Article, shall be made by personally delivering to and leaving with the Clerk duplicate copies of such process together with a fee of ten dollars ($10.00). The Clerk shall promptly send one of such copies to the foreign legal consultant to whom the process is directed, by certified mail, return receipt requested, addressed to the foreign legal consultant at the address specified by the foreign legal consultant in his or her application under G.S. 84A-2, as updated pursuant to G.S. 84A-5(5). (1995, c. 427, s. 1.)

§ 84A-7. Delegation of duties.

The North Carolina State Bar may delegate any of its duties under this Chapter to the North Carolina Board of Law Examiners. (1995, c. 427, s. 1.)

§ 84A-8. Adoption of rules.

The North Carolina State Bar is authorized to adopt and amend such rules, subject to approval of the North Carolina Supreme Court, as are appropriate to accomplish the provisions of this Chapter. (1995, c. 427, s. 1.)

Chapter 85.

Auctions and Auctioneers.

§§ 85-1 through 85-27. Repealed by Session Laws 1973, c. 552, s. 9.

Chapter 85A.

Bail Bondsmen and Runners.

§§ 85A-1 through 85A-34. Recodified as §§ 85C-1 to 85C-41.

Chapter 85B.

Auctions and Auctioneers.

§ 85B-1. Definitions.

For the purposes of this Chapter the following definitions shall apply:

(1) "Auction" means the sale of goods or real estate by means of exchanges between an auctioneer and members of an audience, the exchanges consisting of a series of invitations for offers made by the auctioneer, offers by members of the audience, and the acceptance by the auctioneer of the highest or most favorable offer.

(2) "Auctioneer" means any person who conducts or offers to conduct auctions and includes apprentice auctioneers except as stricter standards are specified by this Chapter for apprentice auctioneers.

(3) "Owner" means the bona fide owner of the property being offered for sale; in the case of partnerships, "owner" means a general partner in a partnership that owns the property being offered for sale, provided that in the case of a limited partnership it has filed a certificate of limited partnership as

required by Chapter 59 of the General Statutes; in the case of corporations, "owner" means an officer or director or employee or someone acting on behalf of the employee of a corporation that owns the property being offered for sale provided that the corporation is registered to do business in the State.

(4) "Absolute Auction" means the sale of real or personal property at auction in which the item offered for auction is sold to the highest bidder without reserve, without the requirement of any minimum bid, and without competing bids of any type by the owner, or agent of the owner, of the property.

(5) "Estate Sale" means the liquidation by sale at auction of real or personal property of a specified person.

(6) "Auction Firm" means a sole proprietorship of which the owner is not a licensed auctioneer, or any partnership, association, or corporation, not otherwise exempt from this Chapter, that sells either directly or through agents, real or personal property at auction, or that arranges, sponsors, manages, conducts or advertises auctions, or that in the regular course of business uses or allows the use of its facilities for auctions. This definition applies whether or not an owner or officer of the business acts as an auctioneer.

(7) "Fund" means Auctioneer Recovery Fund.

(8) "Auctioneering", "conduct of auction", or "conduct of business" means, in addition to the actual calling of bids, any of the following:

a. Contracting for auction.

b. Accepting consignments of items for sale at auction.

c. Advertising an auction.

d. Offering items for sale at auction.

e. Accepting payment or disbursing monies for items sold at auction.

f. Otherwise soliciting, arranging, sponsoring, or managing an auction or holding oneself out as an auctioneer or auction firm.

(9) "Consignment" means, unless otherwise modified by written agreement, the act of delivering or transferring goods or real estate in fact or constructively

to an auctioneer or the auctioneer's agent in trust for the purpose of resale at auction whereby title does not pass to the buyer until there is an action indicating a sale. For purposes of this section, consignment may also mean a bailment for sale.

(10)   "Designated person" means any person approved by the Board to have the authority to transact business for a licensed auction firm. (1973, c. 552, s. 1; 1983, c. 751, s. 1; 1991 (Reg. Sess., 1992), c. 819, s. 1; 2005-330, s. 1.)

§ 85B-2. Activities governed by Chapter.

(a)   This Chapter shall apply to all auctions held in this State except the following:

(1)   Sales at auction conducted by the owner of all of the goods or real estate being offered, or an attorney representing the owner, unless the owner's regular course of business includes engaging in the sale of goods or real estate by means of auction or unless the owner originally acquired the goods for the purposes of resale at auction;

(2)   Sales at auction conducted by or under the direction of any public authority;

(3)   Sales conducted by a receiver, trustee, guardian, administrator or executor or any similarly appointed person under order of any court or any person conducting a sale pursuant to an order of a United States Bankruptcy Court or the agent or attorney of such person, receiver, trustee, guardian, administrator or executor;

(4)   Any sale required by law to be at auction;

(5)   Sale of livestock at a public livestock market authorized and regulated by the Commissioner of Agriculture;

(6)   Leaf tobacco sales conducted in accordance with the provisions of Chapter 106 of the General Statutes;

(7) Sale at auction of automobiles conducted under the provisions of G.S. 20-77, or sale at auction of motor vehicles by a motor vehicle dealer licensed under Article 12, Chapter 20 of the General Statutes;

(8) Sale at auction of a particular breed of livestock conducted by an auctioneer who specializes in the sale of that breed when such sale is conducted under the auspices of a livestock trade association; provided that the sale is regulated by the Packers and Stockyards Act and the auctioneer is required to be bonded by the United States Department of Agriculture;

(9) Sales conducted by and on behalf of any charitable or religious organization;

(9a) Sales conducted by and on behalf of a civic club, not exceeding one sale per year;

(10) Sales conducted by a trustee pursuant to a power of sale contained in a deed of trust on real property;

(11) Sales of collateral, sales conducted to enforce carriers' or warehousemen's liens, sales of goods by a presenting bank following dishonor of a documentary draft, resales of rightfully rejected goods, resales of goods by an aggrieved seller, or other resales conducted pursuant to authority in Articles 2, 4, 7, and 9 of Chapter 25 of the General Statutes (the Uniform Commercial Code).

(b) The exceptions provided in subdivisions (2), (4), (9), (9a) and (11) of subsection (a) of this section shall not apply to any person or entity engaged in the business of organizing, arranging, or conducting auction sales for compensation or any person who or entity that accepts consignments to be sold at auction where the consignor receives any proceeds from the sale.

(c) The exceptions provided in subdivision (7) of subsection (a) of this section shall not apply to any auctioneer licensed pursuant to this Chapter employed to be an auctioneer of motor vehicles for a licensed motor vehicle dealer, while conducting an auction for that dealer. (1973, c. 552, s. 2; 1977, c. 1115; 1983, c. 751, ss. 2, 3; 1991 (Reg. Sess., 1992), c. 819, s. 2; 2004-190, s. 5; 2005-330, ss. 2, 3.)

§ 85B-3. Auctioneers Commission.

(a) There shall be a five-member North Carolina Auctioneers Commission having the powers and responsibilities set out in this Chapter. The Governor shall appoint the members of the Commission, at least three of whom, and their successors, may be from nominations submitted by the Auctioneers Association of North Carolina. The Auctioneers Association shall submit, within 45 days of when the vacancy occurs, at least three names for each position for which it is entitled to make a nomination. Of the initial five members of the Commission one shall be appointed for a one-year term, two shall be appointed for two-year terms and two for three-year terms; thereafter, each new member shall be appointed for a term of three years. Any vacancy shall be filled for the remainder of the unexpired term only. Each member shall continue in office until his successor is appointed and qualified. No member shall serve more than two complete consecutive terms.

(b) At least three members of the Commission shall be experienced auctioneers who are licensed under this Chapter. One member shall be a person who shall represent the public at large and shall not be licensed under this Chapter.

(c) The Commission shall employ an executive director and other employees as needed to carry out the duties of this Chapter. All employees shall serve at the pleasure of the Commission.

(d) Any action that may be taken by the Commission may be taken by vote of any three of its members.

(e) The members of the Commission shall elect from among themselves a chairman to serve a one-year term. No person shall serve more than two consecutive terms as chairman.

(f) Repealed by Session Laws 1999-142, s. 1, effective October 1, 1999.

(g) Members of the Commission shall receive the compensation set for members of occupational licensing boards by G.S. 93B-5. (1973, c. 552, s. 3; 1975, c. 648, s. 1; 1983, c. 751, ss. 4, 5; 1991 (Reg. Sess., 1992), c. 819, s. 3; 1999-142, s. 1; 2008-138, s. 1.)

§ 85B-3.1. Auctioneers Commission; powers and duties.

(a) The Commission shall have the following powers and duties:

(1) To receive and act upon applications for licenses.

(2) To issue licenses.

(3) To deny, suspend, and revoke licenses pursuant to G.S. 85B-8.

(4) To issue declaratory rulings.

(5) To adopt rules for auctioneers and auctions that are consistent with the provisions of this Chapter and the General Statutes.

(b) The Commission may assess a civil penalty not in excess of two thousand dollars ($2,000) for acts prohibited in G.S. 85B-8. All civil penalties collected by the Commission shall be remitted to the school fund of the county in which the violation occurred. Before imposing and assessing a civil penalty and fixing the amount thereof, the Commission shall, as a part of its deliberations, take into consideration the following factors:

(1) The nature, gravity, and persistence of the particular violation.

(2) The appropriateness of the imposition of a civil penalty when considered alone or in combination with other punishment.

(3) Whether the violation was willful.

(4) Any other factors that would tend to mitigate or aggravate the violations found to exist.

(c) The Commission shall have the power to acquire, hold, rent, encumber, alienate, and otherwise deal with real property in the same manner as a private person or corporation, subject only to approval of the Governor and the Council of State. Collateral pledged by the Commission for an encumbrance is limited to the assets, income, and revenues of the Commission.

(d) The Commission may purchase, rent, or lease equipment and supplies and purchase liability insurance or other insurance to cover the activities of the

Commission, its operations, or its employees. (1999-142, s. 2; 1999-456, s. 23; 2001-198, s. 3.)

§ 85B-3.2. Criminal history record checks of applicants for licensure.

(a) Definitions. - The following definitions shall apply in this section:

(1) Applicant - An applicant for initial licensure as an auctioneer, apprentice auctioneer, or auction firm.

(2) Criminal history - A State or federal history of conviction of a crime, whether a misdemeanor or felony, that bears upon an applicant's fitness to be licensed as an auctioneer, apprentice auctioneer, or auction firm.

(b) The Commission shall ensure that the State criminal history of an applicant is checked. National criminal history checks are authorized for an applicant who has not resided in the State of North Carolina during the past five years. The Commission shall provide to the North Carolina Department of Justice the fingerprints of the applicant to be checked, a form signed by the applicant to be checked consenting to the check of the criminal history and to the use of fingerprints and other identifying information required by the State or National Repositories, and any additional information required by the Department of Justice.

(c) All releases of criminal history information to the Commission shall be subject to, and in compliance with, rules governing the dissemination of criminal history record checks as adopted by the North Carolina Division of Criminal Information. All of the information the Commission receives through the checking of the criminal history is for the exclusive use of the Commission and shall be kept confidential.

(d) If the applicant's verified criminal history record check reveals one or more convictions of a crime that is punishable as a felony offense, or the conviction of any crime involving fraud or moral turpitude, the Commission may deny the applicant's license. However, the conviction shall not automatically prohibit licensure, and the following factors shall be considered by the Commission in determining whether licensure shall be denied:

(1) The level and seriousness of the crime.

(2) The date of the crime.

(3) The age of the person at the time of the crime.

(4) The circumstances surrounding the commission of the crime, if known.

(5) The nexus between the criminal conduct of the applicant and the applicant's duties as an auctioneer, apprentice auctioneer, or auction firm.

(6) The prison, jail, probation, parole, rehabilitation, and employment records of the applicant since the date the crime was committed.

(7) The subsequent commission by the person of a crime.

(e) The Commission may deny licensure to an applicant who refuses to consent to a criminal history record check or use of fingerprints or other identifying information required by the State or National Repositories of Criminal Histories.

(f) The Commission shall notify the applicant of the applicant's right to review the criminal history information, the procedure for challenging the accuracy of the criminal history, and the applicant's right to contest the Commission's denial of licensure.

(g) The Commission shall collect any fees required by the Department of Justice and shall remit the fees to the Department of Justice for expenses associated with conducting the criminal history record check. (1999-142, s. 3; 2000-140, ss. 59(a), 59(b); 2001-198, s. 1.)

§ 85B-4. Licenses required.

(a) No person who is not exempt under G.S. 85B-2, shall sell, or offer to sell, goods or real estate at auction in this State or perform any act for which an auction firm license is required unless the person holds a currently valid license issued under this Chapter.

(b) No person shall be licensed as an apprentice auctioneer, auctioneer, or receive an auction firm license if the person:

(1)   Is under 18 years of age.

(1a)   Is not a high school graduate or the equivalent. However, a person licensed under this Chapter prior to July 1, 1999, does not need to meet this requirement.

(2)   Repealed by Session Laws 1983, c. 751, s. 6.

(3)   Has within the preceding five years pleaded guilty to, entered a plea of nolo contendere or been convicted of any felony, or committed or been convicted of any act involving fraud or moral turpitude.

(4)   Has had an auctioneer or apprentice auctioneer or auction firm license revoked.

(5)   Has, within the preceding five years, committed any act that constitutes grounds for license suspension or revocation under this Chapter or a Commission rule.

(c)   Each applicant for an apprentice auctioneer license shall submit a written application in a form approved by the Commission and containing at least two statements by residents of the community in which the applicant resides attesting to the applicant's good moral character.

(c1)   Each apprentice auctioneer application and license shall name a licensed auctioneer to serve as the supervisor of the apprentice. No apprentice auctioneer may enter into an agreement to conduct an auction, or conduct an auction, without the express approval of his supervisor. The supervisor shall review all contracts before approving them and shall regularly review the records his apprentice is required to maintain under G.S. 85B-7 to see that they are accurate and current, and shall perform such other supervisory duties as may be required by the Commission.

(d)   No person shall be licensed as an auctioneer unless the person has held an apprentice auctioneer license and served as an apprentice auctioneer for the two preceding years, accumulated sufficient knowledge and experience in such areas of the auctioneer profession as the Commission may deem appropriate, and has taken an examination approved by the Commission and performed on it to the satisfaction of the Commission. The examination shall test the applicant's understanding of the law relating to auctioneers and auctions, ethical practices for auctioneers, the mathematics applicable to the auctioneer business, and such other matters relating to auctions as the Commission considers appropriate. The examination shall be given at least twice each year in North Carolina, and at other times and places the Commission designates, but no person shall be allowed to take the examination within six months after having failed it a second time.

Any person who has successfully completed the equivalent of at least 80 hours of classroom instruction in a course in auctioneering at an institution whose curriculum and instructors meet the qualifications approved or established by the Commission may be licensed as an auctioneer without holding an apprentice license and serving as an apprentice for two years, but shall take the examination required by this subsection and perform on it to the satisfaction of the Commission.

Each applicant for an auctioneer license shall submit a written application in a form approved by the Commission, pay all applicable fees, and consent in writing to a criminal history check as required by G.S. 85B-3.2. If the applicant has been previously licensed as an apprentice auctioneer, the application shall contain an evaluation by the applicant's supervisor of the applicant's performance as an apprentice auctioneer and the applicant's performance in specific areas as required by the Commission. If the applicant is exempted from apprenticeship after completion of the equivalent of at least 80 hours of classroom instruction in auctioneering, the application shall contain a transcript of the applicant's course work in auctioneering. Each application shall be accompanied by statements of at least two residents of the community in which the applicant resides attesting to the applicant's good moral character. The Commission may require verification of any information included in an application for an auctioneer license and may request other information or verification of information provided to determine whether the applicant possesses the good moral character or other qualifications for licensure.

(e)   Each license issued under this Chapter shall be valid from July 1 of the year issued, or from the date issued, whichever is later, to the following June 30 unless sooner revoked or suspended pursuant to this Chapter or a rule of the Commission. A license may be renewed for one year at a time, except an apprentice auctioneer license may not be renewed for more than three times. No examination shall be required for renewal of an auctioneer license if the application for renewal is made within 24 months of the expiration of the previous license.

(e1) The Commission may require licensees to complete annually not more than six hours of Commission-approved continuing education courses prior to license renewal. The Commission may impose different continuing education requirements, including no such requirements, upon the classes of licensees under this Chapter. The Commission may waive any or all continuing education requirements in cases of hardship, disability, or illness, or under other circumstances as the Commission deems appropriate. The Commission may adopt rules not inconsistent with the provisions of this Chapter to establish continuing education requirements, including rules that govern any of the following:

(1) The content and subject matter of continuing education courses.

(2) The curriculum of required continuing education courses.

(3) The criteria, standards, and procedures for the approval of courses, course sponsors, and course instructors.

(4) The methods of instruction for continuing education courses.

(5) The computation of course credit.

(6) The number of credit hours needed annually.

(7) The ability to carry forward course credit from one year to another.

(8) The waiver of the continuing education requirement for hardship or other reasons to be determined by the Commission.

(9) The procedures for compliance and noncompliance with continuing education requirements.

(f) No person shall be issued an auctioneer or apprentice auctioneer license until the person has made the contribution to the Fund as required by G.S. 85B-4.1.

(g) An auction firm must be licensed by the Board even though no owner or officer of the firm acts as an auctioneer. To be licensed an auction firm must make the contribution to the Fund as required by G.S. 85B-4.1 and must pay the proper fees as set out in G.S. 85B-6. Auction firms are covered by the provisions of G.S. 85B-8.

An auction firm license issued by the Commission is restricted to the persons named in the license and does not inure to the benefit of any other person. Where a license is issued to an auction firm, authority to transact business under the license is limited to the person or persons designated in the application and named in the license.

The designated person or persons, prior to being licensed, shall be required to take a written examination, approved by the Commission, and demonstrate to the satisfaction of the Commission a thorough understanding of the law relating to the conduct of the auction business and other matters the Commission deems appropriate. An individual who is licensed as an auctioneer and who is the designated person applying for an auction firm license is not required to take the auction firm examination. Licensed real estate brokers and real estate firms may be exempt from the auction firm examination provided they employ or associate themselves with a licensed auctioneer to handle those aspects of the transactions peculiar to the auctioneer profession. Any person or entity, on the effective date of this Chapter, duly licensed as an auction firm in good standing is not required to take any examination in order to maintain or to renew an auction firm license provided that the license does not otherwise expire or lapse and is not suspended or revoked by the Commission.

(h) The Commission shall publish at least once a year a list of names and addresses of all persons, sole proprietorships, partnerships and corporations holding valid apprentice auctioneer, auctioneer, or auction firm licenses.

(i) The Commission may investigate as it deems necessary the ethical background of any applicant for licensure under this Chapter. (1973, c. 552, s. 4; c. 1195, ss. 1, 2; 1975, c. 648, ss. 2-4; 1983, c. 603, s. 4; c. 751, ss. 6-8; 1989, c. 732, s. 1; 1991 (Reg. Sess., 1992), c. 819, s. 4; c. 1030, s. 51.5; 1993, c. 421, s. 3; 1999-142, s. 4; 2001-198, s. 2; 2005-330, s. 4.)

§ 85B-4.1. Auctioneer Recovery Fund.

(a) In addition to license fees, upon application for a license or renewal of a license, the Commission may charge the applicant or licensee up to fifty dollars ($50.00) per year to be included in the Fund.

(b) The Commission shall maintain at least two hundred thousand dollars ($200,000) in the Fund for use as provided in this Chapter. The Fund may be invested by the State Treasurer in interest bearing accounts, and any interest accrued shall be added to the Fund. Sufficient liquidity shall be maintained to insure that funds will be available to satisfy claims processed through the Board. The Fund may be disbursed by a warrant drawn against the State Treasurer or by other method at the discretion of the State Treasurer.

(c) The Commission, in its discretion, may use contents of the Fund in excess of two hundred thousand dollars ($200,000) for the following purposes:

(1) To promote education and research in the auctioneer profession, in order to benefit persons licensed under this Chapter and to improve the efficiency of the profession.

(2) To underwrite educational seminars, training centers, and other forms of educational projects for the use and benefit of licensees.

(3) To sponsor, contract for, or underwrite education and research projects in order to advance the auctioneer profession in North Carolina.

(4) To cooperate with associations of auctioneers, or other groups, in order to promote the enlightenment and advancement of the auctioneer profession in North Carolina. (1983, c. 603, s. 2; 1989, c. 732, s. 2; 1991 (Reg. Sess., 1992), c. 819, s. 5; 1999-142, s. 5.)

§ 85B-4.2. Grounds for payment; notice and application to Commission.

An aggrieved person who has suffered a monetary loss as a direct result of the conversion of funds or property or other fraudulent act or conduct by a licensed auctioneer, apprentice auctioneer, or auction firm shall be eligible to seek compensation from the Fund subject to the limitations of this Chapter and the amount of loss which is otherwise unrecoverable provided that:

(1) The aggrieved person has sued the licensee in a court of competent jurisdiction and has filed with the Commission written notice of such lawsuit within 60 days after its commencement unless the total loss claimed excluding attorneys' fees is less than two thousand five hundred dollars ($2,500), in which

case the notice may be filed within 90 days after the termination of all judicial proceedings, including appeals;

(2) The aggrieved person has obtained final judgment in a court of competent jurisdiction against the licensee based upon conversion or other fraudulent conduct arising out of a transaction which occurred when the licensee was licensed by the Commission and was acting in a capacity for which a North Carolina license is required, which judgment shall show the amount owed the aggrieved person;

(3) The aggrieved person was not engaged in any act or conduct for which an auctioneer license is required and was not acting in violation of any of the laws of the State of North Carolina or of the United States; and

(4) Execution on the judgment has been issued and has been returned unsatisfied in whole or in part.

Upon the termination of all judicial proceedings including appeals, and for a period of one year thereafter, a person eligible for recovery may file a verified application with the Commission for payment out of the Fund of the amount remaining unpaid upon the judgment which represents the actual and direct loss sustained by reason of conversion or other fraudulent conduct. A certified copy of the judgment and return of execution shall be attached to the application and filed with the Commission. The applicant shall serve upon the judgment debtor a copy of the application and shall file with the Commission an affidavit or certificate of service, in accordance with the procedures specified by rule by the Commission. (1983, c. 603, s. 2; 1989, c. 732, s. 3; 1991 (Reg. Sess., 1992), c. 819, s. 6.)

§ 85B-4.3. Hearing; required showing.

Upon application by an aggrieved person, the Commission shall conduct a hearing and the aggrieved person shall be required to show that:

(1) The person is not a spouse of the judgment debtor or a person representing such spouse;

(2) The person gave notice of the lawsuit as required by G.S. 85B-4.2;

(3) The person is making application not more than one year after termination of all judicial proceedings, including appeals, in connection with the judgment;

(4) The person has complied with all requirements of this Article;

(5) The person has obtained a judgment as described in G.S. 85B-4.2;

(6) The person has made all reasonable searches and inquiries to ascertain whether the judgment debtor is possessed of real or personal property or other assets subject to be sold or applied in satisfaction of the judgment;

(7) That by a search the person has discovered no real or personal property or other assets subject to be sold or applied, or has discovered certain of them, describing them, but that the amount realized was insufficient to satisfy the judgment, stating the amount realized and the balance remaining due on the judgment after application of the amount realized; and

(8) The person has diligently pursued available remedies including attempted execution on the judgment against all the judgment debtors and the execution has been returned unsatisfied. In addition to that, the person knows of no assets of the judgment debtor and has attempted collection from all other persons who may be liable in the transaction for which payment is sought from the Fund if there are any other persons. (1991 (Reg. Sess., 1992), c. 819, s. 7.)

§ 85B-4.4. Response and defense by Commission and judgment debtor; proof of conversion or other fraudulent act.

(a) When the Commission proceeds upon an application as set forth in this Article, counsel for the Commission may defend action on behalf of the Fund and shall have recourse to all appropriate means of defense, including the examination of witnesses. The judgment debtor may personally defend the action and shall have recourse to all appropriate means of defense, including the examination of witnesses. Within 30 days after service of the application, counsel for the Commission and the judgment debtor may file responses setting forth answers and defenses. Responses shall be filed with the Commission and copies shall be served upon every party by the filing party. If at any time it appears there are no triable issues of fact and the application for payment from the Fund is without merit, the Commission shall dismiss the application. A motion to dismiss may be supported by affidavit of any person having knowledge of the facts and may be made on the basis that the application or the judgment referred to does not form a basis for meritorious recovery under G.S. 85B-4.2, that the applicant has not complied with the provisions of this Article, or that the liability of the Fund with regard to the particular licensee or transaction has been exhausted; provided, however, notice of such motion shall be given at least 10 days prior to the time fixed for hearing.

(b)   Whenever the judgment obtained by an applicant is by default, stipulation, or consent, or whenever the action against the licensee was defended by a trustee in bankruptcy, the applicant, for purposes of this Article, shall have the burden of proving the cause of action for conversion of funds or property or other fraudulent conduct. Otherwise, the judgment shall create a rebuttable presumption of conversion or other fraudulent conduct. (1991 (Reg. Sess., 1992), c. 819, s. 8.)

§ 85B-4.5. Determination of certain small claims without a prior judicial determination.

Notwithstanding any other provisions of this Chapter, the Commission may, in its discretion, order that payment be made from the Fund, without requiring a prior judicial determination in any case where:

(1)   The total loss claimed by the claimant is two thousand five hundred dollars ($2,500) or less;

(2)   The amount of alleged loss is readily ascertainable rather than speculative in nature;

(3)   The alleged loss is one that is otherwise compensable under this Chapter;

(4)   The claimant filed a properly notarized complaint with the Commission not more than one year following the date of the alleged wrongful act or conduct of the licensee; and

(5)   The Commission, in its discretion, determines that, based upon the evidence presented, justice would be better served by allowing compensation to

be paid without first requiring the aggrieved party to obtain a judgment from a court of competent jurisdiction. (1991 (Reg. Sess., 1992), c. 819, s. 9.)

§ 85B-4.6. Order directing payment out of Fund; compromise of claims.

(a) Applications for payment from the Fund shall be heard and decided by a majority of the members of the Commission. If, after a hearing, the Commission finds that the claim should be paid from the Fund, the Commission shall enter an order requiring payment from the Fund of whatever sum the Commission shall find to be payable upon the claim in accordance with the limitations contained in this Article.

(b) Subject to Commission approval, a claim based upon the application of an aggrieved person may be compromised; however, the Commission shall not be bound in any way by any compromise or stipulation of the judgment debtor. (1991 (Reg. Sess., 1992), c. 819, s. 10.)

§ 85B-4.7. Limitations; pro rata distribution; attorneys' fees.

(a) Payments from the Fund shall be subject to the following limitations:

(1) The right to recovery under this Article shall be forever barred unless timely notice is given as required by G.S. 85B-4.2(a)(1) and application is made within one year after termination of all proceedings, including appeals, in connection with the judgment.

(2) The Fund shall not be liable for more than ten thousand dollars ($10,000) per transaction regardless of the number of persons aggrieved.

(3) The liability of the Fund shall not exceed in the aggregate ten thousand dollars ($10,000) for any one licensee within a single calendar year, and in no event shall it exceed in the aggregate twenty thousand dollars ($20,000) for any one licensee.

(4) The Fund shall not be liable for payment of any judgment awards of consequential damages, multiple or punitive damages, civil penalties, incidental

damages, special damages, interest, costs of court or action, or other similar awards.

(b)   If the maximum of the Fund is insufficient to pay in full the valid claims of all aggrieved persons whose claims relate to the same transaction or to the same licensee, the amount for which the Fund is liable shall be distributed among the claimants in a ratio that their respective claims bear to the total of such valid claims or in a manner the Commission deems equitable. Upon petition of the Commission, the Commission may require all claimants and prospective claimants to be joined in one proceeding so that the respective rights of all claimants to the Fund may be equitably resolved. (1991 (Reg. Sess., 1992), c. 819, s. 11.)

§ 85B-4.8. Repayment to Fund; automatic suspension of license.

Should the Commission pay from the Fund any amount in settlement of a claim or toward satisfaction of a judgment against a licensee, the license of the licensee shall be automatically suspended upon the effective date of the order authorizing payment from the Fund. The licensee shall not be eligible for consideration for reinstatement until repayment in full, plus interest at the legal rate as provided for in G.S. 24-1, the amount paid from the Fund. (1991 (Reg. Sess., 1992), c. 819, s. 12.)

§ 85B-4.9. Subrogation of rights.

When the Commission has paid from the Fund any sum to the judgment creditor, the Commission shall be subrogated to all of the rights of the judgment creditor to the extent of the amount paid and the judgment creditor shall assign all his right, title, and interest in the judgment to the extent of the amount paid to the Commission and any amount and interest recovered by the Commission on the judgment shall be deposited in the Fund. (1991 (Reg. Sess., 1992), c. 819, s. 13.)

§ 85B-4.10. Waiver of rights.

The failure of an aggrieved person to comply with this Chapter shall constitute a waiver of any rights hereunder. (1991 (Reg. Sess., 1992), c. 819, s. 14.)

§ 85B-4.11. Persons ineligible to recover from Fund.

No licensee who suffers the loss of any commission from any transaction in which the licensee was acting in the capacity of an auctioneer, apprentice auctioneer, or auction firm shall be entitled to make application for payment from the Fund for the loss. Likewise, any person who suffers any monetary loss as a result of a joint business venture of any sort with a licensee shall not be entitled to be compensated from the Fund for the loss. (1991 (Reg. Sess., 1992), c. 819, s. 15.)

§ 85B-4.12. Disciplinary action against licensee.

Nothing contained in this Article shall limit the authority of the Commission to take disciplinary action against any licensee under this Chapter, nor shall the repayment in full of all obligations to the Fund by any licensee nullify or modify the effect of any other disciplinary proceeding brought under this Chapter. (1991 (Reg. Sess., 1992), c. 819, s. 16.)

§ 85B-5. Licensing of nonresidents.

(a) Any person who holds a valid auctioneer license in another state may apply for and be granted a reciprocal North Carolina license if the resident state in which the person is licensed has minimum training or experience standards which are acceptable to the Commission but are not more lenient than those required by this Chapter, if the resident state extends similar reciprocal privileges to auctioneers who are residents of and licensed by the State of North Carolina.

(b) An applicant under this section shall submit an application and other documentation and proof of eligibility for licensure as may be required by the Commission, but shall not be required to take the examination required under G.S. 85B-4. Applicants shall pay the appropriate fee under G.S. 85B-6 and shall file with the Commission an irrevocable consent that service on the Executive Director of the Commission shall be sufficient service of process for actions against the applicant by a resident of this State arising out of his auctioneering activities.

(c) An applicant under this section shall make the contribution to the Fund as required by G.S. 85B-4.1. Any license issued under this section shall be marked to indicate that its holder is a nonresident reciprocal licensee.

(d) A license issued pursuant to this section shall be valid from the date of issuance to the following June 30 and may be renewed from year to year unless suspended or revoked pursuant to the provisions of this Chapter or rule of the Commission, provided that the licensee continues to be a resident of and duly licensed in good standing in the licensee's resident state.

(e) Any person licensed under this section shall notify the Commission of the lapse, surrender, suspension, revocation, or any other act amounting to a loss of license in the person's resident state. The notice must be sent to the Commission, by certified mail, return receipt requested, within 10 days of the occurrence.

(f) Any person licensed under this section shall provide the Commission with written notice of any change of business address or residence within 10 days of the occurrence.

(g) Any license issued under this section shall be immediately suspended or revoked based upon the occurrence of any of the events set out in subsection (e) of this section or based upon a change of principal state residence of the reciprocal licensee.

(h) Any person whose license is terminated as a result of a change of principal state residence may reapply for reciprocal status provided the person is otherwise eligible for a license based upon the new state residence, and submits with the application the fees required by the Commission.

(i) Notwithstanding any other provision of this section, a reciprocal licensee who subsequently becomes a domiciliary of the State of North Carolina may request, by application, that the reciprocal license be converted to that of an in-State licensee without having to take the State exam required by G.S. 85B-4. The Commission may, however, require an applicant to pay processing and application fees it deems appropriate. (1973, c. 552, s. 5; 1983, c. 603, s. 5; c. 751, ss. 9-11; 1989, c. 732, s. 4; 1991 (Reg. Sess., 1992), c. 819, s. 17.)

§ 85B-6. Fees; local governments not to charge fees or require licenses.

(a) The Commission shall collect and remit to the State Treasurer fees in an amount not to exceed the following:

Item
Maximum Fee

Apprentice Auctioneers:

  Application for license..
$ 125.00

  Issuance or renewal of license..
125.00

Auctioneers:

  Application for license..
125.00

  Examination..
75.00

  Issuance or renewal of license..
250.00

Auction Firms:

  Application for license..
125.00

  Examination..
75.00

Issuance or renewal of license...
250.00

Reinstatement of License...
75.00.

An application fee for a license and an examination fee are nonrefundable. The amount payable by a nonresident under G.S. 85B-5 to obtain a nonresident reciprocal auctioneer license is the greater of the amount set in the above table for an examination for and the issuance of an auctioneer's license and the amount the nonresident's state would charge a resident auctioneer of this State to obtain a comparable license from that state.

A reinstatement fee is payable when a person applies for renewal of a license after the license has lapsed for failure to renew it before it expired. The reinstatement of a lapsed license is not retroactive in effect and does not limit the authority of the courts or of the Commission to take disciplinary action against a person who engages in the auctioneer profession with a lapsed license.

(b)   No local government or agency of local government may charge any fees or require any licenses for auctioneers, apprentice auctioneers, or auction firms in addition to those set out in this Chapter. (1973, c. 552, s. 6; c. 1195, s. 3; 1975, c. 648, s. 5; 1977, 2nd Sess., c. 1219, s. 43.7; 1983, c. 751, s. 12; 1991 (Reg. Sess., 1992), c. 819, s. 18; 1993, c. 421, s. 1; 1999-142, s. 6.)

§ 85B-7. Conduct of auction; records.

(a)   No licensee shall conduct an auction in this State without first having a written agreement with the owner of any property to be sold. The agreement must contain the terms and conditions upon which the auctioneer received the goods for sale. The licensee shall provide the owner with a signed copy of the agreement and shall keep at least one copy for his own records for two years from the date of the agreement. Copies of all contracts shall be made available to the Commission or its designated agent upon request.

(b)   Each licensee shall maintain consignment records and enter in them, upon receipt of goods for auction and before sale, the name and address of the person who employed the licensee to sell the goods at auction and the name and address of the owner of the goods to be sold. The consignment record shall contain an adequate description of the goods to be sold and shall be sufficient to positively identify each item. Consignment records shall be open for inspection by the Commission or its designated agent at reasonable times.

(c)   All licensees shall have their licenses available at each auction they conduct.

(d)   Each licensee shall maintain sales records, which identify the purchaser of all goods sold by name, address, and when possible, telephone number. The sales records shall contain an adequate description of the items sold and must be sufficient to positively identify the owner of the property. Sales records shall be maintained for a period of not less than two years from the date of sale. Sales records shall be open for inspection by the Commission or its designated agent at reasonable times. (1973, c. 552, s. 7; 1991 (Reg. Sess., 1992), c. 819, s. 19; 2005-330, s. 5.)

§ 85B-7.1. Handling clients' funds.

(a)   Each licensee who does not disburse all funds to the seller on auction day shall maintain a trust or escrow account and shall deposit in the account all funds that are received for the benefit of another person and are not disbursed to the seller on auction day. The licensee shall deposit funds that are not disbursed on auction day with an insured bank or savings and loan association located in North Carolina. At or before the time of all final settlements, the auctioneer shall provide the seller or consignor with a settlement statement, which includes a description of all goods sold, the selling price of the goods sold, the net proceeds due to the seller or consignor, the name and address of the person receiving the disbursement, and the amount of the disbursement. All settlement statements shall be signed by the licensee or the licensee's agent and by the person receiving the disbursement.

(b)   Each licensee shall maintain, for not less than five years, complete records showing the deposit, maintenance, and withdrawal of trust or escrow funds and the disbursement of funds on auction day. Records of the disbursement of funds on auction day shall include a copy of each receipt or settlement statement issued when the funds were disbursed. The Commission or its designated agent may inspect these records periodically, without prior notice, and may also inspect these records whenever the Commission determines that they are pertinent to an investigation of any specific complaint against a licensee. (1991 (Reg. Sess., 1992), c. 819, s. 20; 1993, c. 421, s. 2; 2005-330, s. 6.)

§ 85B-8. Prohibited acts; assessment of civil penalty; denial, suspension, or revocation of license.

(a) The following shall be grounds for the assessment of a civil penalty in accordance with G.S. 85B-3.1(b) or the denial, suspension, or revocation of an auctioneer, auctioneer apprentice, or auction firm license:

(1) Any violation of this Chapter or any violation of a rule or regulation duly adopted by the Commission.

(2) A continued and flagrant course of misrepresentation or making false promises, either by the licensee, an employee of the licensee, or by someone acting on behalf of and with the licensee's consent.

(3) Any failure to account for or to pay over within a reasonable time, not to exceed 30 days, funds belonging to another which have come into the licensee's possession through an auction sale.

(4) Any false, misleading, or untruthful advertising.

(5) Any act of conduct in connection with a sales transaction which demonstrates bad faith or dishonesty.

(6) Knowingly using false bidders, cappers or pullers, or knowingly making a material false statement or representation.

(7) Commingling the funds or property of a client with the licensee's own or failing to maintain and deposit in a trust or escrow account in an insured bank or savings and loan association located in North Carolina funds received for another person through sale at auction.

(8) Failure to make the required contribution to the Fund.

(9) The commission or conviction of a crime that is punishable as a felony offense under the laws of North Carolina or the laws of the jurisdiction where

committed or convicted, or the commission of any act involving fraud or moral turpitude.

(10) Failure to properly make any disclosures or to provide documents or information required by this Chapter or by the Commission.

(11) A demonstrated lack of financial responsibility.

(b) through (d) Repealed by Session Laws 1973, c. 1195, s. 5.

(e) The Commission may investigate complaints and conduct hearings as follows:

(1) The Commission may upon its own motion or upon the complaint in writing of any person, provided the complaint and any evidence presented with it establishes a prima facie case, hold a hearing and investigate the actions of any auctioneer, apprentice auctioneer, or auction firm, or any person who holds himself or herself out as an auctioneer or apprentice auctioneer, and shall have the power to impose a civil penalty on any licensee, suspend or revoke any license issued under the provisions of this Chapter, or to reprimand or censure any licensee. In all proceedings for the imposition of a civil penalty or the denial, suspension, or revocation of licenses, the provisions of Chapter 150B of the General Statutes including provisions relating to summary suspension shall be applicable. Any person who desires to appeal the denial of an application for any license authorized to be issued under this Chapter shall file a written appeal with the Commission not later than 30 days following notice of denial.

(2) The Commission may, upon its own motion, summarily suspend a license when the health, safety, or welfare of the public is at risk, such as in the event of a potential loss of consigned items or potential loss of funds.

(f) A person whose license has been denied, suspended, or revoked may not apply in that person's name or in any other manner within the period during which the order of denial, suspension, or revocation is in effect, and no firm, partnership, or corporation in which any person has a substantial interest or exercises management responsibility or control may be licensed during the period. (1973, c. 552, s. 8; c. 1195, ss. 4, 5; c. 1331, s. 3; 1975, c. 648, s. 6; 1983, c. 603, s. 6; 1989, c. 732, s. 5; 1991 (Reg. Sess., 1992), c. 819, s. 21; 1999-142, s. 7; 2005-330, s. 7.)

§ 85B-9. Penalties and enforcement.

(a) Any person, corporation or association of persons violating the provisions of G.S. 85B-4(a) shall be guilty of a Class 1 misdemeanor. The Attorney General of North Carolina, or the Attorney General's designee, shall have concurrent jurisdiction with the district attorneys of this State to prosecute violations of this Chapter.

(b) The Commission may in its own name seek injunctive relief in the General Court of Justice to restrain any violation or anticipated violation of the provisions of G.S. 85B-4(a) or any violation of this Chapter.

(c) The Commission shall be entitled to the services of the Attorney General of North Carolina in enforcing the provisions of this Chapter or may employ an attorney to assist and represent it in enforcement of specific matters. (1973, c. 1195, s. 6; 1975, c. 648, s. 7; 1991 (Reg. Sess., 1992), c. 819, s. 22; 1993, c. 539, s. 600; 1994, Ex. Sess., c. 24, s. 14(c); 1999-142, s. 8.)

Chapter 85C.

Bail Bondsmen and Runners.

§§ 85C-1 through 85C-41: Recodified as Article 71 of Chapter 58.

Chapter 86.

Barbers.

§§ 86-1 through 86-25. Recodified as §§ 86A-1 to 86A-26.

Chapter 86A.

Barbers.

§ 86A-1. Necessity for certificate of registration and shop or school permit.

No person or combination of persons shall, either directly or indirectly, practice or attempt to practice barbering in the State of North Carolina without first obtaining a certificate of registration either as a registered apprentice or as a registered barber issued pursuant to provisions of this Chapter by the State Board of Barber Examiners. No person or combination of persons, or corporation, shall operate, manage or attempt to operate or manage a barber school, barbershop, or any other place where barber services are rendered, after July 1, 1945, without first obtaining a shop permit, or school permit, issued by the State Board of Barber Examiners, pursuant to the provisions of this Chapter. (1929, c. 119, s. 1; 1941, c. 375, s. 1; 1945, c. 830, s. 1; 1979, c. 695, s. 1.)

§ 86A-2. What constitutes practice of barbering.

Any one or combination of the following practices constitutes the practice of barbering in the purview of this Chapter:

(1)   Shaving or trimming the beard, or cutting the hair;

(2)   Dyeing the hair or applying hair tonics, permanent waving or marcelling the hair;

(3)   Giving facial or scalp massages, or treatments with oils, creams, lotions or other preparations either by hand or mechanical appliances. (1929, c. 119, s. 2; 1941, c. 375, s. 2; 1979, c. 695, s. 1.)

§ 86A-3. Qualifications for certificate as a registered barber.

A certificate of registration as a registered barber shall be issued by the Board to any person who meets all of the following qualifications:

(1)   Has attended an approved barber school for at least 1528 hours.

(2)   Has completed a 12-month apprenticeship under the supervision of a licensed barber, as provided in G.S. 86A-24.

(3)   Has passed a clinical examination conducted by the Board.

(4)   Has submitted to the Board the affidavit required by G.S. 86A-24(c) certifying that the applicant has served the apprenticeship required by

subdivision (2). (1929, c. 119, ss. 3, 4, 11; 1941, c. 375, s. 3; 1961, c. 577, s. 1; 1979, c. 695, s. 1; 1981, c. 457, s. 1; 1995 (Reg. Sess., 1996), c. 605, s. 1.)

§ 86A-4. State Board of Barber Examiners; appointment and qualifications; term of office; removal.

(a) The State Board of Barber Examiners is established to consist of five members appointed by the Governor. Four shall be licensed barbers; the other shall be a person who is not licensed under this Chapter and who shall represent the interest of the public at large.

(b) No member appointed to the Board on or after July 1, 1981, shall serve more than three complete consecutive three-year terms, except that each member shall serve until the member's successor is appointed and qualifies.

No person who has been employed by the North Carolina State Board of Barber Examiners and has been removed for just cause shall be appointed within five years of the removal to serve as a Board member.

(c) The Governor may remove any member for good cause shown and may appoint members to fill unexpired terms.

(d) Expired effective July 1, 2007. (1929, c. 119, s. 6; 1979, c. 695, s. 1; 1981, c. 457, s. 2; 1995 (Reg. Sess., 1996), c. 605, s. 2; 2001-486, s. 2.2; 2004-146, s. 1(a).)

§ 86A-5. Powers and duties of the Board.

(a) The Board has the following powers and duties:

(1) To see that inspections of barbershops and schools are conducted to determine compliance with sanitary regulations. The Board may appoint inspectors as necessary.

(2) To adopt sanitary regulations concerning barber schools and shops and procedural rules in accordance with the guidelines established in G.S. 86A-15.

(3) To review the barber licensing laws of other states and to determine which are the substantive equivalent of the laws of North Carolina for purposes of G.S. 86A-12.

(4) To conduct examinations of applicants for certificate of registration as registered barber, registered apprentice and barber school instructor.

(5) To employ and fix the compensation of personnel that the Board deems necessary to carry out the provisions of this Chapter.

(6) To assess civil penalties pursuant to G.S. 86A-27.

(b) The Board shall adopt regulations:

(1) Prohibiting the use of commercial chemicals of unknown content by persons registered under this Chapter. For purposes of this section, "commercial chemicals" are those products sold only through beauty and barber supply houses and not available to the general public;

(2) Instructing persons registered under this Chapter in the proper use and application of commercial chemicals where no manufacturer's instructions are included. In the alternative, the Board shall prohibit the use of such commercial chemicals by persons registered under this Chapter.

(c) Each Board member shall submit periodic reports to the Board concerning his activities in carrying out duties as a Board member. (1929, c. 119, ss. 10, 12, 16; 1931, c. 32; 1933, c. 95, s. 2; 1941, c. 375, ss. 5, 7; 1945, c. 830, s. 8; 1947, c. 1024; 1961, c. 577, ss. 2, 3, 5; 1973, c. 1331, s. 3; 1979, c. 695, s. 1; 1981, c. 457, ss. 3, 4; 2004-146, s. 2.)

§ 86A-6. Office; seal; officers and executive director; funds.

The Board shall maintain a suitable office in Raleigh, and shall adopt and use a common seal for the authentication of its orders and records. The Board shall annually elect its own officers, and in addition, may elect or appoint a full-time executive director who shall not be a member of the Board, and whose salary shall be fixed by the Board. The executive director shall turn over to the State Treasurer to be credited to the State Board of Barber Examiners all funds collected or received under this Chapter, the funds to be held and expended under the supervision of the Director of the Budget, exclusively for the enforcement and administration of the provisions of this Chapter. Nothing herein shall be construed to authorize any expenditure in excess of the amount available from time to time in the hands of the State Treasurer derived from fees collected under the provisions of this Chapter and received by the State Treasurer pursuant to the provisions of this section. (1929, c. 119, ss. 7, 14; 1937, c. 138, s. 4; 1941, c. 375, s. 4; 1943, c. 53, s. 1; 1945, c. 830, ss. 2, 4; 1951, c. 821, s. 1; 1957, c. 813, ss. 1, 3; 1965, c. 513; 1971, c. 826, ss. 1, 2; 1973, c. 1398; 1979, c. 695, s. 1; 1981, c. 884, s. 5; 1983, c. 717, s. 15; 1995 (Reg. Sess., 1996), c. 605, s. 3; 2004-146, s. 3.)

§ 86A-7. Salary and expenses; employees; audits; annual reports to the Governor.

(a)   Each member of the Board of Barber Examiners shall be reimbursed for his actual expenses and shall receive compensation and travel allowance according to G.S. 93B-5 for the distance traveled in performance of his duties. The expenses, compensation and all other salaries and expenses in connection with the administration of this Chapter, shall be paid upon warrant drawn on the State Treasurer, solely from the funds derived from fees collected and received under this Chapter.

(b)   The Board shall employ such agents, assistants and attorneys as it deems necessary.

(c)   Repealed by Session Laws 1981, c. 884, s. 6.

(d)   Repealed by Session Laws 1983, c. 913, s. 8.

(e)   The Board shall report annually to the Governor, a full statement of its receipts and expenditures, and also a full statement of its work during the year, together with such recommendations as it may deem expedient. (1929, c. 119, s. 8; 1943, c. 53, s. 2; 1945, c. 830, s. 3; 1957, c. 813, s. 2; 1979, c. 695, s. 1; 1981, c. 884, s. 6; 1983, c. 913, s. 8.)

§ 86A-8. Application for examinations; payment of fee.

Each applicant for an examination shall:

(1) Make application to the Board on forms prepared and furnished by the Board, and the application shall contain proof under applicant's oath of the particular qualifications of the applicant. All applications for examination must be filed with the Board at least 30 days prior to the actual taking of such examination by applicants;

(2) Pay to the Board the required fee. (1929, c. 119, s. 9; 1979, c. 695, s. 1.)

§ 86A-9. Board to conduct examinations not less than four times each year.

The Board shall conduct examinations of applicants for certificates of registration to practice as registered barbers and registered apprentices, not less than four times each year, at such times and places as will prove most convenient and as the Board may determine. The Board may adopt rules establishing procedures for the administration of examinations. (1929, c. 119, s. 10; 1979, c. 695, s. 1; 2004-146, s. 4.)

§ 86A-10. Issuance of certificates of registration.

Whenever the provisions of this Chapter have been complied with, the Board shall issue, or have issued, a certificate of registration as a registered barber or as a registered apprentice, as the case may be. (1929, c. 119, s. 11; 1979, c. 695, s. 1; 1981, c. 457, s. 5.)

§ 86A-11. Temporary permits.

(a) The Board may grant a temporary permit to work to a graduate of a barber school in North Carolina provided application for examination has been filed and fee paid. The permit is valid only until the date of the next succeeding Board examination of applicants for apprenticeship registration except in cases of undue hardship as the Board may determine, unless it is revoked or suspended earlier by the Board. In no event shall a temporary permit be issued or remain valid after the holder has twice failed the apprentice examination required by G.S. 86A-24(a). The permittee may operate only under the supervision of a licensed barber and may work only at the registered barbershop specified in the permit.

(b)   The Board may grant a temporary permit to work to one whose license has been expired for more than five years in North Carolina provided application for examination to restore has been filed and fee paid. The permit is valid only until the date of the next succeeding Board examination of applicants for barber licenses except in cases of undue hardship as the Board may determine, unless it is revoked or suspended earlier by the Board.

(c)   The Board may grant a temporary permit to persons licensed in another state who come to North Carolina for the purpose of teaching or demonstrating barber skills. The Board shall also inspect and approve the area where the demonstration is to be given if it is not an already approved shop or school. This permit shall be limited to the specific days of demonstration and shall be of no validity before or after.

(d)   The Board may grant a temporary permit to work to persons licensed in another state and seeking permanent licensure in North Carolina under G.S. 86A-12. (1929, c. 119, s. 12; 1941, c. 375, s. 5; 1947, c. 1024; 1961, c. 577, s. 2; 1979, c. 695, s. 1; 1981, c. 457, ss. 6, 7; 1995 (Reg. Sess., 1996), c. 605, s. 4.)

§ 86A-12. Applicants licensed in other states.

(a)   The Board shall issue, without examination, a license to applicants already licensed in another state provided the applicant presents evidence satisfactory to the Board that:

(1)   He is currently an active, competent practitioner in good standing; and

(2)   He has practiced at least three out of the five years immediately preceding his application; and

(3)   He currently holds a valid license in another state; and

(4) There is no disciplinary proceeding or unresolved complaint pending against him at the time a license is to be issued by this State; and

(5) The licensure requirements in the other state are the substantive equivalent of those required by this State.

(b) The requirements in subdivisions (1) or (5), or both, of subsection (a) of this section may be waived by the Board provided that the applicant presents evidence satisfactory to the Board that the applicant:

(1) Has met the licensure requirements of the state in which he received his license;

(2) Has at least five years practical experience; and

(3) Demonstrates his knowledge of barbering skills and of the sanitary regulations in North Carolina by passing a practical, written or oral examination.

(c) Any license granted pursuant to this section is subject to the same duties and obligations and entitled to the same rights and privileges as a license issued under G.S. 86A-3. (1929, c. 119, s. 12; 1941, c. 375, s. 5; 1947, c. 1024; 1961, c. 577, s. 2; 1979, c. 695, s. 1; 1981, c. 457, s. 8; 1987, c. 210.)

§ 86A-13. Barbershop and barber school permits.

(a) Any person, firm or corporation, before establishing or opening a barbershop or barber school not heretofore licensed by the State or the Board shall make application to the Board on forms to be furnished by the Board, for a permit to operate a barbershop or barber school, and the shop or school of the applicant shall be inspected and approved by the State Board of Barber Examiners or an agent designated for that purpose by the Board, before the barbershop or barber school may open for business. It is unlawful to open a new or reopened barbershop or barber school until that shop or school has been inspected and determined by the Board to be in compliance with the requirements of G.S. 86A-15 in the case of shops and G.S. 86A-15 and 86A-22 in the case of schools. Upon compliance by the applicant with all requirements set forth in G.S. 86A-15, and the payment of the prescribed fee the Board shall issue to the applicant the permit applied for. Notwithstanding any other provision of this Chapter, no person, firm, or corporation shall be issued a permit to operate a barbershop in a location registered as a barber school, nor shall any person, firm, or corporation be issued a permit to operate a barber school in a location registered as a barbershop.

(b) The owners of every registered barbershop and barber school shall annually, on or before May 31 of each year, renew the barbershop's or barber school's certificate of registration and pay the required renewal fee. Every certificate of registration for any barbershop or barber school shall expire on the 31st day of May in each year. Any certificate of registration issued under this Chapter shall be suspended automatically by operation of law after failure to renew the certificate of registration by the expiration date. The owner of any barbershop or barber school whose certificate of registration has expired may, after the barbershop or barber school has been inspected as required in subsection (a) of this section, have the certificate restored immediately upon paying all lapsed renewal fees and the required late fee. (1929, c. 119, ss. 1, 16; 1931, c. 32; 1933, c. 95, s. 2; 1941, c. 375, ss. 1, 7; 1945, c. 830, ss. 1, 8; 1961, c. 577, ss. 3, 5; 1973, c. 1331, s. 3; 1979, c. 695, s. 1; 1995 (Reg. Sess., 1996), c. 605, s. 5.)

§ 86A-14. Persons exempt from the provisions of this Chapter.

The following persons are exempt from the provisions of this Chapter while engaged in the proper discharge of their duties:

(1) Persons authorized under the laws of the State to practice medicine and surgery, and those working under their supervision;

(2) Commissioned medical or surgical officers of the United States Army or other components of the Armed Forces of the United States, and those working under their supervision;

(3) Registered nurses and licensed practical nurses and those working under their supervision;

(4) Licensed embalmers and funeral directors and those working under their supervision;

(5) Persons who are working in licensed cosmetic shops or beauty schools and are licensed by the State Board of Cosmetic Art Examiners pursuant to Chapter 88B of the General Statutes; and

(6) Persons who are working in licensed barber shops and are licensed by the State Board of Cosmetic Art Examiners pursuant to Chapter 88B of the General Statutes, provided that those persons shall comply with G.S. 86A-15. (1929, c. 119, s. 15; 1937, c. 138, s. 2; 1941, c. 375, s. 6; 1979, c. 695, s. 1; 1995 (Reg. Sess., 1996), c. 605, s. 6; 1998-230, s. 2.2; 2011-183, s. 51.)

§ 86A-15. Sanitary rules and regulations; inspections.

(a) Each barber and each owner or manager of a barbershop, barber school or college, or any other place where barber service is rendered, shall comply with the following sanitary rules and regulations:

(1) Proper quarters. -

a. Every barbershop, or other place where barber service is rendered, shall be located in buildings or rooms of such construction that they may be easily cleaned, well lighted, well ventilated and kept in an orderly and sanitary condition.

b. Each area where barber service is rendered or where a combination of barber service and cosmetology service is rendered shall be separated by a substantial partition or wall from areas used for purposes other than barber services, cosmetology services, or shoe shining services.

c. Walls, floor and fixtures where barber service is rendered are to be kept sanitary.

d. Running water, hot and cold, shall be provided, and sinks shall be located at a convenient place in each barbershop so that barbers may wash their hands after each haircut. Tanks and lavatories shall be of such construction that they may be easily cleaned. The lavatory must have a drain pipe to drain all waste water out of the building.

e.   Every barbershop or other place where barber service is rendered, and every building or structure used as a part of a barber school, shall comply with applicable building and fire codes and regulations.

(2)   Equipment and instruments. -

a.   Each person serving as a barber shall, immediately before using razors, tweezers, combs, contact cup or pad, sterilize the instruments by immersing them in a solution of fifty percent (50%) alcohol, five percent (5%) carbolic acid, twenty percent (20%) formaldehyde, or ten percent (10%) lysol or other product or solution that the Board may approve. Every owner or manager of a barbershop shall supply a separate container for the use of each barber, adequate to provide for a sufficient supply of the above solutions.

b.   Each barber shall maintain combs and hair brushes in a clean and sanitary condition at all times and shall thoroughly clean mug and lather brush before each separate use.

c.   The headrest of every barber chair shall be protected with clean paper or a clean laundered towel. Each barber chair shall be covered with a smooth nonporous surface, such as vinyl or leather, that is cleaned easily.

d.   Every person serving as a barber shall use a clean towel for each patron. All clean towels shall be placed in closed cabinets until used. Receptacles composed of material that can be washed and cleansed shall be provided to receive used towels, and all used towels must be placed in receptacles until laundered. Towels shall not be placed in a sterilizer or tank or rinsed in the barbershop. All wet and used towels shall be removed from the workstand or lavatory after serving each patron.

e.   Whenever a hair cloth is used in cutting the hair, shampooing, etc., a newly laundered towel or paper neckstrap shall be placed around the patron's neck so as to prevent the hair cloth from touching the skin. Hair cloths shall be replaced when soiled.

(3)   Barbers. -

a.   Every person serving as a barber shall thoroughly cleanse his or her hands immediately before serving each patron.

b. Each person working as a barber shall be clean both as to person and dress.

c. No barber shall serve any person who has an infectious or communicable disease, and no barber shall undertake to treat any patron's infectious or contagious disease.

(4) Any person, other than a registered barber, shall before undertaking to give shampoos in a barbershop furnish the Board with a health certificate on a form provided by the Board.

(5) The owner or manager of a barbershop or any other place where barber service is rendered shall post a copy of these rules and regulations in a conspicuous place in the shop or other place where the services are rendered.

(b) All barbershops, barber schools and colleges, and any other place where barber service is rendered, shall be open for inspection at all times during business hours to any members of the Board of Barber Examiners or its agents or assistants. A copy of the sanitary rules and regulations set out in this section shall be furnished by the Board to the owner or manager of each barbershop or barber school, or any other place where barber service is rendered in the State, and that copy shall be posted in a conspicuous place in each barbershop or barber school. The Board shall have the right to make additional rules and regulations governing barbers and barbershops and barber schools for the proper administration and enforcement of this section, but no such additional rules or regulations shall be in effect until those rules and regulations have been furnished to each barbershop within the State.

(c) Notwithstanding any other provision of law, a registered barber may practice barbering in a client's home out of medical necessity without meeting the requirements of subsection (b) of this section. The Board of Barber Examiners shall adopt rules to allow this exception. (1929, c. 119, s. 16; 1931, c. 32; 1933, c. 95, s. 2; 1941, c. 375, s. 7; 1961, c. 577, s. 3; 1979, c. 695, s. 1; 1995 (Reg. Sess., 1996), c. 605, s. 7; 2009-471, s. 1.)

§ 86A-16. Certificates to be displayed.

Every holder of a certificate of registration as a registered barber, registered apprentice, shop permit, school permit, instructor's certificate, or temporary permit issued pursuant to G.S. 86A-11 shall display it in a conspicuous place adjacent to or near the person's work chair. (1929, c. 119, s. 17; 1979, c. 695, s. 1; 1995 (Reg. Sess., 1996), c. 605, s. 8.)

§ 86A-17. Renewal or restoration of certificate.

(a)   Registered barbers who continue in practice shall annually, on or before May 31 of each year, renew their certificates of registration and furnish such health certificate as the Board may require and pay the required renewal fee. Every certificate of registration shall expire on the 31st day of May in each year. Any certificate of registration issued under this Chapter is automatically suspended by operation of law after failure to renew the certificate of registration by the expiration date.

(b)   A registered barber whose certificate of registration has expired may have the certificate restored immediately upon paying all lapsed renewal fees and the required late fee and furnishing a health certificate if required by the Board. Where a registered barber's certificate of registration has expired for a period greater than six months, the Board may impose civil penalties pursuant to G.S. 86A-27. A registered barber whose certificate has expired for a period of five years shall be required to take the clinical examination prescribed by the State Board of Barber Examiners and otherwise comply with the provisions of this Chapter before engaging in the practice of barbering. No registered barber who is reissued a certificate under this subsection shall be required to serve an apprenticeship as a prerequisite to reissuance of the certificate.

(c)   All persons serving in the Armed Forces of the United States and persons whose certificates of registration as a registered barber were in force one year prior to entering service may, without taking the required examination, renew their certificates within 90 days after receiving an honorable discharge, by paying the current annual license fee and furnishing the State Board of Barber Examiners with a satisfactory health certificate if required by the Board. (1929, c. 119, s. 18; 1937, c. 138, s. 5; 1945, c. 830, s. 5; 1973, c. 605; 1979, c. 695, s. 1; 1981, c. 457, s. 11; 1995 (Reg. Sess., 1996), c. 605, s. 9; 2004-146, s. 5; 2011-183, s. 52.)

§ 86A-18. Disqualifications for certificate.

The Board may either refuse to issue or to renew, or may suspend or revoke any certificate of registration or barbershop permit or barber school permit for any one or combination of the following causes:

(1) Conviction of the applicant or certificate holder of a felony proved by certified copy of the record of the court conviction;

(2) Gross malpractice or gross incompetence;

(3) Continued practice by a person knowingly having an infectious or contagious disease after being warned in writing by the Board to cease practice;

(4) Habitual drunkenness or habitual addiction to the use of morphine, cocaine or other habit forming drugs;

(5) The commission of any of the offenses described in subdivisions (3), (5), and (6) of G.S. 86A-20;

(6) The violation of any one or more of the sanitary rules and regulations established by statute or rule or regulation of the Board, provided that the Board has previously given two written warnings to the individual committing the violation;

(7) The violation of the rules and regulations pertaining to barber schools, provided that the Board has previously given two written warnings to the school. (1929, c. 119, s. 19; 1941, c. 375, s. 8; 1945, c. 830, s. 6; 1961, c. 477, s. 4; 1979, c. 695, s. 1; 1981, c. 457, s. 9.)

§ 86A-19. Refusal, revocation or suspension of certificates or permits.

The Board may neither refuse to issue nor refuse to renew, or suspend or revoke any certificate of registration, barbershop permit, or barber school permit, for any of these causes except in accordance with the provisions of Chapter 150B of the General Statutes. (1929, c. 119, s. 20; 1939, c. 218, s. 1; 1945, c. 830, s. 7; 1953, c. 1041, s. 2; 1973, c. 1331, s. 3; 1979, c. 695, s. 1.)

§ 86A-20. Misdemeanors.

Each of the following acts constitutes a Class 3 misdemeanor:

(1)   Violation of any of the provisions of G.S. 86A-1;

(2)   Obtaining or attempting to obtain a certificate of registration for money other than the required fee or any other thing of value, or by fraudulent misrepresentations;

(3)   Practicing or attempting to practice by fraudulent misrepresentations;

(4)   Willful failure to display a certificate of registration as required by G.S. 86A-16;

(5)   Practicing or attempting to practice barbering during the period of suspension or revocation of any certificate of registration granted under this Chapter. Each day's operation during a period of suspension or revocation shall be deemed a separate offense;

(6)   Permitting any person in one's employ, supervision or control to practice as a barber unless that person holds a certificate as a registered barber or registered apprentice. (1929, c. 119, s. 21; 1933, c. 95, s. 1; 1937, c. 138, s. 6; 1941, c. 375, ss. 9, 10; 1951, c. 821, s. 2; 1971, c. 819; 1979, c. 695, s. 1; 1981, c. 457, s. 10; 1993, c. 539, s. 601; 1994, Ex. Sess., c. 24, s. 14(c).)

§ 86A-20.1. Enjoining illegal practices.

The Board, the Department of Health and Human Services, or any county or district health director may apply to the superior court for an injunction to restrain any person from violating the provisions of this Chapter or the Board's rules. Actions under this section shall be brought in the county where the defendant resides or maintains his or her principal place of business or where the alleged acts occurred. (2004-146, s. 6.)

§ 86A-21. Board to keep record of proceedings; data on registrants.

The Board shall keep a record of its proceedings relating to the issuance, refusal, renewal, suspension, and revocation of certificates of registration. This record shall contain the name, place of business and residence of each registered barber and registered apprentice, and the date and number of his certificate of registration. This record shall be open to public inspection at all reasonable times. (1929, c. 119, s. 22; 1979, c. 695, s. 1.)

§ 86A-22. Licensing and regulating barber schools and colleges.

The North Carolina State Board of Barber Examiners may approve barber schools or colleges in the State, and may prescribe rules and regulations for their operation. The Board shall adopt rules establishing criteria for barber schools and colleges to maintain their accreditation. No barber school or college shall be approved by the Board unless the school or college meets all of the following requirements:

(1) Each school shall provide a course of instruction of at least 1528 hours.

(2) Each school shall employ at least two instructors for the first 40 enrolled students and employ at least one additional instructor for every additional 20 enrolled students. Schools that are organized as nonprofits and have obtained a ruling from the Internal Revenue Service recognizing their tax-exempt status shall have at least one instructor for every 20 enrolled students. No school, whether for profit or nonprofit, shall provide practical training and theoretical training simultaneously unless at least two instructors are present.

(3) An application for a student's permit, on a form prescribed by the Board, must be filed with the Board before the student enters school. No student may enroll without having obtained a student's permit.

(4) Each student enrolled shall be given a complete course of instruction on the following subjects: hair cutting; shaving; shampooing, and the application of creams and lotions; care and preparation of tools and implements; scientific massaging and manipulating the muscles of the scalp, face, and neck; sanitation and hygiene; shedding and regrowth of hair; elementary chemistry relating to sterilization and antiseptics; instruction on common skin and scalp diseases to the extent that they may be recognized; pharmacology as it relates to preparations commonly used in barbershops; instruction in the use of electrical appliances and the effects of the use of these on the human skin;

structure of the skin and hair; nerve points of the face; the application of hair dyes and bleaches; permanent waving; marcelling or hair pressing; frosting and streaking; and the statutes and regulations relating to the practice of barbering in North Carolina. The Board shall specify the minimum number of hours of instruction for each subject required by this subsection.

(5) Each school shall file an up-to-date list of its students with the Board at least once a month. If a student withdraws or transfers, the school shall file a report with the Board stating the courses and hours completed by the withdrawing or transferring student. The school shall also file with the Board a list of students who have completed the amount of work necessary to meet the licensing requirements.

(6) Each school shall comply with the sanitary requirements of G.S. 86A-15.

(7) a. Each school shall provide a guaranty bond unless the school has already provided a bond or an alternative to a bond under G.S. 115D-95.

The North Carolina State Board of Barber Examiners may revoke the approval of a school that fails to maintain a bond or an alternative to a bond pursuant to this subdivision or G.S. 115D-95.

b. When application is made for approval or renewal of approval, the applicant shall file a guaranty bond with the clerk of the superior court of the county in which the school will be located. The bond shall be in favor of the students. The bond shall be executed by the applicant as principal and by a bonding company authorized to do business in this State. The bond shall be conditioned to provide indemnification to any student, or his parent or guardian, who has suffered a loss of tuition or any fees by reason of the failure of the school to offer or complete student instruction, academic services, or other goods and services related to course enrollment for any reason, including the suspension, revocation, or nonrenewal of a school's approval, bankruptcy, foreclosure, or the school ceasing to operate.

The bond shall be in an amount determined by the Board to be adequate to provide indemnification to any student, or his parent or guardian, under the terms of the bond. The bond amount for a school shall be at least equal to the maximum amount of prepaid tuition held at any time during the last fiscal year by the school. The bond amount shall also be at least ten thousand dollars ($10,000).

Each application for approval shall include a letter signed by an authorized representative of the school showing in detail the calculations made and the method of computing the amount of the bond pursuant to this subpart and the rules of the Board. If the Board finds that the calculations made and the method of computing the amount of the bond are inaccurate or that the amount of the bond is otherwise inadequate to provide indemnification under the terms of the bond, the Board may require the applicant to provide an additional bond.

The bond shall remain in force and effect until cancelled by the guarantor. The guarantor may cancel the bond upon 30 days notice to the Board. Cancellation of the bond shall not affect any liability incurred or accrued prior to the termination of the notice period.

c. An applicant that is unable to secure a bond may seek a waiver of the guaranty bond from the Board and approval of one of the guaranty bond alternatives set forth in this subpart. With the approval of the Board, an applicant may file with the clerk of the superior court of the county in which the school will be located, in lieu of a bond:

1. An assignment of a savings account in an amount equal to the bond required (i) which is in a form acceptable to the Board; (ii) which is executed by the applicant; and (iii) which is executed by a state or federal savings and loan association, state bank, or national bank, that is doing business in North Carolina and whose accounts are insured by a federal depositors corporation; and (iv) for which access to the account in favor of the State of North Carolina is subject to the same conditions as for a bond in subpart b. above.

2. A certificate of deposit (i) which is executed by a state or federal savings and loan association, state bank, or national bank, which is doing business in North Carolina and whose accounts are insured by a federal depositors corporation; and (ii) which is either payable to the State of North Carolina, unrestrictively endorsed to the Board; in the case of a negotiable certificate of deposit, is unrestrictively endorsed to the Board; or in the case of a nonnegotiable certificate of deposit, is assigned to the Board in a form satisfactory to the Board; and (iii) for which access to the certificate of deposit in favor of the State of North Carolina is subject to the same conditions as for a bond in subpart b. above. (1945, c. 830, s. 8; 1961, c. 577, s. 5; 1973, c. 1331, s. 3; 1979, c. 695, s. 1; 1981, c. 457, s. 12; 1989 (Reg. Sess., 1990), c. 824, s. 3; 1995, c. 397, s. 1; 1995 (Reg. Sess., 1996), c. 605, ss. 10, 11; 2004-146, s. 7.)

§ 86A-23. Instructors.

(a) The Board shall issue an instructor's certificate to any currently registered barber who has passed an instructor's examination given by the Board. This examination shall cover the subjects listed in G.S. 86A-22(4) and in the Textbook of Barber Styling approved by the Board.

(b) A person desiring to take an instructor's examination must make application to the Board for examination on forms to be furnished by the Board and pay the instructor's examination fee. Each person who passes the instructor's examination shall be issued a certificate of registration as a registered instructor by paying the issuance fee. Every instructor's certificate shall expire on May 31 of each year. Any instructor's certificate issued under this Chapter is automatically suspended by operation of law after failure to renew the instructor's certificate by the expiration date and may be renewed only upon payment of all lapsed renewal fees and the required late fee. Any person whose instructor's certificate has expired for a period of three years or more shall be required to take and pass the instructor's examination before the certificate can be renewed. (1945, c. 830, s. 8; 1961, c. 577, s. 5; 1973, c. 1331, s. 3; 1979, c. 695, s. 1; 1981, c. 457, s. 13; 1995 (Reg. Sess., 1996), c. 605, s. 12.)

§ 86A-24. Apprenticeship.

(a) Before being issued an apprentice license, an applicant must pass an examination conducted by the Board to determine his competence, including his knowledge of barbering, sanitary rules and regulations, and knowledge of diseases of the face, skin and scalp.

(b) An apprentice license expires on May 31 of each year. Every holder of an apprentice license shall annually renew the apprentice license by the expiration date and pay the required renewal fee. An apprentice license issued under this Chapter is automatically suspended by operation of law after failure to renew the apprentice license by the expiration date. An apprentice whose apprentice license has expired may have the certificate restored immediately upon paying all lapsed renewal fees and the required late fee. The certificate of registration of an apprentice is valid only so long as the apprentice works under the supervision of a registered barber. The registered barber shall remain present on the premises of the barbershop at all times while the apprentice is working. No apprentice shall operate a barbershop.

(c)   On completion of at least one year's apprenticeship, evidenced by affidavit of the supervising registered licensed barber or barbers, and upon meeting the other requirements of G.S. 86A-3, the apprentice shall be issued a license as a registered barber, pursuant to G.S. 86A-10. No registered apprentice may practice for a period exceeding three years without retaking and passing the required examination to receive a certificate as a registered apprentice. (1929, c. 119, ss. 4, 5; 1941, c. 375, s. 3; 1975, c. 68, ss. 1, 2; 1979, c. 695, s. 1; 1981, c. 457, s. 14; 1995 (Reg. Sess., 1996), c. 605, s. 13; 2004-146, s. 8.)

§ 86A-25. Fees collectible by Board.

The State Board of Barber Examiners shall charge fees not to exceed the following:

Certificate of registration or renewal as a barber .... $ 50.00

Certificate of registration or renewal as an apprentice barber 50.00

Barbershop permit or renewal 50.00

Examination to become a registered barber 85.00

Examination to become a registered apprentice barber 85.00

Late fee for restoration of an expired barber certificate within

   first year after expiration 35.00

Late fee for restoration of an expired barber certificate after first

year after expiration but within five years after expiration ....
70.00

Late fee for restoration of an expired apprentice certificate

within first year after expiration ....
35.00

Late fee for restoration of an expired apprentice certificate after

first year after expiration but within three years of first

issuance of the certificate ....
45.00

Late fee for restoration of an expired barbershop certificate ....
45.00

Examination to become a barber school instructor ....
165.00

Student permit ....
25.00

Issuance of any duplicate copy of a license, certificate, or permit ....
10.00

Barber school permit or renewal ....
130.00

Late fee for restoration of an expired barber school certificate ....
85.00

Barber school instructor certificate or renewal ....
85.00

Late fee for restoration of an expired barber school instructor

certificate within first year after expiration ....
45.00

Late fee for restoration of an expired barber school instructor

   certificate after first year after expiration but within

      three years after expiration ....
85.00

Inspection of newly established barbershop ....
120.00

Inspection of newly established barber school ....
220.00

Issuance of a registered barber or apprentice certificate

      by certification ....
120.00

Barbers 70 years and older certificate or renewal ....
No charge

Reasonable charges for certified copies of public documents

Reasonable charges for duplication services and material.

(1929, c. 119, s. 14; 1937, c. 138, s. 4; 1945, c. 830, ss. 4, 8; 1951, c. 821, s. 1; 1957, c. 813, s. 3; 1961, c. 577, s. 5; 1965, c. 513; 1971, c. 826, ss. 1, 2; 1973, c. 1331, s. 3; c. 1398; 1979, c. 695, s. 1; 1981, c. 753; 1989 (Reg. Sess., 1990), c. 1029, s. 1; 1995 (Reg. Sess., 1996), c. 605, s. 14; 2004-146, s. 11.)

§ 86A-26. Barbering among members of same family.

This Chapter shall not prohibit a member of a family from practicing barbering on a member of his or her family. For purposes of this section, "a member of his or her family" means a spouse, brother, sister, parent, grandparent, child, grandchild, mother-in-law, father-in-law, daughter-in-law, son-in-law, stepparent, or stepchild. (1941, c. 375, s. 12; 1979, c. 695, s. 1; 2004-146, s. 9.)

§ 86A-27. Civil penalties; disciplinary costs.

(a) Authority to Assess Civil Penalties. - The Board may assess a civil penalty not in excess of five hundred dollars ($500.00) per offense for the violation of any section of this Chapter or the violation of any rules adopted by the Board. The clear proceeds of any civil penalty assessed under this section shall be remitted to the Civil Penalty and Forfeiture Fund in accordance with G.S. 115C-457.2.

(b) Consideration Factors. - Before imposing and assessing a civil penalty, the Board shall consider the following factors:

(1) The nature, gravity, and persistence of the particular violation.

(2) The appropriateness of the imposition of a civil penalty when considered alone or in combination with other punishment.

(3) Whether the violation was willful and malicious.

(4) Any other factors that would tend to mitigate or aggravate the violations found to exist.

(c) Schedule of Civil Penalties. - The Board shall establish a schedule of civil penalties for violations of this Chapter and rules adopted by the Board.

(d) Costs. - The Board may in a disciplinary proceeding charge costs, including reasonable attorneys' fees, to the licensee against whom the proceedings were brought. (2004-146, s. 10.)

Chapter 87.

Contractors.

Article 1.

General Contractors.

§ 87-1. "General contractor" defined; exceptions.

(a) For the purpose of this Article any person or firm or corporation who for a fixed price, commission, fee, or wage, undertakes to bid upon or to construct or who undertakes to superintend or manage, on his own behalf or for any person, firm, or corporation that is not licensed as a general contractor pursuant to this Article, the construction of any building, highway, public utilities, grading or any improvement or structure where the cost of the undertaking is thirty thousand dollars ($30,000) or more, or undertakes to erect a North Carolina labeled manufactured modular building meeting the North Carolina State Building Code, shall be deemed to be a "general contractor" engaged in the business of general contracting in the State of North Carolina.

(b) This section shall not apply to the following:

(1) Persons, firms, or corporations furnishing or erecting industrial equipment, power plan equipment, radial brick chimneys, and monuments.

(2) Any person, firm, or corporation who constructs or alters a building on land owned by that person, firm, or corporation provided (i) the building is intended solely for occupancy by that person and his family, firm, or corporation after completion; and (ii) the person, firm, or corporation complies with G.S. 87-14. If the building is not occupied solely by the person and his family, firm, or corporation for at least 12 months following completion, it shall be presumed that the person, firm, or corporation did not intend the building solely for occupancy by that person and his family, firm, or corporation.

(3) Any person engaged in the business of farming who constructs or alters a building on land owned by that person and used in the business of farming, when the building is intended for use by that person after completion. (1925, c. 318, s. 1; 1931, c. 62, s. 1; 1937, c. 429, s. 1; 1949, c. 936; 1953, c. 810; 1971, c. 246, s. 1; 1975, c. 279, s. 1; 1981, c. 783, s. 1; 1989, c. 109, s. 1; c. 653, s. 1; 1991 (Reg. Sess., 1992), c. 840, s. 1; 2011-376, s. 1.)

§ 87-1.1. Exception for licensees under Article 2 or 4.

G.S. 87-1 shall not apply to a licensee under Article 2 or 4 of this Chapter of the General Statutes, G.S. 87-43 shall not apply to a licensee under Article 2 of this Chapter of the General Statutes, and G.S. 87-21(a)(5) shall not apply to a licensee under Article 4 of this Chapter of the General Statutes when the licensee is bidding and contracting directly with the owner of a public building project if: (i) a licensed general contractor performs all work that falls within the classifications in G.S. 87-10(b) and the State Licensing Board of General Contractor's rules; and (ii) the total amount of the general contracting work so classified does not exceed a percentage of the total bid price pursuant to rules established by the. Board; and (iii) a licensee with the appropriate license under Article 2 or Article 4 of this Chapter performs all work that falls within the classifications in Article 2 and Article 4 of this Chapter. (2003-231, s. 1; 2006-241, s. 2; 2006-259, s. 43; 2006-261, s. 3.)

§ 87-1.2. Exception for specified Department of Transportation contractors.

The letting of contracts for the types of projects specified in G.S. 136-28.14 shall not be subject to the licensing requirement of this Article. (2006-261, s. 2.)

§ 87-2. Licensing Board; organization.

There is created the State Licensing Board for General Contractors consisting of nine members appointed by the Governor for staggered five-year terms. Five of the members shall be general contractors, one member shall be a registered engineer who practices structural engineering, and three shall be public members. Of the general contractor members, one shall have as the larger part of his business the construction of highways; one shall have as the larger part of his business the construction of public utilities; one shall have as the larger part of his business the construction of buildings; and two shall have as a larger part of their businesses the construction of residences, one of whom shall be the holder of an unlimited general contractor's license. The public members shall have no ties with the construction industry and shall represent the interests of the public at large. Members shall serve until the expiration of their respective terms and until their successors are appointed and qualified. Vacancies occurring during a term shall be filled by appointment of the Governor for the remainder of the unexpired term. The Governor may remove any member of the Board for misconduct, incompetency, or neglect of duty. No Board member shall serve more than two complete consecutive terms. (1925, c. 318, s. 2; 1979, c. 713, s. 1; 1991, c. 124, s. 1.)

§ 87-3. Members of Board to take oath.

Each member of the Board shall, before entering upon the discharge of the duties of his office, take and file with the Secretary of State an oath in writing to properly perform the duties of his office as a member of said Board and to uphold the Constitution of North Carolina and the Constitution of the United States. (1925, c. 318, s. 3.)

§ 87-4. First meeting of Board; officers; secretary-treasurer and assistants.

The said Board shall, within 30 days after its appointment by the Governor, meet in the City of Raleigh, at a time and place to be designated by the Governor, and organize by electing a chairman, a vice-chairman, and a secretary-treasurer, each to serve for one year. Said Board shall have power to make such bylaws, rules and regulations as it shall deem best, provided the same are not in conflict with the laws of North Carolina. The secretary-treasurer shall give bond in such sum as the Board shall determine, with such security as shall be approved by the Board, said bond to be conditioned for the faithful performance of the duties of his office and for the faithful accounting of all moneys and other property as shall come into his hands. The secretary-treasurer need not be a member of the Board, and the Board is hereby authorized to employ a full-time secretary-treasurer, and such other assistants and make such other expenditures as may be necessary to the proper carrying out of the provisions of this Article. Payment of compensation and reimbursement of expenses of board members shall be governed by G.S. 93B-5. (1925, c. 318, s. 4; 1941, c. 257, s. 4; 1947, c. 611; 1951, c. 453; 1979, c. 713, s. 6.)

§ 87-5. Seal of Board.

The Board shall adopt a seal for its own use. The seal shall have the words "North Carolina Licensing Board for General Contractors" and the secretary shall have charge, care and custody thereof. (1925, c. 318, s. 5; 1979, c. 713, s. 7.)

§ 87-6. Meetings; notice; quorum.

The Board shall meet twice each year, once in April and once in October, for the purpose of transacting such business as may properly come before it. At the April meeting in each year the Board shall elect officers. Special meetings may be held at such times as the Board may provide in the bylaws it shall adopt. Due notice of each meeting and the time and place thereof shall be given to each member in such manner as the bylaws may provide. Five members of the Board shall constitute a quorum. (1925, c. 318, s. 6; 1979, c. 713, s. 8.)

§ 87-7. Records of Board; disposition of funds.

The secretary-treasurer shall keep a record of the proceedings of the said Board and shall receive and account for all moneys derived from the operation of this Article. Any funds remaining in the hands of the secretary-treasurer to the credit of the Board after the expenses of the Board for the current year have been paid shall be paid over to the Greater University of North Carolina for the use of the School of Engineering through the North Carolina Engineering Foundation. The Board has the right, however, to retain at least ten percent (10%) of the total expense it incurs for a year's operation to meet any emergency that may arise. As an expense of the Board, said Board is authorized to expend such funds as it deems necessary to provide retirement and disability compensation for its employees. (1925, c. 318, s. 7; 1953, c. 805, s. 1; 1959, c. 1184.)

§ 87-8. Records; roster of licensed contractors; report to Governor.

The secretary-treasurer shall keep a record of the proceedings of the Board and a register of all applicants for license showing for each the date of application, name, qualifications, place of business, place of residence, and whether license was granted or refused. The books and register of this Board shall be prima facie evidence of all matters recorded therein. A roster showing the names and places of business and of residence of all licensed general contractors shall be prepared by the secretary of the Board during the month of March of each year; the roster shall be printed by the Board out of funds of the Board as provided in G.S. 87-7, with copies being made available to contractors and members of the public, at cost, upon request, or furnished without cost, as directed by the Board. On or before the last day of March of each year the Board shall submit to the Governor a report of its transactions for the preceding year, and shall file with the Secretary of State a copy of the report, together with a complete statement of the receipts and expenditures of the Board, attested by the affidavits of the chairman and the secretary, and a copy of the roster of licensed general contractors. (1925, c. 318, s. 8; 1937, c. 429, s. 2; 1985, c. 630, s. 1; 1993, c. 148, s. 1.)

§ 87-9. Compliance with Federal Highway Act, etc.; contracts financed by federal road funds; contracts concerning water or waste water systems.

Nothing in this Article shall operate to prevent the Department of Transportation from complying with any act of Congress and any rules and regulations promulgated pursuant thereto for carrying out the provisions of the Federal Highway Act, or shall apply to any person, firm or corporation proposing to submit a bid or enter into contract for any work to be financed in whole or in part with federal aid road funds in such manner as will conflict with any act of Congress or any such rules and regulations promulgated pursuant thereto.

Neither shall anything in this Article prevent the State of North Carolina or any of its political subdivisions or their contractors from complying with any act of Congress and any rules and regulations promulgated pursuant thereto for carrying out the provisions of any federal program to assist in the planning, financing, or construction of drinking water or waste water processing, collection, and disposal systems and facilities. (1939, c. 230; 1971, c. 246, s. 2; 1973, c. 507, s. 5; 1977, c. 464, s. 34; 1989, c. 159.)

§ 87-9.1. Ownership of real property; equipment; liability insurance.

(a) The Board shall have the power to acquire, hold, rent, encumber, alienate, and otherwise deal with real property in the same manner as a private person or corporation, subject only to approval of the Governor and the Council of State as to the acquisition, rental, encumbering, leasing, and sale of real property. Collateral pledged by the Board for an encumbrance is limited to the assets, income, and revenues of the Board.

(b) The Board may purchase or rent equipment and supplies and purchase liability insurance or other insurance to cover the activities of the Board, its operations, or its employees. (1999-349, s. 1.)

§ 87-10. Application for license; examination; certificate; renewal.

(a) Anyone seeking to be licensed as a general contractor in this State shall file an application for an examination on a form provided by the Board, at least 30 days before any regular or special meeting of the Board. The Board may require the applicant to pay the Board or a provider contracted by the Board an examination fee not to exceed one hundred dollars ($100.00) and pay to the Board a license fee not to exceed one hundred twenty-five dollars ($125.00) if the application is for an unlimited license, one hundred dollars ($100.00) if the application is for an intermediate license, or seventy-five dollars ($75.00) if the application is for a limited license. The fees accompanying any application or examination shall be nonrefundable. The holder of an unlimited license shall be entitled to act as general contractor without restriction as to value of any single project; the holder of an intermediate license shall be entitled to act as general contractor for any single project with a value of up to one million dollars ($1,000,000); the holder of a limited license shall be entitled to act as general contractor for any single project with a value of up to five hundred thousand dollars ($500,000); and the license certificate shall be classified in accordance with this section. Before being entitled to an examination an applicant must show to the satisfaction of the Board from the application and proofs furnished that the applicant is possessed of a good character and is otherwise qualified as to competency, ability, integrity, and financial responsibility, and that the applicant has not committed or done any act, which, if committed or done by any licensed contractor would be grounds under the provisions hereinafter set forth for the suspension or revocation of contractor's license, or that the applicant has not committed or done any act involving dishonesty, fraud, or deceit, or that the applicant has never been refused a license as a general contractor nor had such license revoked, either in this State or in another state, for reasons that should preclude the granting of the license applied for, and that the applicant has never been convicted of a felony involving moral turpitude, relating to building or contracting, or involving embezzlement or misappropriation of funds or property entrusted to the applicant: Provided, no applicant shall be refused the right to an examination, except in accordance with the provisions of Chapter 150B of the General Statutes.

(b) The Board shall conduct an examination, either oral or written, of all applicants for license to ascertain, for the classification of license for which the applicant has applied: (i) the ability of the applicant to make a practical application of the applicant's knowledge of the profession of contracting; (ii) the qualifications of the applicant in reading plans and specifications, knowledge of relevant matters contained in the North Carolina State Building Code, knowledge of estimating costs, construction, ethics, and other similar matters pertaining to the contracting business; (iii) the knowledge of the applicant as to the responsibilities of a contractor to the public and of the requirements of the laws of the State of North Carolina relating to contractors, construction, and liens; and (iv) the applicant's knowledge of requirements of the Sedimentation Pollution Control Act of 1973, Article 4 of Chapter 113A of the General Statutes, and the rules adopted pursuant to that Article. If the results of the examination of the applicant shall be satisfactory to the Board, then the Board shall issue to the applicant a certificate to engage as a general contractor in the State of North Carolina, as provided in said certificate, which may be limited into five classifications as follows:

(1) Building contractor, which shall include private, public, commercial, industrial and residential buildings of all types.

(1a) Residential contractor, which shall include any general contractor constructing only residences which are required to conform to the residential building code adopted by the Building Code Council pursuant to G.S. 143-138.

(2) Highway contractor.

(3) Public utilities contractors, which shall include those whose operations are the performance of construction work on the following subclassifications of facilities:

a. Water and sewer mains, water service lines, and house and building sewer lines as defined in the North Carolina State Building Code, and water storage tanks, lift stations, pumping stations, and appurtenances to water storage tanks, lift stations, and pumping stations.

b. Water and wastewater treatment facilities and appurtenances thereto.

c. Electrical power transmission facilities, and primary and secondary distribution facilities ahead of the point of delivery of electric service to the customer.

d. Public communication distribution facilities.

e. Natural gas and other petroleum products distribution facilities; provided the General Contractors Licensing Board may issue license to a public utilities contractor limited to any of the above subclassifications for which the general contractor qualifies.

(4) Specialty contractor, which shall include those whose operations as such are the performance of construction work requiring special skill and involving the use of specialized building trades or crafts, but which shall not include any operations now or hereafter under the jurisdiction, for the issuance of license, by any board or commission pursuant to the laws of the State of North Carolina.

(b1) Public utilities contractors constructing house and building sewer lines as provided in sub-subdivision a. of subdivision (3) of subsection (b) of this section shall, at the junction of the public sewer line and the house or building sewer line, install as an extension of the public sewer line a cleanout at or near the property line that terminates at or above the finished grade. Public utilities contractors constructing water service lines as provided in sub-subdivision a. of subdivision (3) of subsection (b) of this section shall terminate the water service lines at a valve, box, or meter at which the facilities from the building may be connected. Public utilities contractors constructing fire service mains for connection to fire sprinkler systems shall terminate those lines at a flange, cap, plug, or valve inside the building one foot above the finished floor. All fire service mains shall comply with the NFPA standards for fire service mains as incorporated into and made applicable by Volume V of the North Carolina Building Code.

(c) If an applicant is an individual, examination may be taken by his personal appearance for examination, or by the appearance for examination of one or more of his responsible managing employees, and if a copartnership or corporation, or any other combination or organization, by the examination of one or more of the responsible managing officers or members of the personnel of the applicant, and if the person so examined shall cease to be connected with the applicant, then in such event the license shall remain in full force and effect for a period of 90 days thereafter, and then be canceled, but the applicant shall then be entitled to a reexamination, all pursuant to the rules to be promulgated by the Board: Provided, that the holder of such license shall not bid on or undertake any additional contracts from the time such examined employee shall cease to be connected with the applicant until said applicant's license is reinstated as provided in this Article.

(d) Anyone failing to pass this examination may be reexamined at any regular meeting of the Board upon payment of an examination fee. Anyone requesting to take the examination a third or subsequent time shall submit a new application with the appropriate examination and license fees.

(e) A certificate of license shall expire on the thirty-first day of December following its issuance or renewal and shall become invalid 60 days from that date unless renewed, subject to the approval of the Board. Renewals may be effected any time during the month of January without reexamination, by the payment of a fee to the secretary of the Board. The fee shall not exceed one hundred twenty-five dollars ($125.00) for an unlimited license, one hundred dollars ($100.00) for an intermediate license, and seventy-five dollars ($75.00) for a limited license. No later than November 30 of each year, the Board shall mail written notice of the amount of the renewal fees for the upcoming year to the last address of record for each general contractor licensed pursuant to this Article. Renewal applications shall be accompanied by evidence of continued financial responsibility satisfactory to the Board. Renewal applications received by the Board after January shall be accompanied by a late payment of ten dollars ($10.00) for each month or part after January. After a lapse of four years no renewal shall be effected and the applicant shall fulfill all requirements of a new applicant as set forth in this section. (1925, c. 318, s. 9; 1931, c. 62, s. 2; 1937, c. 328; c. 429, s. 3; 1941, c. 257, s. 1; 1953, c. 805, s. 2; c. 1041, s. 3; 1971, c. 246, s. 3; 1973, c. 1036, ss. 1, 2; c. 1331, s. 3; 1975, c. 279, ss. 2, 3; 1979, c. 713, s. 2; 1981, c. 739, ss. 1, 2; 1985, c. 630, ss. 2, 3; 1989, c. 431; 1993, c. 112, ss. 1, 2; c. 553, s. 26; 1999-123, s. 1; 1999-379, s. 7; 1999-427, s. 1; 2001-140, s. 1; 2001-296, s. 1; 2005-381, ss. 1, 2, 3; 2006-241, s. 1; 2007-247, s. 3; 2011-376, s. 5.)

§ 87-10.1. Licensing of nonresidents.

(a) Definitions. - The following definitions apply in this section:

(1) Delinquent income tax debt. - The amount of income tax due as stated in a final notice of assessment issued to a taxpayer by the Secretary of Revenue when the taxpayer no longer has the right to contest the amount.

(2) Foreign corporation. - Defined in G.S. 55-1-40.

(3) Foreign entity. - A foreign corporation, a foreign limited liability company, or a foreign partnership.

(4) Foreign limited liability company. - Has the same meaning as the term "foreign LLC" in G.S. 57D-1-03.

(5) Foreign partnership. - Either of the following that does not have a permanent place of business in this State:

a. A foreign limited partnership as defined in G.S. 59-102.

b. A general partnership formed under the laws of a jurisdiction other than this State.

(b) Licensing. - The Board shall not issue a certificate of license for a foreign corporation unless the corporation has obtained a certificate of authority from the Secretary of State pursuant to Article 15 of Chapter 55 of the General Statutes. The Board shall not issue a certificate of license for a foreign limited liability company unless the company has obtained a certificate of authority from the Secretary of State pursuant to Article 7 of Chapter 57D of the General Statutes.

(c) Information. - Upon request, the Board shall provide the Secretary of Revenue on an annual basis the name, address, and tax identification number of every nonresident individual and foreign entity licensed by the Board. The information shall be provided in the format required by the Secretary of Revenue.

(d) Delinquents. - If the Secretary of Revenue determines that any nonresident individual or foreign corporation licensed by the board, a member of any foreign limited liability company licensed by the Board, or a partner in any foreign partnership licensed by the Board, owes a delinquent income tax debt, the Secretary of Revenue may notify the Board of these nonresident individuals and foreign entities and instruct the Board not to renew their certificates of license. The Board shall not renew the certificate of license of such a nonresident individual or foreign entity identified by the Secretary of Revenue unless the Board receives a written statement from the Secretary that the debt either has been paid or is being paid pursuant to an installment agreement. (1998-162, ss. 4, 10; 2013-157, s. 20.)

§ 87-11. Revocation of license; charges of fraud, negligence, incompetency, etc.; hearing thereon; reissuance of certificate.

(a) The Board shall have the power to refuse to issue or renew or revoke, suspend, or restrict a certificate of license or to issue a reprimand or take other disciplinary action if a general contractor licensed under this Article is found guilty of any fraud or deceit in obtaining a license, or gross negligence, incompetency, or misconduct in the practice of his or her profession, or willful violation of any provision of this Article. The Board shall also have the power to revoke, suspend, or otherwise restrict the ability of any person to act as a qualifying party for a license to practice general contracting, as provided in G.S. 87-10(c), for any copartnership, corporation or any other organization or combination, if that person committed any act in violation of the provisions of this section and the Board may take disciplinary action against the individual license held by that person.

(a1) Any person may prefer charges of fraud, deceit, negligence, or misconduct against any general contractor licensed under this Article. The charges shall be in writing and sworn to by the complainant and submitted to the Board. The charges, unless dismissed without hearing by the Board as unfounded or trivial, shall be heard and determined by the Board in accordance with the provisions of Chapter 150B of the General Statutes.

(b) The Board shall adopt and publish guidelines, consistent with the provisions of this Article, governing the suspension and revocation of licenses.

(c) The Board shall establish and maintain a system whereby detailed records are kept regarding complaints against each licensee. This record shall include, for each licensee, the date and nature of each complaint, investigatory action taken by the Board, any findings by the Board, and the disposition of the matter.

(d) The Board may reissue a license to any person, firm or corporation whose license has been revoked: Provided, five or more members of the Board vote in favor of such reissuance for reasons the Board may deem sufficient.

The Board shall immediately notify the Secretary of State of its findings in the case of the revocation of a license or of the reissuance of a revoked license.

A certificate of license to replace any certificate lost, destroyed or mutilated may be issued subject to the rules and regulations of the Board.

(e) The Board shall be entitled to recover its reasonable administrative costs associated with the investigation and prosecution of a violation of this Article or rules or regulations of the Board up to a maximum of five thousand dollars ($5,000) for any licensee or qualifying party found to have committed any of the following:

(1) Fraud or deceit in obtaining a license.

(2) Gross negligence, incompetency, or misconduct in the practice of general contracting.

(3) Willful violation of any provision of this Article. (1925, c. 318, s. 10; 1937, c. 429, s. 4; 1953, c. 1041, s. 4; 1973, c. 1331, s. 3; 1979, c. 713, s. 3; 1987, c. 827, s. 1; 1991, c. 124, s. 2; 1999-427, s. 2; 2005-381, s. 4.)

§ 87-12. Certificate evidence of license.

The issuance of a certificate of license or limited license by this Board shall be evidence that the person, firm, or corporation named therein is entitled to all the rights and privileges of a licensed or limited licensed general contractor while said license remains unrevoked or unexpired. A licensed general contractor holding a license which qualifies him for work as described in G.S. 87-10 shall be authorized to perform the said work without any additional occupational license, notwithstanding the provisions of any other occupational licensing statute. A license issued by any other occupational licensing board having jurisdiction over any work described in G.S. 87-10 shall qualify such licensee to perform the work for which the license qualifies him without obtaining the license from the General Contractors Licensing Board. Nothing contained herein shall operate to relieve any general contractor from the necessity of compliance with other provisions of the law requiring building permits and construction in accordance with appropriate provisions of the North Carolina State Building Code. (1925, c. 318, s. 11; 1937, c. 429, s. 5; 1975, c. 279, s. 4.)

§ 87-13. Unauthorized practice of contracting; impersonating contractor; false certificate; giving false evidence to Board; penalties.

Any person, firm, or corporation not being duly authorized who shall contract for or bid upon the construction of any of the projects or works enumerated in G.S. 87-1, without having first complied with the provisions hereof, or who shall attempt to practice general contracting in the State, except as provided for in this Article, and any person, firm, or corporation presenting or attempting to file as his own the licensed certificate of another or who shall give false or forged evidence of any kind to the Board or to any member thereof in maintaining a certificate of license or who falsely shall impersonate another or who shall use an expired or revoked certificate of license, and any architect or engineer who recommends to any project owner the award of a contract to anyone not properly licensed under this Article, shall be deemed guilty of a Class 2 misdemeanor. And the Board may, in its discretion, use its funds to defray the expense, legal or otherwise, in the prosecution of any violations of this Article. No architect or engineer shall be guilty of a violation of this section if his recommendation to award a contract is made in reliance upon current written information received by him from the appropriate Contractor Licensing Board of this State which information erroneously indicates that the contractor being recommended for contract award is properly licensed. (1925, c. 318, s. 12; 1931, c. 62, s. 3; 1937, c. 429, s. 6; 1983 (Reg. Sess., 1984), c. 970, s. 2; 1993, c. 539, s. 602; 1994, Ex. Sess., c. 24, s. 14(c).)

§ 87-13.1. Board may seek injunctive relief.

Whenever the Board determines that any person, firm or corporation has violated or is violating any of the provisions of this Article or rules and regulations of the Board promulgated under this Article, the Board may apply to the superior court for a restraining order and injunction to restrain the violation; and the superior courts have jurisdiction to grant the requested relief, irrespective of whether or not criminal prosecution has been instituted or administrative sanctions imposed by reason of the violation. The court may award the Board its reasonable costs associated with the investigation and prosecution of the violation. (1979, c. 713, s. 4; 2003-97, s. 2; 2005-381, s. 5.)

§ 87-14. Regulations as to issue of building permits.

(a) Any person, firm, or corporation, upon making application to the building inspector or such other authority of any incorporated city, town, or county in North Carolina charged with the duty of issuing building or other permits for the construction of any building, highway, sewer, grading, or any improvement or structure where the cost thereof is to be thirty thousand dollars ($30,000) or more, shall, before being entitled to the issuance of a permit, satisfy the following:

(1) Furnish satisfactory proof to the inspector or authority that the person seeking the permit or another person contracting to superintend or manage the construction is duly licensed under the terms of this Article to carry out or superintend the construction or is exempt from licensure under G.S. 87-1(b). If an applicant claims an exemption from licensure pursuant to G.S. 87-1(b)(2), the applicant for the building permit shall execute a verified affidavit attesting to the following:

a. That the person is the owner of the property on which the building is being constructed or, in the case of a firm or corporation, is legally authorized to act on behalf of the firm or corporation.

b. That the person will personally superintend and manage all aspects of the construction of the building and that the duty will not be delegated to any other person not duly licensed under the terms of this Article.

c. That the person will be personally present for all inspections required by the North Carolina State Building Code, unless the plans for the building were drawn and sealed by an architect licensed pursuant to Chapter 83A of the General Statutes.

The building inspector or other authority shall transmit a copy of the affidavit to the Board, who shall verify that the applicant was validly entitled to claim the exemption under G.S. 87-1(b)(2). If the Board determines that the applicant was not entitled to claim the exemption under G.S. 87-1(b)(2), the building permit shall be revoked pursuant to G.S. 153A-362 or G.S. 160A-422.

(2) Furnish proof that the person has in effect Workers' Compensation insurance as required by Chapter 97 of the General Statutes.

(3) Any person, firm, or corporation, upon making application to the building inspector or such other authority of any incorporated city, town, or county in

North Carolina charged with the duty of issuing building permits pursuant to G.S. 160A-417(a)(1) or G.S. 153A-357(a)(1) for any improvements for which the combined cost is to be thirty thousand dollars ($30,000) or more, other than for improvements to an existing single-family residential dwelling unit as defined in G.S. 87-15.5(7) that the owner occupies as a residence, or for the addition of an accessory building or accessory structure as defined in the North Carolina Uniform Residential Building Code, the use of which is incidental to that residential dwelling unit, shall be required to provide to the building inspector or other authority the name, physical and mailing address, telephone number, facsimile number, and electronic mail address of the lien agent designated by the owner pursuant to G.S. 44A-11.1(a).

(b) It shall be unlawful for the building inspector or other authority to issue or allow the issuance of a building permit pursuant to this section unless and until the applicant has furnished evidence that the applicant is either exempt from the provisions of this Article and, if applicable, fully complied with the provisions of subdivision (a)(1) of this section, or is duly licensed under this Article to carry out or superintend the work for which permit has been applied; and further, that the applicant has in effect Workers' Compensation insurance as required by Chapter 97 of the General Statutes. Any building inspector or other authority who is subject to and violates the terms of this section shall be guilty of a Class 3 misdemeanor and subject only to a fine of not more than fifty dollars ($50.00). (1925, c. 318, s. 13; 1931, c. 62, s. 4; 1937, c. 429, s. 7; 1949, c. 934; 1953, c. 809; 1969, c. 1063, s. 6; 1971, c. 246, s. 4; 1981, c. 783, s. 2; 1989, c. 109, s. 2; 1991 (Reg. Sess., 1992), c. 840, s. 2; 1993, c. 539, s. 603; 1994, Ex. Sess., c. 24, s. 14(c); 2011-376, s. 2; 2012-158, s. 4; 2013-117, s. 4.)

§ 87-15. Copy of Article included in specifications; bid not considered unless contractor licensed.

All architects and engineers preparing plans and specifications for work to be contracted in the State of North Carolina shall include in their invitations to bidders and in their specifications a copy of this Article or such portions thereof as are deemed necessary to convey to the invited bidder, whether he be a resident or nonresident of this State and whether a license has been issued to him or not, the information that it will be necessary for him to show evidence of a license before his bid is considered. (1925, c. 318, s. 14; 1937, c. 429, s. 8; 1941, c. 257, s. 2.)

§ 87-15.1. Reciprocity of licensing.

To the extent that other states which provide for the licensing of general contractors provide for similar action, the Board in its discretion may grant licenses of the same or equivalent classification to general contractors licensed by other states, without written examination upon satisfactory proof furnished to the Board that the qualifications of such applicants are equal to the qualifications of holders of similar licenses in North Carolina and upon payment of the required fee. (1971, c. 246, s. 5.)

§ 87-15.2. Public awareness program.

The Board shall establish and implement a public awareness program to inform the general public of the purpose and function of the Board. (1979, c. 713, s. 4.)

§ 87-15.3. Identity of complaining party confidential.

Once a complaint has been filed with the Board against a licensee or an unlicensed general contractor, the Board may, in its discretion, keep the identity of a complaining party confidential and not a public record within the meaning of Chapter 132 of the General Statutes until a time no later than the receipt of the complaint by the full Board for a disciplinary hearing or injunctive action. (2003-97, s. 1)

§ 87-15.4. Builder designations created.

(a) A licensee who successfully completes the educational requirements for accredited builder or accredited master builder, as established by the North Carolina Builders Institute (Institute), shall be designated by the Board as a "North Carolina Certified Accredited Residential Builder" or "North Carolina Certified Accredited Master Residential Builder," respectively. The Institute shall provide to the Board written certification of those licensees who have successfully completed the requirements for the designations. The certification shall remain in effect as long as: (i) the licensee's license is in effect pursuant to G.S. 87-10; and (ii) the licensee completes at least eight hours of continuing education each calendar year as certified by the Institute.

(b) The Board shall approve for designation a licensee who has successfully completed a course of study, deemed by the Board to be equivalent to the educational requirements under subsection (a) of this section, offered by a community college or by another provider, and who completes the requisite number of hours of continuing education required by the Board.

(c) The Board may use all powers granted to it under this Article to enforce the provisions of this section and ensure that the designations created by this section are conferred upon and used only by a licensee who complies with the provisions of this section and any rules adopted by the Board. (2007-417, s. 1.)

Article 1A.

Homeowners Recovery Fund.

§ 87-15.5. Definitions.

The following definitions apply in this Article:

(1) Applicant. - The owner or former owner of a single-family residential dwelling unit who has suffered a reimbursable loss and has filed an application for reimbursement from the Fund.

(2) Board. - The State Licensing Board for General Contractors.

(3) Dishonest conduct. - Fraud or deceit in either of the following:

a. Obtaining a license under Article 1 of Chapter 87 of the General Statutes.

b. The practice of general contracting by a general contractor.

(4) Fund. - The Homeowners Recovery Fund.

(5) General contractor. - A person or other entity who meets any of the following descriptions:

a. Is licensed under Article 1 of Chapter 87 of the General Statutes.

b. Fraudulently procures any building permit by presenting the license certificate of a general contractor.

c. Fraudulently procures any building permit by falsely impersonating a licensed general contractor.

(6) Reimbursable loss. - A monetary loss that meets all of the following requirements:

a. Results from dishonest or incompetent conduct by a general contractor in constructing or altering a single-family residential dwelling unit.

b. Is not paid, in whole or in part, by or on behalf of the general contractor whose conduct caused the loss.

c. Is not covered by a bond, a surety agreement, or an insurance contract.

(7) Single-family residential dwelling unit. - A separately owned residence for use of one or more persons as a housekeeping unit with space for eating, living, and permanent provisions for cooking and sanitation, whether or not attached to other such residences. (1991, c. 547, s. 1.)

§ 87-15.6. Homeowners Recovery Fund.

(a) The Homeowners Recovery Fund is established as a special account of the Board. The Board shall administer the Fund. The purpose of the Fund is to reimburse homeowners who have suffered a reimbursable loss in constructing or altering a single-family residential dwelling unit.

(b) Whenever a general contractor applies for the issuance of a permit for the construction of any single-family residential dwelling unit or for the alteration of an existing single-family residential dwelling unit, a city or county building inspector shall collect from the general contractor a fee in the amount of ten dollars ($10.00) for each dwelling unit to be constructed or altered under the permit. The city or county inspector shall forward nine dollars ($9.00) of each fee collected to the Board on a quarterly basis and the city or county may retain one dollar ($1.00) of each fee collected. The Board shall deposit the fees received into the Fund. The Board may accept donations and appropriations to the Fund. G.S. 87-7 shall not apply to the Fund.

The Board may suspend collection of this fee for any year upon a determination that the amount in the Fund is sufficient to meet likely disbursements from the Fund for that year. The Board shall notify city and county building inspectors when it suspends collection of the fee.

(c) The Board may adopt rules to implement this Article. (1991, c. 547, s. 1; 2003-372, s. 1.)

§ 87-15.7. Fund administration.

(a) The Board shall determine the procedure for applying to the Board for reimbursement from the Fund, for processing applications, for granting requests for reimbursement, and for the subrogation or assignment of the rights of any reimbursed applicant. The Board shall submit annually a report to the State Treasurer accounting for all monies credited to and expended from the Fund.

(b) The Board may use monies in the Fund only for the following purposes:

(1) To reimburse an applicant's reimbursable loss after approval by the Board.

(2) To purchase insurance to cover reimbursable losses when the Board finds it appropriate to do so.

(3) To invest amounts in the Fund that are not currently needed to reimburse losses and maintain adequate reserves in the manner in which State law allows fiduciaries to invest funds.

(4) To pay the expenses of the Board to administer the Fund, including employment of counsel to prosecute subrogation claims. (1991, c. 547, s. 1.)

§ 87-15.8. Application for reimbursement.

(a) The Board shall prepare a form to be used to apply for reimbursement from the Fund. Only a person whom the Board determines to meet all of the following requirements may be reimbursed from the Fund:

(1) Has suffered a reimbursable loss in the construction or alteration of a single-family residential dwelling unit owned or previously owned by that person.

(2) Did not, directly or indirectly, obtain the building permit in the person's own name or did use a general contractor.

(3) Has exhausted all civil remedies against the general contractor whose conduct caused the loss and, if applicable, the general contractor's estate, and has obtained a judgment against the general contractor that remains unsatisfied. This requirement is waived if the person is prevented from filing suit or obtaining a judgment against the contractor due to the automatic stay provision of section 362 of the U.S. Bankruptcy Code.

(4) Has complied with the applicable rules of the Board.

(b) The Board shall investigate all applications for reimbursement and may reject or allow part or all of a claim based on the amount of money in the Fund. The Board shall have complete discretion to determine the order, amount, and manner of payment of approved applications. All payments are a matter of privilege and not of right and no person has a right to reimbursement from the Fund as a third party beneficiary or otherwise. No attorney shall be compensated by the Board for prosecuting an application before it. (1991, c. 547, s. 1.)

§ 87-15.9. Subrogation for reimbursement made.

The Board is subrogated to an applicant who is reimbursed from the Fund in the amount reimbursed and may bring an action against the general contractor whose conduct caused the reimbursable loss, the general contractor's assets, or the general contractor's estate. The Board may enforce any claims it may have for restitution or otherwise, and may employ and compensate consultants, agents, legal counsel, and others it finds necessary and appropriate to carry out its authority under this section. (1991, c. 547, s. 1.)

Article 2.

Plumbing and Heating Contractors.

§ 87-16. Board of Examiners; appointment; term of office.

There is created the State Board of Examiners of Plumbing, Heating, and Fire Sprinkler Contractors consisting of seven members appointed by the Governor: one member from a school of engineering of the Greater University of North Carolina, one member who is a plumbing or mechanical inspector from a city in North Carolina, one licensed air conditioning contractor, one licensed plumbing contractor, one licensed heating contractor, one licensed fire sprinkler contractor, and one person who has no tie with the construction industry to represent the interests of the public at large. Members serve for terms of seven years, with the term of one member expiring each year. The term of the member initially appointed to fill the position of licensed fire sprinkler contractor shall commence April 25, 1991. No member appointed after June 7, 1979, shall serve more than one complete consecutive term. Vacancies occurring during a term are filled by appointment of the Governor for the remainder of the unexpired term. (1931, c. 52, s. 1; 1939, c. 224, s. 1; 1971, c. 768, s. 1; 1973, c. 476, s. 128; 1979, c. 834, s. 1; 1989 (Reg. Sess., 1990), c. 842, s. 1; c. 978, s. 1.)

§ 87-17. Removal, qualifications and compensation of members; allowance for expenses.

The Governor may remove any member of the Board for misconduct, incompetency or neglect of duty. Each member of the Board shall be a resident of this State at the time of his appointment. Each member of the Board shall receive for attending sessions of the Board or of its committees the amount of per diem, and for the time spent in necessary traveling in carrying out the provisions of this Article, and in addition to the per diem compensation, each member shall be reimbursed by the Board from funds in its hands for necessary traveling expenses and for such expenses incurred in carrying out the provisions hereof as shall be approved by a majority of the members of the

Board. Payment of compensation and reimbursement of expenses of Board members shall be governed by G.S. 93B-5. (1931, c. 52, s. 2; 1969, c. 445, s. 8; 1979, c. 834, ss. 2, 3.)

§ 87-18. Organization meeting; officers; seal; rules; employment of personnel; acquire property.

The Board shall, within 30 days after its appointment, meet in the City of Raleigh and organize, and elect a chairman, secretary, and treasurer, each to serve for one year. Thereafter the officers shall be elected annually. The secretary and treasurer shall give bond approved by the Board for the faithful performance of their duties in the sum as the Board may, from time to time, determine. The Board shall have a common seal, shall formulate rules to govern its actions, and is hereby authorized to employ personnel as it may deem necessary to carry out the provisions of this Article. The Board shall have the power to acquire, hold, rent, encumber, alienate, and otherwise deal with real property in the same manner as a private person or corporation, subject only to the approval of the Governor and the Council of State. Collateral pledged by the Board for an encumbrance is limited to the assets, income, and revenues of the Board. (1931, c. 52, s. 3; 1939, c. 224, s. 2; 1953, c. 254, s. 1; 2001-270, s. 1.)

§ 87-19. Regular and special meetings; quorum.

The Board after holding its first meeting as hereinbefore provided, shall thereafter hold at least two regular meetings each year. Special meetings may be held at such times and places as the bylaws and/or rules of the Board provide; or as may be required in carrying out the provisions hereof. A quorum of the Board shall consist of not less than four members. (1931, c. 52, s. 4; 1989 (Reg. Sess., 1990), c. 842, s. 2.)

§ 87-20. Record of proceedings and register of applicants; reports.

The Board shall keep a record of its proceedings and a register of all applicants for examination, showing the date of each application, the name, age and other qualifications, place of business and residence of each applicant. The books and records of the Board shall be prima facie evidence of the correctness of the contents thereof. On or before the first day of March of each year the Board shall submit to the Governor a report of its activities for the preceding year, and file with the Secretary of State a copy of such report, together with a statement of receipts and expenditures of the Board attested by the chairman and secretary. (1931, c. 52, s. 5.)

§ 87-21. Definitions; contractors licensed by Board; examination; posting license, etc.

(a) Definitions. - For the purpose of this Article:

(1) The word "plumbing" is hereby defined to be the system of pipes, fixtures, apparatus and appurtenances, installed upon the premises, or in a building, to supply water thereto and to convey sewage or other waste therefrom.

(2) The phrase "heating, group number one" shall be deemed and held to be the heating system of a building, which requires the use of high or low pressure steam, vapor or hot water, including all piping, ducts, and mechanical equipment appurtenant thereto, within, adjacent to or connected with a building, for comfort heating.

(3) The phrase "heating, group number two" means an integral system for heating or cooling a building consisting of an assemblage of interacting components producing conditioned air to raise or lower the temperature, and having a mechanical refrigeration capacity in excess of fifteen tons, and which circulates air. Systems installed in single-family residences are included under heating group number three, regardless of size. Holders of a heating group number three license who have heretofore installed systems classified as heating group number two systems may nevertheless service, replace, or make alterations to those installed systems until June 30, 2004.

(4) The phrase "heating, group number three" shall be deemed and held to be a direct heating or cooling system of a building that raises or lowers the temperature of the space within the building for the purpose of comfort in which electric heating elements or products of combustion exchange heat either directly with the building supply air or indirectly through a heat exchanger using an air distribution system of ducts and having a mechanical refrigeration

capacity of 15 tons or less. A heating system requiring air distribution ducts and supplied by ground water or utilizing a coil supplied by water from a domestic hot water heater not exceeding 150 degrees Fahrenheit requires either plumbing or heating group number one license to extend piping from valved connections in the domestic hot water system to the heating coil and requires either heating group number one or heating group number three license for installation of coil, duct work, controls, drains and related appurtenances.

(5)   Any person, firm or corporation, who for a valuable consideration, (i) installs, alters or restores, or offers to install, alter or restore, either plumbing, heating group number one, or heating group number two, or heating group number three, or (ii) lays out, fabricates, installs, alters or restores, or offers to lay out, fabricate, install, alter or restore fire sprinklers, or any combination thereof, as defined in this Article, shall be deemed and held to be engaged in the business of plumbing, heating, or fire sprinkler contracting; provided, however, that nothing herein shall be deemed to restrict the practice of qualified registered professional engineers. Any person who installs a plumbing, heating, or fire sprinkler system on property which at the time of installation was intended for sale or to be used primarily for rental is deemed to be engaged in the business of plumbing, heating, or fire sprinkler contracting without regard to receipt of consideration, unless exempted elsewhere in this Article.

(6)   The word "contractor" is hereby defined to be a person, firm or corporation engaged in the business of plumbing, heating, or fire sprinkler contracting.

(7)   The word "heating" shall be deemed and held to mean heating group number one, heating group number two, heating group number three, or any combination thereof.

(8)   Repealed by Session Laws 1997-298, s. 1.

(9)   The word "Board" means the State Board of Examiners of Plumbing, Heating, and Fire Sprinkler Contractors.

(10)   The word "experience" means actual and practical work directly related to the category of plumbing, heating group number one, heating group number two, heating group number three, or fire sprinkler contracting, and includes related work for which a license is not required.

(11) The phrase "fire sprinkler" means an automatic or manual sprinkler system designed to protect the interior or exterior of a building or structure from fire, and where the primary extinguishing agent is water. These systems include wet pipe and dry pipe systems, preaction systems, water spray systems, foam water sprinkler systems, foam water spray systems, nonfreeze systems, and circulating closed-loop systems. These systems also include the overhead piping, combination standpipes, inside hose connections, thermal systems used in connection with the sprinklers, tanks, and pumps connected to the sprinklers, and controlling valves and devices for actuating an alarm when the system is in operation. This subsection shall not apply to owners of property who are building or improving farm outbuildings. This subsection shall not include water and standpipe systems having no connection with a fire sprinkler system. Nothing herein shall prevent licensed plumbing contractors, utility contractors, or fire sprinkler contractors from installing underground water supplies for fire sprinkler systems.

(b) Classes of Licenses; Eligibility and Examination of Applicant; Necessity for License. -

(1) In order to protect the public health, comfort and safety, the Board shall establish two classes of licenses: Class I covering all plumbing, heating, and fire sprinkler systems for all structures, and Class II covering plumbing and heating systems in single-family detached residential dwellings.

(2) Restricted licenses or classifications. -

a. The Board shall establish and issue a fuel piping license for use by persons who do not possess the required Class I or Class II plumbing or heating license, but desire to engage in the contracting or installing of fuel piping extending from an approved fuel source at or near the premises, which piping is used or may be used to supply fuel to any systems, equipment, or appliances located inside the premises.

b. The Board shall establish and issue a limited plumbing contractor license for use by persons who do not possess the required Class I or Class II plumbing license but desire to engage in the contracting or installation, repair, or replacement of either of the following:

1. Exterior potable water service lines or backflow preventers serving irrigation systems or domestic water service systems of two inch diameter or smaller.

2. Exterior building sewer or water service piping of two inch diameter or smaller.

c. The Board may also establish additional restricted classifications to provide for: (i) the licensing of any person, partnership, firm, or corporation desiring to engage in a specific phase of heating, plumbing, or fire sprinkling contracting; (ii) the licensing of any person, partnership, firm, or corporation desiring to engage in a specific phase of heating, plumbing, or fire sprinkling contracting that is an incidental part of their primary business, which is a lawful business other than heating, plumbing, or fire sprinkling contracting; or (iii) the licensing of persons desiring to engage in contracting and installing fuel piping from an approved fuel source on the premises to a point inside the residence.

(3) The Board shall prescribe the standard of competence, experience and efficiency to be required of an applicant for license of each class, and shall give an examination designed to ascertain the technical and practical knowledge of the applicant concerning the analysis of plans and specifications, estimating costs, fundamentals of installation and design, codes, fire hazards, and related subjects as these subjects pertain to plumbing, heating, or fire sprinkler systems. The examination for a fire sprinkler contractor's license shall include such materials as would test the competency of the applicant and which may include the minimum requirements of certification for Level III, subfield of Automatic Sprinkler System Layout, National Institute for Certification of Engineering Technologies (NICET). As a result of the examination, the Board shall issue a certificate of license of the appropriate class in plumbing, heating, or fire sprinkler contracting, and a license shall be obtained, in accordance with the provisions of this Article, before any person, firm or corporation shall engage in, or offer to engage in, the business of plumbing, heating, or fire sprinkler contracting, or any combination thereof. The obtaining of a license, as required by this Article, shall not of itself authorize the practice of another profession or trade for which a State qualification license is required. Prior to taking the examination, the applicant may be required by the Board to establish that the applicant is at least 18 years of age and is of good moral character. The Board may require experience as a condition of examination, provided that (i) the experience required may not exceed two years, (ii) that up to one-half the experience may be in the form of academic or technical courses of study, and (iii) that registration is not required at the commencement of the period of experience.

(4) Conditions of examination set by the Board shall be uniformly applied to each applicant within each license classification. It is the purpose and intent of this section that the Board shall provide an examination for plumbing, heating group number one, or heating group number two, or heating group number three, or each restricted classification, and may provide an examination for fire sprinkler contracting or may accept a current certification of the National Institute for Certification in Engineering Technologies for Fire Protection Engineering Technician, Level III, subfield of Automatic Sprinkler System Layout.

(5) The Board is authorized to issue a certificate of license limited to either plumbing or heating group number one, or heating group number two, or heating group number three, or fire sprinkler contracting, or any combination thereof. The Board is also authorized to issue a certificate of license limited to one or more restricted classifications that are established pursuant to this section.

(6) Examinations shall be given at least twice each year, and additional examinations may be given as the Board deems wise and necessary. The examination shall be conducted in two parts to include a business and law portion and a technical portion. Requests for examination applications and information shall be made available online without charge and supplied at no cost to the potential examinee. The Board may offer written examinations or administer examinations by computer within 30 days after approving an application. Applicants shall be permitted to obtain the test score from each part of computerized examinations immediately upon completion of the examination. Upon passing the examination and paying the annual license fee, the applicant shall be issued a license. A person who fails to pass any examination shall not be reexamined until after 90 days from the date the person was last examined. An applicant who fails to pass any examination may take the failed portion within six months of the date approved to take the examination without retaking the portion passed. The Board may require applicants who fail any part of the examination three times to receive additional education before the applicant is allowed to retake the examination or wait one year before retaking any portion of the examination.

(c) To Whom Article Applies. - The provisions of this Article shall apply to all persons, firms, or corporations who engage in, or attempt to engage in, the business of plumbing, heating, or fire sprinkler contracting, or any combination thereof as defined in this Article. The provisions of this Article shall not apply to those who make minor repairs or minor replacements to an already installed system of plumbing, heating or air conditioning, but shall apply to those who make repairs, replacements, or modifications to an already installed fire sprinkler system. Minor repairs or minor replacements within the meaning of this subsection shall include the replacement of parts in an installed system which do not require any change in energy source, fuel type, or routing or sizing of venting or piping. Parts shall include a compressor, coil, contactor, motor, or capacitor.

(c1) Exemption. - The provisions of this Article shall not apply to a person who performs the on-site assembly of a factory designed drain line system for a manufactured home, as defined in G.S. 143-143.9(6), if the person (i) is a licensed manufactured home retailer, a licensed manufactured home set-up contractor, or a full-time employee of either, (ii) obtains an inspection by the local inspections department and (iii) performs the assembly according to the State Plumbing Code.

(c2) Exemption. - The provisions of this Article shall not apply to electric generating facilities that are subject to G.S. 62-110.1 or that provide power sold at wholesale that is regulated by the Federal Energy Regulatory Commission.

(d) Repealed by Session Laws 1979, c. 834, s. 7.

(d1) Expired December 31, 1991.

(e) Posting License; License Number on Contracts, etc. - The current license issued in accordance with the provisions of this Article shall be posted in the business location of the licensee, and its number shall appear on all proposals or contracts and requests for permits issued by municipalities. The initial qualified licensee on a license is the permanent possessor of the license number under which that license is issued, except that a licensee, or the licensee's legal agent, personal representative, heirs or assigns, may designate in writing to the Board a qualified licensee to whom the Board shall assign the license number upon the payment of a ten dollar ($10.00) assignment fee. Upon such assignment, the qualified licensee becomes the permanent possessor of the assigned license number. Notwithstanding the foregoing, the license number may be assigned only to a qualified licensee who has been employed by the initial licensee's plumbing and heating company for at least 10 years or is a lineal relative, sibling, first cousin, nephew, niece, daughter-in-law, son-in-law, brother-in-law, or sister-in-law of the initial licensee. Each successive licensee to whom a license number is assigned under this subsection may assign the license number in the same manner as provided in this subsection.

(f) Repealed by Session Laws 1971, c. 768, s. 4.

(g) The Board may, in its discretion, grant to plumbing, heating, or fire sprinkler contractors licensed by other states license of the same or equivalent classification without written examination upon receipt of satisfactory proof that the qualifications of such applicants are substantially equivalent to the qualifications of holders of similar licenses in North Carolina and upon payment of the usual license fee.

(h) Expired December 31, 1993.

(i) The provisions of this Article shall not apply to a retailer, as defined in G.S. 105-164.3(35), who, in the ordinary course of business, enters into a transaction with a buyer in which the retailer of a water heater sold for installation in a one- or two-family residential dwelling contracts with a licensee under this Article to provide the installation services for the water heater if the retail sales and installation contract with the buyer is signed by the buyer, the retailer, and the licensee and bears the licensee's license number and telephone number. All installation services rendered by the licensee in connection with any such contract must be performed in compliance with all building code, permit, and inspection requirements.

(j) The provisions of this Article shall not apply to a person primarily engaged in the retail sale of goods and services who contracts for or arranges financing for the sale and installation of a single-family residential heating or cooling system for which a license to install such system is required under this Article, provided all of the following requirements are met:

(1) No contract or proposal for sale or installation may be presented to or signed by the buyer unless either (i) the specifications for and design of the system have been first reviewed and approved by an employee of the retail seller who is licensed under this Article or (ii) the specifications for and design of the system have been first reviewed and approved by the person licensed under this Article who will install the system, if the installer is not an employee of the retail seller. This subdivision does not prohibit the retailer from providing a written estimate to a potential buyer so long as no contract or proposal for contract is presented or signed prior to the review and approval required by this subsection.

(2) The person installing the system is licensed under this Article.

(3) The contract for sale and for installation is signed by the buyer, by an authorized representative of the retail seller, and by the licensed contractor and contains the contractor's name, license number, and telephone number and the license number of the person approving the system design specifications.

(4) Installation services are performed in compliance with all applicable building codes, manufacturer's installation instructions, and permit and inspection requirements.

(5) The retailer provides, in addition to any other warranties it may offer with respect to the system itself, a warranty for a period of at least one year for any defects in installation.

(k) The provisions of subsections (i) and (j) of this section shall not apply to a system meeting the definition of subdivision (a)(11) of this section. (1931, c. 52, s. 6; 1939, c. 224, s. 3; 1951, c. 953, ss. 1, 2; 1953, c. 254, s. 2; 1967, c. 770, ss. 1-6; 1971, c. 768, ss. 2-4; 1973, c. 1204; 1979, c. 834, ss. 4-7; 1981, c. 332, s. 1; 1983, c. 569, ss. 1, 2; 1989, c. 623, s. 1; 1989 (Reg. Sess., 1990), c. 842, s. 3; c. 978, s. 2; 1991, c. 355, s. 1; c. 507, s. 1; c. 761, s. 13; 1993, c. 78, s. 1; 1997-298, s. 1; 1997-382, ss. 1, 4; 2001-270, s. 2; 2002-159, s. 36(a); 2003-2, s. 1; 2003-31, ss. 1-3.1; 2004-203, s. 69; 2005-131, s. 1; 2005-289, s. 3; 2013-332, s. 1.)

§ 87-22. License fee; expiration and renewal; reinstatement.

All persons, firms, or corporations engaged in the business of either plumbing or heating contracting, or both, shall pay an annual license fee not to exceed one hundred fifty dollars ($150.00). The annual fee for a piping or restricted classification license shall not exceed that for a plumbing or heating license. All persons, firms, or corporations engaged in the business of fire sprinkler contracting shall pay an initial application fee not to exceed seventy-five dollars ($75.00) and an annual license fee not to exceed three hundred dollars ($300.00). In the event the Board refuses to license an applicant, the license fee deposited shall be returned by the Board to the applicant. All licenses shall expire on the last day of December in each year following their issuance or renewal. Persons who obtain a license by passing an examination on or after October 1 of any year may receive a license for the remainder of the year by paying one-half of the usual license fee for that classification of license. It shall be the duty of the secretary and treasurer to send by United States mail or e-mail to every licensee registered with the Board, notice to the licensee's last known address reflected on the records of the Board of the amount of fee required for renewal of license, the notice to be mailed at least one month in advance of the expiration of the license. The Board may require payment of all unpaid annual fees before reissuing a license. In the event of failure on the part of any person, firm or corporation to renew the license certificate annually and pay the required fee during the month of January in each year, the Board shall increase the license fee by twenty-five dollars ($25.00) to cover any additional expense associated with late renewal. The Board shall require reexamination upon failure of a licensee to renew license within three years after expiration. The Board may adopt regulations requiring attendance at programs of continuing education as a condition of license renewal. A licensee employed full time as a local government plumbing, heating, or mechanical inspector and holding qualifications from the Code Officials Qualifications Board may renew the license at a fee not to exceed twenty-five dollars ($25.00). (1931, c. 52, s. 7; 1939, c. 224, s. 4; 1971, c. 768, s. 5; 1979, c. 834, s. 8; 1981, c. 332, s. 2; 1989, c. 623, s. 2; 1989 (Reg. Sess., 1990), c. 842, s. 4; 1997-382, s. 2; 2001-270, s. 3; 2005-131, s. 2.)

§ 87-22.1. Examination fees; funds disbursed upon warrant of chairman and secretary-treasurer.

The Board shall charge a nonrefundable application and examination fee not to exceed one hundred fifty dollars ($150.00) for each examination or any part of an examination, and the funds collected shall be disbursed upon warrant of the chairman and secretary-treasurer, to partially defray general expenses of the Board. The application and examination fee shall be retained by the Board whether or not the applicant is granted a license. Until changed by the Board pursuant to rules adopted by the Board, the fee for each examination or any part taken on a particular day shall be one hundred dollars ($100.00). (1959, c. 865, s. 2; 1989, c. 623, s. 3; 2001-270, s. 4; 2005-131, s. 3.)

§ 87-22.2. Licensing of nonresidents.

(a) Definitions. - The following definitions apply in this section:

(1) Delinquent income tax debt. - The amount of income tax due as stated in a final notice of assessment issued to a taxpayer by the Secretary of Revenue when the taxpayer no longer has the right to contest the amount.

(2) Foreign corporation. - Defined in G.S. 55-1-40.

(3) Foreign entity. - A foreign corporation, a foreign limited liability company, or a foreign partnership.

(4) Foreign limited liability company. - Has the same meaning as the term "foreign LLC" in G.S. 57D-1-03.

(5) Foreign partnership. - Either of the following that does not have a permanent place of business in this State:

a. A foreign limited partnership as defined in G.S. 59-102.

b. A general partnership formed under the laws of a jurisdiction other than this State.

(b) Licensing. - The Board shall not issue a license for a foreign corporation unless the corporation has obtained a certificate of authority from the Secretary of State pursuant to Article 15 of Chapter 55 of the General Statutes. The Board shall not issue a license for a foreign limited liability company unless the company has obtained a certificate of authority from the Secretary of State pursuant to Article 7 of Chapter 57D of the General Statutes.

(c) Information. - Upon request, the Board shall provide the Secretary of Revenue on an annual basis the name, address, and tax identification number of every nonresident individual and foreign entity licensed by the Board. The information shall be provided in the format required by the Secretary of Revenue.

(d) Delinquents. - If the Secretary of Revenue determines that any nonresident individual or foreign corporation licensed by the Board, a member of any foreign limited liability company licensed by the Board, or a partner in any foreign partnership licensed by the Board, owes a delinquent income tax debt, the Secretary of Revenue may notify the Board of these nonresident individuals and foreign entities and instruct the Board not to renew their licenses. The Board shall not renew the license of such a nonresident individual or foreign entity identified by the Secretary of Revenue unless the Board receives a written statement from the Secretary that the debt either has been paid or is being paid pursuant to an installment agreement. (1998-162, ss. 5, 11; 2013-157, s. 21.)

§ 87-23. Revocation or suspension of license for cause.

(a) The Board shall have power to revoke or suspend the license of or order the reprimand or probation of any plumbing, heating, or fire sprinkler contractor, or any combination thereof, who is guilty of any fraud or deceit in obtaining or renewing a license, or who fails to comply with any provision or requirement of this Article, or the rules adopted by the Board, or for gross negligence, incompetency, or misconduct, in the practice of or in carrying on the business of a plumbing, heating, or fire sprinkler contractor, or any combination thereof, as defined in this Article. Any person may prefer charges of such fraud, deceit, gross negligence, incompetency, misconduct, or failure to comply with any provision or requirement of this Article, or the rules of the Board, against any plumbing, heating, or fire sprinkler contractor, or any combination thereof, who is licensed under the provisions of this Article. All of the charges shall be in writing and investigated by the Board. Any proceedings on the charges shall be carried out by the Board in accordance with the provisions of Chapter 150B of the General Statutes.

(b) The Board shall adopt and publish guidelines, consistent with the provisions of this Chapter, governing the suspension and revocation of licenses.

(c) The Board shall establish and maintain a system whereby detailed records are kept regarding complaints against each licensee. (1931, c. 52, s. 8; 1939, c. 224, s. 5; 1953, c. 1041, s. 5; 1973, c. 1331, s. 3; 1979, c. 834, s. 9; 1987, c. 827, s. 1; 1989 (Reg. Sess., 1990), c. 842, s. 5; 1997-382, s. 3.)

§ 87-24. Reissuance of revoked licenses; replacing lost or destroyed license.

The Board may in its discretion reissue license to any person, firm or corporation whose license may have been revoked: Provided, four or more members of the Board vote in favor of such reissuance for reasons deemed sufficient by the Board. A new certificate of registration to replace any license which may be lost or destroyed may be issued subject to the rules and regulations of the Board. (1931, c. 52, s. 9; 1989 (Reg. Sess., 1990), c. 842, s. 6.)

§ 87-25. Violations made misdemeanor; employees of licensees excepted.

Any person, firm or corporation who shall engage in or offer to engage in, or carry on the business of plumbing, heating, or fire sprinkler contracting, or any combination thereof, as defined in G.S. 87-21, without first having been licensed to engage in such business, or businesses, as required by the provisions of this Article; or any person, firm or corporation holding a limited plumbing or heating license under the provisions of this Article who shall practice or offer to practice or carry on any type of plumbing or heating contracting not authorized by said limited license; or any person, firm or corporation who shall give false or forged evidence of any kind to the Board, or any member thereof, in obtaining a license, or who shall falsely impersonate any other practitioner of like or different name, or who shall use an expired or revoked license, or who shall violate any of the provisions of this Article, shall be guilty of a Class 2 misdemeanor. An employee in the course of his work as a bona fide employee of a licensee of the Board shall not be construed to have engaged in the business of plumbing, heating, or fire sprinkler contracting, as the case may be. (1931, c. 52, s. 10; 1939, c. 224, s. 6; 1989, c. 623, s. 4; 1989 (Reg. Sess., 1990), c. 842, s. 7; 1993, c. 539, s. 604; 1994, Ex. Sess., c. 24, s. 14(c).)

§ 87-25.1. Board may seek injunctive relief.

Whenever it appears to the Board that any person, firm or corporation is violating any of the provisions of this Article or of the rules and regulations of the Board promulgated under this Article, the Board may apply to the superior court for a restraining order and injunction to restrain the violation; and the superior courts have jurisdiction to grant the requested relief, irrespective of whether or not criminal prosecution has been instituted or administrative sanctions imposed by reason of the violation. The court may award the Board its reasonable costs associated with the investigation and prosecution of the violation. (1979, c. 834, s. 11; 2013-332, s. 2.)

§ 87-26. Corporations; partnerships; persons doing business under trade name.

(a) A license may be issued in the name of a corporation, provided, one or more officers, or full time employee or employees, or both, empowered to act for the corporation, are licensed in accordance with the provisions of this Article; and provided such officers or employee or employees shall execute contracts to the extent of their license qualifications in the name of the said corporation and exercise general supervision over the work done thereunder.

(b) A license may be issued in the name of a partnership provided one or more general partners, or full time employee or employees empowered to act for the partnership, are licensed in accordance with the provisions of this Article, and provided such general partners or employee or employees shall execute contracts to the extent of their license qualifications in the name of the said partnership, and exercise general supervision over the work done thereunder.

(c) A license may be issued in an assumed or designated trade name, provided the owner of the business conducted thereunder, or full time employee or employees empowered to act for the owner, are licensed in accordance with the provisions of this Article; and such owner or employee or employees shall execute contracts to the extent of their license qualifications, in the said trade name, and exercise general supervision over the work done thereunder.

(d) A certificate of license may be issued in accordance with the provisions of this Article upon payment of the annual license fee by such corporation, partnership, or owner of the business conducted under an assumed or designated trade name, as the case may be, and the names and qualifications of individual licensee or licensees connected therewith shall be indicated on the aforesaid license.

(e) It shall be necessary that persons licensed in accordance with the provisions of this section shall exercise general supervision over contracts to completion. (1931, c. 52, s. 12; 1939, c. 224, s. 8; 1957, c. 815; 1967, c. 770, s. 7.)

§ 87-27. License fees payable in advance; application of.

All license fees shall be paid in advance to the secretary and treasurer of the Board and by him held as a fund for the use of the Board. The compensation and expenses of the members of the Board as herein provided, the salaries of its employees, the costs of continuing educational programs for licensees and applicants, and all expenses incurred in the discharge of its duties under this Article shall be paid out of such fund, upon the warrant of the chairman and secretary and treasurer. (1931, c. 52, s. 13; 1933, c. 57; 1939, c. 224, s. 9; 1953, c. 254, s. 3; 1959, c. 865, s. 1; 1979, c. 834, s. 10.)

§ 87-27.1. Public awareness program.

The Board shall establish and implement a public awareness program to inform the general public of the purpose and function of the Board. (1979, c. 834, s. 11.)

Article 3.

Tile Contractors.

§§ 87-28 through 87-38: Repealed by Session Laws 1977, c. 143.

Article 4.

Electrical Contractors.

§ 87-39. Board of Examiners; appointment; terms; chairman; meetings; quorum; principal office; compensation; oath.

(a)   The State Board of Examiners of Electrical Contractors shall continue as the State agency responsible for the licensing of persons engaging in electrical contracting within this State, and shall consist of one member from the North Carolina Department of Insurance to be designated by the Commissioner of Insurance; one member who has satisfied the requirements for an unlimited license as defined in G.S. 87-43.3 and who is a representative of the North Carolina Association of Electrical Contractors to be designated by the governing body of that organization; and five members to be appointed by the Governor: one from the faculty of The Greater University of North Carolina who teaches or does research in the field of electrical engineering, one who is serving as a chief electrical inspector of a municipality or county in North Carolina, one who has satisfied the requirements for an unlimited license as defined in G.S. 87-43.3 and who is a representative of the Carolinas Electrical Contractors Association operating a sole proprietorship, partnership or corporation located in North Carolina which is actively engaged in the business of electrical contracting, and two who have no ties with the construction industry and who represent the interest of the public at large.

(b)   Members of the Board shall serve staggered seven-year terms. Each member shall serve until his or her successor is designated or appointed, and is duly qualified. Vacancies occurring during a term shall be filled for the remainder of that term by the authority that designated or appointed the departing member.

(c)   Members of the Board shall not serve consecutive, complete terms. For purposes of this subsection, only a term of less than seven years that results from the filling of a vacancy is an incomplete term; a term of less than seven years that results from the successor's late designation or appointment is not an incomplete term.

(d)   All members shall be residents of North Carolina during their tenure on the Board. Any member of the Board may be removed by the authority that designated or appointed that member for misconduct, incompetency, or neglect of duty.

(e)   The Board shall hold regular meetings quarterly and may hold meetings on call of the chair. The chair shall be required to call a special meeting upon written request by two members of the Board. At its regular first quarter meeting, the Board shall elect from its membership a chair and a vice-chair, each to serve for one year. Four members of the Board shall constitute a quorum. The principal office of the Board shall be at such place as shall be designated by a majority of the members thereof. Payment of compensation and reimbursement of expenses of Board members shall be governed by G.S. 93B-5.

(f)   Before entering upon the performance of his or her duties hereunder, each member of the Board shall take and file with the Secretary of State an oath in writing to properly perform the duties of his or her office as a member of the Board, and to uphold the Constitution of North Carolina and the Constitution of the United States. (1937, c. 87, s. 1; 1969, c. 669, s. 1; 1979, c. 904, ss. 1-3; 1989, c. 709, s. 1; 1995, c. 114, s. 1.)

§ 87-40. Secretary-treasurer.

At its regular first quarter meeting, the Board shall appoint a secretary-treasurer to serve for one year. The secretary-treasurer need not be a member of the Board, and the Board is authorized to employ a full-time secretary-treasurer and such other assistants and to make such other expenditures as may be necessary to the proper performance of the duties of the Board under this Article. The compensation and the duties of the secretary-treasurer shall be fixed by the Board, and the secretary-treasurer shall give bond in such sum and form as the Board shall require for the faithful performance of duty. The secretary-treasurer shall keep a record of the proceedings of said Board and shall receive and account for all moneys derived from the operations of the Board under this Article. (1937, c. 87, ss. 2, 3; 1969, c. 669, s. 1; 1995, c. 114, s. 2.)

§ 87-41. Seal of Board.

The Board shall adopt a seal for its own use, and the secretary-treasurer shall have charge and custody thereof. The seal shall have inscribed thereon the words "Board of Examiners of Electrical Contractors, State of North Carolina." (1937, c. 87, s. 3; 1969, c. 669, s. 1.)

§ 87-41.1. Definitions.

As used in this Article, unless the context requires otherwise:

(1)   A "qualified individual" is an individual who is qualified in a specific license classification as a result of having taken and passed the qualifying examination required by this Article for such a classification and who has been certified as such by the Board pursuant to G.S. 87-42.

(2) A "listed qualified individual" is a qualified individual whose name is listed on a license issued by the Board. A listed qualified individual has the specific duty and authority to supervise and direct electrical contracting done by or in the name of a licensee of the Board on whose license the qualified individual is so listed.

(3) A licensee of the Board is a person listed pursuant to subsection (2), or a partnership, firm or corporation that regularly employs at least one listed qualified individual and which has been issued a license by the Board. (1989, c. 709, s. 2.)

§ 87-42. Duties and powers of Board.

In order to protect the life, health and property of the public, the State Board of Examiners of Electrical Contractors shall provide for the written examination of all applicants for certification as a qualified individual, as defined in G.S. 87-41.1. The Board shall receive all applications for certification as a qualified individual and all applications for licenses to be issued under this Article, shall examine all applicants to determine that each has met the requirements for certification and shall discharge all duties enumerated in this Article. Applicants for certification as a qualified individual must be at least 18 years of age and shall be required to demonstrate to the satisfaction of the Board their good character and adequate technical and practical knowledge concerning the safe and proper installation of electrical work and equipment. The examination to be given for this purpose shall include, but not be limited to, the appropriate provisions of the National Electrical Code as incorporated in the North Carolina State Building Code, the analysis of electrical plans and specifications, estimating of electrical installations, and the fundamentals of the installation of electrical work and equipment. Certification of qualified individuals shall be issued in the same classifications as provided in this Article for license classifications. The Board shall prescribe the standards of knowledge, experience and proficiency to be required of qualified individuals, which may vary for the various license classifications. The Board shall issue certifications and licenses to all applicants meeting the requirements of this Article and of the Board upon the receipt of the fees prescribed by G.S. 87-44. The Board shall have power to make rules and regulations necessary to the performance of its duties and for the effective implementation of the provisions of this Article. The Board shall have the power to administer oaths and issue subpoenas requiring the attendance of persons and the production of papers and records before the

Board in any hearing, investigation, or proceeding conducted by it. Members of the Board's staff or the sheriff or other appropriate official of any county of this State shall serve all notices, subpoenas, and other papers given to them by the Chairman for service in the same manner as process issued by any court of record. Any person who neglects or refuses to obey a subpoena issued by the Board shall be guilty of a Class 1 misdemeanor. The Board shall have the power to acquire, rent, encumber, alienate, and otherwise deal with real property in the same manner as a private person or corporation, subject only to approval of the Governor and the Council of State. Collateral pledged by the Board for an encumbrance is limited to the assets, income, and revenues of the Board. The Board shall keep minutes of all its proceedings and shall keep an accurate record of receipts and disbursements which shall be audited at the close of each fiscal year by a certified public accountant, and the audit report shall be filed with the State of North Carolina in accordance with Chapter 93B of the General Statutes. (1937, c. 87, s. 4; 1969, c. 669, s. 1; 1989, c. 709, s. 3; 1993, c. 539, s. 605; 1994, Ex. Sess., c. 24, s. 14(c); 2001-159, s. 1.)

§ 87-43. Electrical contracting defined; licenses.

Electrical contracting shall be defined as engaging or offering to engage in the business of installing, maintaining, altering or repairing any electric work, wiring, devices, appliances or equipment. No person, partnership, firm or corporation shall engage, or offer to engage, in the business of electrical contracting within the State of North Carolina without having received a license in the applicable classification described in G.S. 87-43.3 from the State Board of Examiners of Electrical Contractors in compliance with the provisions of this Article, regardless of whether the offer was made or the work was performed by a qualified individual as defined in G.S. 87-41.1. In each separate place of business operated by an electrical contractor at least one listed qualified individual shall be regularly on active duty and shall have the specific duty and authority to supervise and direct all electrical wiring or electrical installation work done or made by such separate place of business. Every person, partnership, firm or corporation engaging in the business of electrical contracting shall display a current certificate of license in his principal place of business and in each branch place of business which he operates. Licenses issued hereunder shall be signed by the chairman and the secretary-treasurer of the Board, under the seal of the Board. A registry of all licenses issued to electrical contractors shall be kept by the secretary-treasurer of the Board, and said registry shall be open for public inspection during ordinary business hours. (1937, c. 87, s. 5;

1951, c. 650, ss. 1-2 1/2; 1953, c. 595; 1961, c. 1165; 1969, c. 669, s. 1; 1989, c. 709, s. 4.)

§ 87-43.1. Exceptions.

The provisions of this Article shall not apply:

(1) To the installation, construction or maintenance of facilities for providing electric service to the public ahead of the point of delivery of electric service to the customer;

(2) To the installation, construction, maintenance, or repair of telephone, telegraph, or signal systems, by public utilities, or their corporate affiliates, when said work pertains to the services furnished by said public utilities;

(3) To any person in the course of his work as a bona fide employee of a licensee of this Board;

(4) To the installation, construction or maintenance of electrical equipment and wiring for temporary use by contractors in connection with the work of construction;

(5) To the installation, construction, maintenance or repair of electrical wiring, devices, appliances or equipment by persons, firms or corporations, upon their own property when such property is not intended at the time for rent, lease, sale or gift, who regularly employ one or more electricians or mechanics for the purpose of installing, maintaining, altering or repairing of electrical wiring, devices or equipment used for the conducting of the business of said persons, firms or corporations;

(5a) To any person who is himself and for himself installing, maintaining, altering or repairing electric work, wiring, devices, appliances or equipment upon his own property when such property is not intended at the time for rent, lease, or sale;

(6) To the installation, construction, maintenance or repair of electrical wiring, devices, appliances or equipment by State institutions and private educational institutions which maintain a private electrical department;

(7) To the replacement of lamps and fuses and to the installation and servicing of cord-connected appliances and equipment connected by means of attachment plug-in devices to suitable receptacles which have been permanently installed or to the servicing of appliances connected to a permanently installed junction box. This exception does not apply to permanently installed receptacles or to the installation of the junction box.

(8) To the bonding of corrugated stainless steel tubing (CSST) gas piping systems as required under Section 310.1.1 of the 2012 N.C. Fuel Gas Code.

(9) To the installation, maintenance, or replacement of any load control device or equipment by an electric power supplier, as defined in G.S. 62-133.8, or an electrical contractor contracted by the electric power supplier, so long as the work is subject to supervision by an electrical contractor licensed under this Article. The electric power supplier shall provide such installation, maintenance, or replacement in accordance with (i) an activity or program ordered, authorized, or approved by the North Carolina Utilities Commission pursuant to G.S. 62-133.8 or G.S. 62-133.9 or (ii) a similar program undertaken by a municipal electric service provider, whether the installation, modification, or replacement is made before or after the point of delivery of electric service to the customer. The exemption under this subdivision applies to all existing installations. (1937, c. 87, s. 5; 1951, c. 650, ss. 1-21/2; 1953, c. 595; 1961, c. 1165; 1969, c. 669, s. 1; 1979, c. 904, ss. 4-7; 2013-36, s. 1; 2013-58, s. 1.)

§ 87-43.2. Issuance of license.

(a) A person, partnership, firm, or corporation shall be eligible to be licensed as an electrical contractor and to have such license renewed, subject to the provisions of this Article, provided:

(1) At least one listed qualified individual shall be regularly employed by the applicant at each separate place of business to have the specific duty and authority to supervise and direct electrical contracting done by or in the name of the licensee;

(2) An application is filed with the Board which contains a statement of ownership, states the names and official positions of all employees who are listed qualified individuals and provides such other information as the Board may reasonably require;

(3) The applicant, through an authorized officer or owner, shall agree in writing to report to the Board within five days any additions to or loss of the employment of listed qualified individuals; and

(4) The applicant furnishes, upon the initial application for a license, a bonding ability statement completed by a bonding company licensed to do business in North Carolina, verifying the applicant's ability to furnish performance bonds for electrical contracting projects having a value in excess of the project value limit for a limited license established pursuant to G.S. 87-43.3 for the intermediate license classification and in excess of the project value limit for an intermediate license established pursuant to G.S. 87-43.3 for the unlimited license classification. In lieu of furnishing the bonding ability statement, the applicant may submit for evaluation and specific approval of the Board other information certifying the adequacy of the applicant's financial ability to engage in projects of the license classification applied for. The bonding ability statement or other financial information must be submitted in the same name as the license to be issued. If the firm for which a license application is filed is owned by a sole proprietor, the bonding ability statement or other financial information may be furnished in either the firm name or the name of the proprietor. However, if the application is submitted in the name of a sole proprietor, the applicant shall submit information verifying that the person in whose name the application is made is in fact the sole proprietor of the firm.

(5) Repealed by Session Laws 1989, c. 709, s. 5.

(b) A license shall indicate the names and classifications of all listed qualified individuals employed by the applicant. A license shall be cancelled if at any time no listed qualified individual is regularly employed by the applicant; provided, that work begun prior to such cancellation may be completed under such conditions as the Board shall direct; and provided further that no work for which a license is required under this Article may be bid for, contracted for or initiated subsequent to such cancellation until said license is reinstated by the Board. (1937, c. 87, s. 5; 1951, c. 650, ss. 1-2½; 1953, c. 595; 1961, c. 1165; 1969, c. 669, s. 1; 1989, c. 709, s. 5; 1995, c. 509, s. 135.2(e); 2007-247, s. 2.)

§ 87-43.3. Classification of licenses.

An electrical contracting license shall be issued in one of the following classifications: Limited, under which a licensee shall be permitted to engage in a single electrical contracting project of a value, as established by the Board, not in excess of one hundred thousand dollars ($100,000) and on which the equipment or installation in the contract is rated at not more than 600 volts; Intermediate, under which a licensee shall be permitted to engage in a single electrical contracting project of a value, as established by the Board, not in excess of two hundred thousand dollars ($200,000); Unlimited, under which a licensee shall be permitted to engage in any electrical contracting project regardless of value; and such other special Restricted classifications as the Board may establish from time to time to provide, (i) for the licensing of persons, partnerships, firms or corporations wishing to engage in special restricted electrical contracting, under which license a licensee shall be permitted to engage only in a specific phase of electrical contracting of a special, limited nature, and (ii) for the licensing of persons, partnerships, firms or corporations wishing to engage in electrical contracting work as an incidental part of their primary business, which is a lawful business other than electrical contracting, under which license a licensee shall be permitted to engage only in a specific phase of electrical contracting of a special, limited nature directly in connection with said primary business. The Board may establish appropriate standards for each classification, such standards not to be inconsistent with the provisions of G.S. 87-42. The Board may, by rule, modify the project value limitations up to the maximum amounts set forth in this section for limited and intermediate licenses no more than once every three years based upon an increase or decrease in the project cost index for electrical projects in this State. (1969, c. 669, s. 1; 1973, c. 1228, s. 1; 1975, c. 29; 1989, c. 709, s. 6; 1995, c. 114, s. 6; 2007-247, s. 1.)

§ 87-43.4. Residential dwelling license.

There is hereby created a separate license for electrical contractors which shall permit an electrical contractor to engage in electrical contracting projects pertaining to single-family detached residential dwellings. The value of a single project pertaining to a single-family detached residential dwelling shall not be in excess of the maximum value, established in G.S. 87-43.3, of a single project engaged in by a licensee with a license classified as limited. The Board shall establish appropriate standards for this new license. The standards of knowledge, experience and proficiency shall be those appropriate for that license. (1973, c. 1343; 1995, c. 114, s. 3.)

§ 87-44. Fees; license term.

The Board shall collect a fee from each applicant before granting or renewing a license under the provisions of this Article; the annual license fee for the limited classification shall not exceed one hundred dollars ($100.00) for each principal and each branch place of business; the annual license fee for the intermediate classification shall not exceed one hundred fifty dollars ($150.00) for each principal and each branch place of business; the annual license fee for the unlimited classification shall not exceed two hundred dollars ($200.00) for each principal and each branch place of business; and the annual license fee for the special restricted classifications and for the single-family detached residential dwelling license shall not exceed one hundred dollars ($100.00) for each principal and each branch place of business.

The Board shall establish a system for the renewal of licenses with varying expiration dates. However, all licenses issued by the Board shall expire one year after the date of issuance. Licenses shall be renewed by the Board, subject to G.S. 87-44.1 and G.S. 87-47, after receipt and evaluation of a renewal application from a licensee and the payment of the required fee. The application shall be upon a form provided by the Board and shall require such information as the Board may prescribe. Renewal applications and fees shall be due 30 days prior to the license expiration date.

Upon failure to renew by the expiration date established by the Board, the license shall be automatically revoked. This license may be reinstated by the Board, subject to G.S. 87-44.1 and G.S. 87-47, upon payment of the license fee, an administrative fee of twenty-five dollars ($25.00), and all fees for the lapsed period during which the person, partnership, firm or corporation engaged in electrical contracting, and, further, upon the satisfaction of such experience requirements during the lapse as the Board may prescribe by rule.

The Board may collect fees from applicants for examinations in an amount not to exceed one hundred twenty-five dollars ($125.00), except the fee for a specially arranged examination shall not exceed two hundred dollars ($200.00). In addition, the Board may collect an examination review fee, not to exceed twenty-five dollars ($25.00), from failed examinees who apply for a supervised review of their failed examinations. (1937, c. 87, ss. 6, 7, 10; 1953, c. 1041, s. 7;

1969, c. 669, s. 1; 1973, c. 1228, s. 2; 1979, c. 904, ss. 8-10; 1985, c. 317; 1989, c. 709, s. 7; 2001-159, s. 2.)

§ 87-44.1. Continuing education courses required.

Beginning July 1, 1991, the Board may require as prerequisite to the annual renewal of a license that every listed qualified individual complete continuing education courses in subjects relating to electrical contracting to assure the safe and proper installation of electrical work and equipment in order to protect the life, health, and property of the public. The listed qualified individual shall complete, during the 12 months immediately preceding license renewal, a specific number of hours of continuing education courses approved by the Board prior to enrollment. The Board shall not require more than 10 hours of continuing education courses per 12 months and such continuing education courses shall include those taught at a community college as approved by the Board. The listed qualified individual may accumulate and carry forward not more than two additional years of the annual continuing education requirement. Attendance at any course or courses of continuing education shall be certified to the Board on a form provided by the Board and shall be submitted at the time the licensee makes application to the Board for its license renewal and payment of its license renewal fee. This continuing education requirement may be waived by the Board in cases of certified illness or undue hardship as provided for in the Rules of the Board. (1989, c. 709, s. 8.)

§ 87-44.2. Licensing of nonresidents.

(a) Definitions. - The following definitions apply in this section:

(1) Delinquent income tax debt. - The amount of income tax due as stated in a final notice of assessment issued to a taxpayer by the Secretary of Revenue when the taxpayer no longer has the right to contest the amount.

(2) Foreign corporation. - Defined in G.S. 55-1-40.

(3) Foreign entity. - A foreign corporation, a foreign limited liability company, or a foreign partnership.

(4) Foreign limited liability company. - Has the same meaning as the term "foreign LLC" in G.S. 57D-1-03.

(5) Foreign partnership. - Either of the following that does not have a permanent place of business in this State:

a. A foreign limited partnership as defined in G.S. 59-102.

b. A general partnership formed under the laws of a jurisdiction other than this State.

(b) Licensing. - The Board shall not issue a license for a foreign corporation unless the corporation has obtained a certificate of authority from the Secretary of State pursuant to Article 15 of Chapter 55 of the General Statutes. The Board shall not issue a license for a foreign limited liability company unless the company has obtained a certificate of authority from the Secretary of State pursuant to Article 7 of Chapter 57D of the General Statutes.

(c) Information. - Upon request, the Board shall provide the Secretary of Revenue on an annual basis the name, address, and tax identification number of every nonresident individual and every foreign entity licensed by the Board. The information shall be provided in the format required by the Secretary of Revenue.

(d) Delinquents. - If the Secretary of Revenue determines that any nonresident individual or foreign corporation licensed by the Board, a member of any foreign limited liability company licensed by the Board, or a partner in any foreign partnership licensed by the Board, owes a delinquent income tax debt, the Secretary of Revenue may notify the Board of these nonresident individuals and foreign entities and instruct the Board not to renew their licenses. The Board shall not renew the license of such a nonresident individual or foreign entity identified by the Secretary of Revenue unless the Board receives a written statement from the Secretary that the debt either has been paid or is being paid pursuant to an installment agreement. (1998-162, ss. 6, 12; 2013-157, s. 22.)

§ 87-45. Funds.

The fees collected for examinations and licenses under this Article shall be used for the expenses of the State Board of Examiners of Electrical Contractors in carrying out the provisions of this Article. No expenses of the Board or compensation of any member or employee of the Board shall be payable out of the treasury of the State of North Carolina; and neither the Board nor any member or employee thereof shall have any power or authority to make or incur any expense, debt or other financial obligation binding upon the State of North Carolina. Any funds remaining in the hands of the secretary-treasurer to the credit of the Board after all expenses of the Board for the current fiscal year have been fully provided for shall be paid over to the North Carolina Engineering Foundation, Inc., for the benefit of the electrical engineering department of the Greater University of North Carolina. Provided, however, the Board shall have the right to maintain an amount, the cumulative total of which shall not exceed twenty percent (20%) of gross receipts for the previous fiscal year of its operation as a maximum contingency or emergency fund. (1937, c. 87, ss. 3, 7; 1969, c. 669, s. 1.)

§ 87-46. Responsibility of licensee; nonliability of Board.

Nothing in this Article shall relieve the holder or holders of licenses issued under the provisions hereof from complying with the building or electrical codes or statutes or ordinances of the State of North Carolina, or of any county or municipality thereof now in force or hereafter enacted. Nothing in this Article shall be construed as relieving the holder of any license issued hereunder from responsibility or liability for negligent acts on the part of such holder in connection with electrical contracting work; nor shall the State Board of Examiners of Electrical Contractors be accountable in damages, or otherwise for the negligent act or acts of any holder of such license. (1937, c. 87, s. 12; 1969, c. 669, s. 1.)

§ 87-47. Penalties imposed by Board; enforcement procedures.

(a) Repealed by Session Laws 1989, c. 709, s. 9.

(a1) The following activities are prohibited:

(1) Offering to engage or engaging in electrical contracting without being licensed.

(2) Selling, transferring, or assigning a license, regardless of whether for a fee.

(3) Aiding or abetting an unlicensed person, partnership, firm, or corporation to offer to engage or to engage in electrical contracting.

(4) Being convicted of a crime involving fraud or moral turpitude.

(5) Engaging in fraud or misrepresentation to obtain a certification, obtain or renew a license, or practice electrical contracting.

(6) Engaging in false or misleading advertising.

(7) Engaging in malpractice, unethical conduct, fraud, deceit, gross negligence, gross incompetence, or gross misconduct in the practice of electrical contracting.

(a2) The Board may administer one or more of the following penalties if the applicant, licensee, or qualified individual has engaged in any activity prohibited under subsection (a1) of this section:

(1) Reprimand.

(2) Suspension from practice for a period not to exceed 12 months.

(3) Revocation of the right to serve as a listed qualified individual on any license issued by the Board.

(4) Revocation of license.

(5) Probationary revocation of license or the right to serve as a listed qualified individual on any license issued by the Board, upon conditions set by the Board as the case warrants, and revocation upon failure to comply with the conditions.

(6) Revocation of certification.

(7) Refusal to certify an applicant or a qualified individual.

(8) Refusal to issue a license to an applicant.

(9) Refusal to renew a license.

(a3) In addition to administering a penalty under subsection (a2) of this section, the Board may assess a civil penalty of not more than one thousand dollars ($1,000) against a licensee or a qualified individual who has engaged in an activity prohibited under subsection (a1) of this section or has violated another provision of this Article or a rule adopted by the Board. The clear proceeds of civil penalties collected under this subsection shall be remitted to the Civil Penalty and Forfeiture Fund in accordance with G.S. 115C-457.2.

In determining the amount of a civil penalty, the Board shall consider:

(1) The degree and extent of harm to the public safety or to property, or the potential for harm.

(2) The duration and gravity of the violation.

(3) Whether the violation was committed willfully or intentionally, or reflects a continuing pattern.

(4) Whether the violation involved elements of fraud or deception either to the public or to the Board, or both.

(5) The violator's prior disciplinary record with the Board.

(6) Whether and the extent to which the violator profited by the violation.

(a4) Any person, including the Board and its staff on their own initiative, may prefer charges pursuant to this section, and such charges must be submitted in writing to the Board. The Board may, without a hearing, dismiss charges as unfounded or trivial. The Board may issue a notice of violation based on the charges, to be served by a member of the Board's staff or in accordance with Rule 4 of the Rules of Civil Procedure, against any person, partnership, firm, or corporation for engaging in an activity prohibited under subsection (a1) of this section or for a violation of the provisions of this Article or any rule adopted by the Board. The person or other entity to whom the notice of violation is issued may request a hearing by notifying the Board in writing within 20 days after being served with the notice of violation. Hearings shall be conducted by the Board or an administrative law judge pursuant to Article 3A of Chapter 150B of the General Statutes. In conducting hearings, the Board may remove the hearings to any county in which the offense, or any part thereof, was committed if in the opinion of the Board the ends of justice or the convenience of witnesses require such removal.

(a5)   If the person or other entity does not request a hearing under subsection (a4) of this section, the Board shall enter a final decision and may impose penalties against the person or other entity. If the person or other entity is not a licensee or a qualified individual, the Board may impose penalties under subsection (a2) of this section. If the person or other entity is a licensee or a qualified individual, the Board may impose penalties under subsection (a2) of this section, subsection (a3) of this section, or both.

(b)   The Board shall adopt and publish rules, in accordance with Chapter 150B of the General Statutes and consistent with the provisions of this Article, governing the matters contained in this section.

(c)   The Board shall establish and maintain a system whereby detailed records are kept regarding charges and notices of violation pursuant to this section. This record shall include, for each person, partnership, firm, and corporation charged or notified of a violation, the date and nature of each charge or notice of violation, investigatory action taken by the Board, any findings by the Board, and the disposition of the matter.

(d)   The Board may reinstate a qualified individual's certification and may reinstate a license after having revoked it, provided that one year has elapsed from revocation until reinstatement and that the vote of the Board for reinstatement is by a majority of its members.

The Board shall immediately notify the Secretary of State and the electrical inspectors within the licensee's county of residence upon the revocation of a license or the reissuance of a license which had been revoked.

(e)   In any case in which the Board is entitled to convene a hearing to consider imposing any penalty provided for in subsection (a2) or (a3) of this section, the Board may accept an offer in compromise of the charge, whereby the accused shall pay to the Board a penalty of not more than one thousand dollars ($1,000). The clear proceeds of penalties collected by the Board under this subsection shall be remitted to the Civil Penalty and Forfeiture Fund in accordance with G.S. 115C-457.2. (1969, c. 669, s. 1; 1973, c. 1331, s. 3; 1979, c. 904, s. 11; 1989, c. 709, s. 9; 1995, c. 114, s. 4; 1998-215, s. 132.)

§ 87-48. Penalty for violation of Article; powers of Board to enjoin violation.

(a) Any person, partnership, firm or corporation who shall violate any of the provisions of this Article or any rule of the Board adopted pursuant to this Article or who shall engage or offer to engage in the business of installing, maintaining, altering or repairing within the State of North Carolina any electric wiring, devices, appliances or equipment without first having obtained a license under the provisions of this Article shall be guilty of a Class 2 misdemeanor.

(b) Whenever it shall appear to the State Board of Examiners of Electrical Contractors that any person, partnership, firm or corporation has violated, is violating, or threatens to violate any provisions of this Article, the Board may apply to the courts of the State for a restraining order and injunction to restrain such practices. If upon such application the court finds that any provision of this Article is being violated, or a violation thereof is threatened, the court shall issue an order restraining and enjoining such violations, and such relief may be granted regardless of whether criminal prosecution is instituted under the provisions of this Article. The venue for actions brought under this subsection shall be the superior court of any county in which such acts are alleged to have been committed or in the county where the defendants in such action reside. (1937, c. 87, s. 13; 1969, c. 669, s. 1; 1979, c. 904, s. 14; 1989, c. 709, s. 10; 1993, c. 539, s. 606; 1994, Ex. Sess., c. 24, s. 14(c).)

§ 87-49. No examination required of licensed contractors.

Any person, firm or corporation licensed in this State as a Class II electrical contractor on the effective date of this Article shall be entitled to be licensed, without examination, in the limited classification upon payment of the required fee and may be licensed in the intermediate or in the unlimited classification without written examination upon satisfactory proof to the Board that such applicant is in fact qualified for such classification. Any person, firm or corporation licensed in this State as a Class I electrical contractor on the effective date of this Article shall be entitled to be licensed without examination in the limited, intermediate or unlimited classification upon payment of the required fee. Provided, that any person who has been once duly licensed by the Board, whose license has expired solely because of failure to apply for renewal, may apply and have a license issued under the provisions of this section if within a period of 12 months preceding such issuance the applicant shall have been primarily actively engaged as an electrical contractor or in an occupation which in the judgment of the Board is similar or equivalent to that of an electrical contractor. (1969, c. 669, s. 1.)

§ 87-50. Reciprocity.

To the extent that other states which provide for the licensing of electrical contractors provide for similar action, the Board may grant licenses of the same or equivalent classification to electrical contractors licensed by other states without written examination upon satisfactory proof furnished to the Board that the qualifications of such applicants are equal to the qualifications of holders of similar licenses in North Carolina and upon payment of the required fee. (1969, c. 669, s. 1.)

§ 87-50.1. Public awareness program.

The Board shall establish and implement a public awareness program to inform the general public of the purpose and function of the Board. (1979, c. 904, s. 13.)

§ 87-51. Severability of provisions.

If any provision of this Article or the application thereof to any person or circumstances is for any reason held invalid, such invalidity shall not affect other provisions or applications of the Article which can be given effect without the invalid provision or application, and to this end the provisions of this Article are declared to be severable. (1969, c. 669, s. 1.)

Article 5.

Refrigeration Contractors.

§ 87-52. State Board of Refrigeration Examiners; appointment; term of office.

For the purpose of carrying out the provisions of this Article, the State Board of Refrigeration Examiners is created, consisting of seven members appointed by the Governor to serve seven-year staggered terms. The Board shall consist of one member who is a wholesaler or a manufacturer of refrigeration equipment; one member from an engineering school of The University of North Carolina, one member from the Division of Public Health of The University of North Carolina, two licensed refrigeration contractors, one member who has no ties with the construction industry to represent the interest of the public at large, and one member with an engineering background in refrigeration. The term of office of one member shall expire each year. Vacancies occurring during a term shall be filled by appointment of the Governor for the unexpired term. Whenever the term "Board" is used in this Article, it means the State Board of Refrigeration Examiners. No Board member shall serve more than one complete consecutive term. (1955, c. 912, s. 1; 1959, c. 1206, s. 2; 1973, c. 476, s. 128; 1979, c. 712, s. 1; 1995, c. 376, s. 1.)

§ 87-53. Removal, qualifications and compensation of members; allowance for expenses.

The Governor may remove any member of the Board for misconduct, incompetency or neglect of duty. Each member of the Board shall be a resident of this State at the time of his appointment. Payment of compensation and reimbursement of expenses of Board members shall be governed by G.S. 93B-5. (1955, c. 912, s. 2; 1969, c. 445, s. 9; 1979, c. 712, ss. 2, 7.)

§ 87-54. Organization meeting; officers; seal; rules.

The Board shall within 30 days after its appointment meet in the City of Raleigh and organize, and shall elect a chairman and secretary and treasurer, each to serve for one year. Thereafter said officer shall be elected annually. The secretary and treasurer shall give bond approved by the Board for the faithful performance of his duties, in such sum as the Board may, from time to time, determine. The Board shall have a common seal, shall formulate rules to govern its actions, and is hereby authorized to employ such personnel as it may deem necessary to carry out the provisions of this Article. (1955, c. 912, s. 3.)

§ 87-55. Regular and special meetings; quorum.

The Board after holding its first meeting, as hereinbefore provided, shall thereafter hold at least two regular meetings each year. Special meetings may be held at such times and places as the bylaws and/or rules of the Board provide; or as may be required in carrying out the provisions hereof. A quorum of the Board shall consist of four members. (1955, c. 912, s. 4.)

§ 87-56. Record of proceedings and register of applicants; reports.

The Board shall keep a record of its proceedings and a register of all applicants for examination, showing the date of each application, the name, age and other qualifications, places of business and residence of each applicant. The books and records of the Board shall be prima facie evidence of the correctness of the contents thereof. On or before the first day of March of each year the Board shall submit to the Governor a report of its activities for the preceding year, and file with the Secretary of State a copy of such report, together with a statement of receipts and expenditures of the Board attested by the chairman and secretary. (1955, c. 912, s. 5.)

§ 87-57. License required of persons, firms or corporations engaged in the refrigeration trade.

In order to protect the public health, safety, morals, order and general welfare of the people of this State, all persons, firms or corporations, whether resident or nonresident of the State of North Carolina, before engaging in refrigeration business or contracting, as defined in this Article, shall first apply to the Board and shall procure a license. (1955, c. 912, s. 6.)

§ 87-58. Definitions; contractors licensed by Board; examinations.

(a) As applied in this Article, "refrigeration trade or business" is defined to include all persons, firms or corporations engaged in the installation, maintenance, servicing and repairing of refrigerating machinery, equipment, devices and components relating thereto and within limits as set forth in the codes, laws and regulations governing refrigeration installation, maintenance, service and repairs within the State of North Carolina or any of its political subdivisions. The provisions of this Article shall not repeal any wording, phrase, or paragraph as set forth in Article 2 of Chapter 87 of the General Statutes. This Article shall not apply to any of the following:

(1) The installation of self-contained commercial refrigeration units equipped with an Original Equipment Manufacturer (OEM) molded plug that does not require the opening of service valves or replacement of lamps, fuses, and door gaskets.

(2) The installation and servicing of domestic household self-contained refrigeration appliances equipped with an OEM molded plug connected to suitable receptacles which have been permanently installed and do not require the opening of service valves.

(3) Employees of persons, firms, or corporations or persons, firms or corporations, not engaged in refrigeration contracting as herein defined, that install, maintain and service their own refrigerating machinery, equipment and devices.

(4) Any person, firm or corporation engaged in the business of selling, repairing and installing any comfort cooling devices or systems.

(b) The term "refrigeration contractor" means a person, firm or corporation engaged in the business of refrigeration contracting.

(b1) The term "transport refrigeration contractor" means a person, firm, or corporation engaged in the business of installation, maintenance, servicing, and repairing of transport refrigeration.

(c) Any person, firm or corporation who for valuable consideration engages in the refrigeration business or trade as herein defined shall be deemed and held to be in the business of refrigeration contracting.

(d) In order to protect the public health, comfort and safety, the Board shall prescribe the standard of experience to be required of an applicant for license and shall give an examination designed to ascertain the technical and practical knowledge of the applicant concerning the analysis of plans and specifications, estimating cost, fundamentals of installation and design as they pertain to refrigeration; and as a result of the examination, the Board shall issue a certificate of license in refrigeration to applicants who pass the required examination and a license shall be obtained in accordance with the provisions of this Article, before any person, firm or corporation shall engage in, or offer to engage in the business of refrigeration contracting. The Board shall prescribe standards for and issue licenses for refrigeration contracting and for transport refrigeration contracting. A transport refrigeration contractor license is a specialty license that authorizes the licensee to engage only in transport refrigeration contracting. A refrigeration contractor licensee is authorized to engage in transport refrigeration and all other aspects of refrigeration contracting.

Each application for examination shall be accompanied by a check, post-office money order or cash in the amount of the annual license fee required by this Article. Regular examinations shall be given in the Board's office by appointment.

(e) Repealed by Session Laws 1979, c. 843, s. 1.

(f) Licenses Granted without an Examination. - Persons who had an established place of business prior to July 1, 1979, and who produce satisfactory evidence that they are engaged in the refrigeration business as herein defined in any city, town or other area in which Article 5 of Chapter 87 of the General Statutes did not previously apply shall be granted a certificate of license, without examination, upon application to the Board and payment of the license fee, provided completed applications shall be made prior to June 30, 1981.

(g) The current license issued in accordance with the provisions of this Article shall be posted in the business location of the licensee, and its number shall appear on all proposals or contracts and requests for permits issued by municipalities.

(h) A transport refrigeration contractor having an established place of business doing transport refrigeration contracting prior to October 1, 1995, shall be granted a transport refrigeration contracting specialty license, without examination, if the person produces satisfactory evidence the person is engaged in transport refrigeration contracting, pays the required license fee, and applies to the Board prior to January 1, 1997. The current specialty license shall be posted in accordance with subsection (g) of this section.

(i)   Nothing in this Article shall relieve the holder of a license issued under this section from complying with the building or electrical codes, statutes, or ordinances of the State or of any county or municipality or from responsibility or liability for negligent acts in connection with refrigeration contracting work. The Board shall not be liable in damages, or otherwise, for the negligent acts of licensees.

(j)   The Board in its discretion upon application may grant a reciprocal license to a person holding a valid, active substantially comparable license from another jurisdiction, but only to the extent the other jurisdiction grants reciprocal privileges to North Carolina licensees. (1955, c. 912, s. 7; 1959, c. 1206, s. 1; 1979, c. 843, ss. 1, 2; 1987 (Reg. Sess., 1988), c. 1082, s. 5; 1989, c. 770, s. 13; 1995, c. 376, s. 2; 1998-216, ss. 1, 2, 2.1; 2009-333, ss. 1, 2.)

§ 87-59. Revocation or suspension of license for cause.

(a)   The Board shall have power to revoke or suspend the license of any refrigeration contractor who is guilty of any fraud or deceit in obtaining a license, or who fails to comply with any provision or requirement of this Article, or for gross negligence, incompetency, or misconduct, in the practice of or in carrying on the business of a refrigeration contractor as defined in this Article. Any person may prefer charges of fraud, deceit, gross negligence, incompetency, misconduct, or failure to comply with any provision or requirement of this Article, against any refrigeration contractor who is licensed under the provisions of this Article. All charges shall be in writing and verified by the complainant, and shall be heard and determined by the Board in accordance with the provisions of Chapter 150B of the General Statutes.

(b)   The Board shall adopt and publish rules and regulations, consistent with the provisions of this Article and Chapter 150B of the General Statutes, governing the suspension and revocation of licenses.

(c)   The Board shall establish and maintain a system whereby detailed records are kept regarding complaints against each licensee. This record shall include, for each licensee, the date and nature of each complaint, investigatory action taken by the Board, any findings of the Board, and the disposition of the matter.

(d) In a case in which the Board is entitled to convene a hearing to consider a charge under this section, the Board may accept an offer to compromise the charge, whereby the accused shall pay to the Board a penalty not to exceed one thousand dollars ($1,000). The funds derived from the penalty shall be remitted to the Civil Penalty and Forfeiture Fund in accordance with G.S. 115C-457.2.

(e) All records, papers, and other documents containing information collected and compiled by the Board, or its members or employees, as a result of investigations, inquiries, or interviews conducted in connection with a licensing or disciplinary matter, shall not be considered public records within the meaning of Chapter 132 of the General Statutes. (1955, c. 912, s. 8; 1973, c. 1331, s. 3; 1979, c. 712, s. 3; 1989, c. 770, s. 14; 1995, c. 376, s. 3; 2009-333, ss. 3, 4.)

§ 87-60. Reissuance of revoked licenses; replacing lost or destroyed licenses.

The Board may in its discretion reissue license to any person, firm or corporation whose license was revoked if a majority of the Board votes in favor of such reissuance for reasons deemed sufficient by the Board. A new certificate of registration to replace any license which may be lost or destroyed may be issued subject to the rules and regulations of the Board. (1955, c. 912, s. 9; 1998-216, s. 3.)

§ 87-61. Violations made misdemeanor; employees of licensees excepted.

Any person, firm or corporation who shall engage in or offer to engage in, or carry on the business of refrigeration contracting as defined in this Article, without first having been licensed to engage in the business, or businesses, as required by the provisions of this Article; or any person, firm or corporation holding a refrigeration license under the provisions of this Article who shall practice or offer to practice or carry on any type of refrigeration contracting not authorized by the license; or any person, firm or corporation who shall give false or forged evidence of any kind to the Board, or any member thereof, in obtaining a license, or who shall falsely impersonate any other practitioner of like or different name, or who shall use an expired or revoked license, or who shall violate any of the provisions of this Article, shall be guilty of a Class 3 misdemeanor. The Board may, in its discretion, use its funds to defray the costs and expenses, legal or otherwise, in the prosecution of any violation of this Article. Employees, while working under the supervision and jurisdiction of a person, firm or corporation licensed in accordance with the provisions of this Article, shall not be construed to have engaged in the business of refrigeration contracting. (1955, c. 912, s. 10; 1993, c. 539, s. 607; 1994, Ex. Sess., c. 24, s. 14(c); 1995, c. 376, s. 4; 2009-333, s. 5.)

§ 87-61.1. Board may seek injunctive relief; retain counsel.

(a)   Whenever it appears to the Board that any person, firm or corporation is violating any of the provisions of this Article or of the rules and regulations promulgated under this Article, the Board may apply to the superior court for a restraining order and injunction to restrain the violation; and the superior courts have jurisdiction to grant the requested relief, irrespective of whether or not criminal prosecution has been instituted or administrative sanctions imposed by reason of the violation.

(b)   The Board may employ or retain legal counsel for matters and purposes the Board deems fit and proper, subject to G.S. 114-2.3. (1979, c. 712, s. 4; 2009-333, s. 6.)

§ 87-62. Only one person in partnership or corporation need have license.

(a)   A corporation or partnership may engage in the business of refrigeration contracting if one or more persons connected with the corporation or partnership is registered and licensed as herein required, and the licensed person executes all contracts, exercises general supervision over the work done thereunder and is responsible for compliance with all the provisions of this Article. The Board may determine the number of businesses and the proximity of the businesses one to another over which the licensed person may be responsible.

(b) For purposes of this section, the licensee's connection to the corporation or partnership shall be in the form of a written contract that is executed prior to the corporation or partnership engaging in refrigeration contracting.

(c) Nothing in this Article shall prohibit any employee from becoming licensed pursuant to the provisions thereof. (1955, c. 912, s. 11; 1998-216, s. 4.)

§ 87-63. License fees payable in advance; application of.

All license fees shall be paid in advance as hereafter provided to the secretary and treasurer of the Board and by him held as a fund for the use of the Board. The compensation and expenses of the members of the Board as herein provided, the salaries of its employees, and all expenses incurred in the discharge of its duties under this Article shall be paid out of such fund, upon the warrant of the chairman and secretary and treasurer: Provided, upon the payment of the necessary expenses of the Board as herein set out, and the retention by it of twenty-five per centum (25%) of the balance of funds collected hereunder the residue, if any, shall be paid to the State Treasurer. (1955, c. 912, s. 12.)

§ 87-63.1. Ownership of real property; equipment; liability insurance.

(a) The Board shall have the power to acquire, hold, rent, encumber, alienate, and otherwise deal with real property in the same manner as a private person or corporation, subject only to the approval of the Governor and the Council of State. Collateral pledged by the Board for an encumbrance is limited to the assets, income, and revenues of the Board.

(b) The Board may purchase or rent equipment and supplies and purchase liability insurance or other insurance to cover the activities of the Board, its operations, or its employees. (2009-333, s. 7.)

§ 87-64. Examination and license fees; annual renewal.

Each applicant for a license by examination shall pay to the Board of Refrigeration Examiners a nonrefundable examination fee in an amount not to exceed the sum of forty dollars ($40.00). In the event the applicant successfully passes the examination, the examination fee shall be applied to the license fee required of licensees for the current year in which the examination was taken and passed.

The license of every person licensed under the provisions of this statute shall be annually renewed. Effective January 1, 2012, the Board may require, as a prerequisite to the annual renewal of a license, that licensees complete continuing education courses in subjects related to refrigeration contracting to ensure the safe and proper installation of commercial and transport refrigeration work and equipment. On or before November 1 of each year the Board shall cause to be mailed an application for renewal of license to every person who has received from the Board a license to engage in the refrigeration business, as heretofore defined. On or before January 1 of each year every licensed person who desires to continue in the refrigeration business shall forward to the Board a renewal fee in an amount not to exceed forty dollars ($40.00) together with the application for renewal. Upon receipt of the application and renewal fee the Board shall issue a renewal certificate for the current year. Failure to renew the license annually shall automatically result in a forfeiture of the right to engage in the refrigeration business. Any licensee who allows the license to lapse may be reinstated by the Board upon payment of a fee not to exceed seventy-five dollars ($75.00). Any person who fails to renew a license for two consecutive years shall be required to take and pass the examination prescribed by the Board for new applicants before being licensed to engage further in the refrigeration business. (1955, c. 912, s. 13; 1969, c. 314; 1979, c. 843, ss. 3, 4; 1998-216, s. 5; 2009-333, s. 8.)

§ 87-64.1. Public awareness program.

The Board shall establish and implement a public awareness program to inform the general public of the purpose and function of the Board. (1979, c. 712, s. 4.)

Article 6.

Water Well Contractors.

§§ 87-65 through 87-82: Repealed by Session Laws 1977, c. 712, s. 2.

Article 7.

North Carolina Well Construction Act.

§ 87-83. Short title.

This Article shall be known and may be cited as the North Carolina Well Construction Act. (1967, c. 1157, s. 1.)

§ 87-84. Findings and policy.

The General Assembly of North Carolina finds that improperly constructed, operated, maintained, or abandoned wells can adversely affect the public health and the groundwater resources of the State. Consistent with the duty to safeguard the public welfare, safety, health and to protect and beneficially develop the groundwater resources of this State, it is declared to be the policy of this State to require that the location, construction, repair, and abandonment of wells, and the installation of pumps and pumping equipment conform to such reasonable requirements as may be necessary to protect the public welfare, safety, health and groundwater resources. (1967, c. 1157, s. 2.)

§ 87-85. Definitions.

As used in this Article, unless the context otherwise requires:

(1)   "Abandoned well" means a well whose use has been discontinued, or which is in such a state of disrepair that continued use for obtaining groundwater or other useful purpose is impracticable.

(2)   "Aquifer" means a geologic formation, group of such formations, or a part of such a formation that is water bearing.

(3) "Artesian well" means a well tapping a confined or artesian aquifer.

(4) "Environmental Management Commission" means the North Carolina Environmental Management Commission or its successor, unless otherwise indicated.

(5) "Construction of wells" means all acts necessary to construct wells for any intended purpose or use, including the location and excavation of the well; placement of casings, screens and fittings; development and testing.

(5a) "Department" means the Department of Environment and Natural Resources unless otherwise indicated.

(6) "Installation of pumps and pumping equipment" means the procedure employed in the placement and preparation for operation of pumps and pumping equipment, including all construction involved in making entrances to the well and establishing seals.

(7) "Municipality" means a city, town, county, district, or other public body created by or pursuant to State law, or any combination thereof acting cooperatively or jointly.

(8) "Nonpotable mineralized water" means brackish, saline, or other water containing minerals of such quantity or type as to render the water unsafe, harmful or generally unsuitable for human consumption and general use.

(9) "Person" shall mean any and all persons, including individuals, firms, partnerships, associations, public or private institutions, municipalities or political subdivisions, governmental agencies, or private or public corporations organized or existing under the laws of this State or any other state or country.

(10) "Polluted water" means water containing organic or other contaminants of such type and quantity as to render it unsafe, harmful or unsuitable for human consumption and general use.

(10a) "Private drinking water well" means any excavation that is cored, bored, drilled, jetted, dug, or otherwise constructed to obtain groundwater for human consumption and that serves or is proposed to serve 14 or fewer service connections or that serves or is proposed to serve 24 or fewer individuals. The term "private drinking water well" includes a well that supplies drinking water to a transient noncommunity water system as defined in 40 Code of Federal Regulations § 141.2 (July 1, 2003 Edition).

(11) "Pumps" and "pumping equipment" means any equipment or materials utilized or intended for use in withdrawing or obtaining groundwater including well seals.

(12) "Repair" means work involved in deepening, reaming, sealing, installing or changing casing depths, perforating, screening, or cleaning, acidizing or redevelopment of a well excavation, or any other work which results in breaking or opening the well seal.

(13) "Water supply well" means any well intended or usable as a source of water supply, but not to include a well constructed by an individual on land which is owned or leased by him, appurtenant to a single-family dwelling, and intended for domestic use (including household purposes, farm livestock, or gardens).

(14) "Well" means any excavation that is cored, bored, drilled, jetted, dug or otherwise constructed for the purpose of locating, testing or withdrawing groundwater or for evaluating, testing, developing, draining or recharging any groundwater reservoirs or aquifer, or that may control, divert, or otherwise cause the movement of water from or into any aquifer.

(15) "Well driller," "driller" or "water well contractor" means any person, firm, or corporation engaged in the business of constructing wells.

(16) "Well seal" means an approved arrangement or device used to cap a well or to establish and maintain a junction between the casing or curbing of a well and the piping or equipment installed therein, the purpose or function of which is to prevent pollutants from entering the well at the upper terminal.

(17) "Operation of wells" means the process, frequency, and duration of withdrawing water or other fluids from a well by any means. (1967, c. 1157, s. 3; 1973, c. 1262, s. 23; 1977, c. 771, s. 4; 1987, c. 496, s. 1; 1989, c. 727, s. 218(21); 1997-358, s. 4; 1997-443, s. 11A.119(a); 2006-202, s. 1.)

§ 87-86. Scope.

No person shall construct, operate, repair, or abandon, or cause to be constructed, operated, repaired, or abandoned, any well, nor shall any person install, repair, or cause to be installed or repaired, any pump or pumping equipment contrary to the provisions of this Article and applicable rules and regulations, provided that this Article shall not apply to any distribution of water beyond the point of discharge from the pump. (1967, c. 1157, s. 4; 1987, c. 496, ss. 2, 3.)

§ 87-87. Authority to adopt rules, regulations, and procedures.

The Environmental Management Commission shall adopt rules governing the location, construction, repair, and abandonment of wells, the operation of water wells or well systems with a designed capacity of 100,000 gallons per day or greater, and the installation and repair of pumps and pumping equipment. The Environmental Management Commission shall be responsible for the administration of this Article and shall:

(1) Hold public hearings, upon not less than 30 days' prior notice setting forth the date, place, and time of hearing, and the proposed rules and regulations to be considered at said public hearing, which notice shall be published in one or more newspapers having general circulation throughout the State, in connection with proposed rules and regulations and amendments thereto.

(2) Enforce the provisions of this Article, and any rules and regulations not inconsistent with the provisions of this Article adopted pursuant thereto.

(3) Establish procedures and forms for the submission, review, approval, and rejection of applications, notifications, and reports required under this Article.

(4) Issue such additional regulations as may be necessary to carry out the provisions of this Article.

(5) Neither adopt nor enforce any rule or regulation that concerns the civil liability of an owner to a well driller for any costs or expenses of drilling and installing a well for the owner.

(6) Adopt rules governing the permitting and inspection by the Commission of private drinking water wells with a designed capacity of 100,000 gallons per day or greater.

(7) Adopt rules governing the permitting and inspection by local health departments of private drinking water wells pursuant to G.S. 87-97. (1967, c. 1157, s. 5; 1973, c. 1262, s. 23; 1985, c. 728, s. 4; 1987, c. 496, s. 4; 2006-202, s. 2.)

§ 87-88. General standards and requirements.

(a) Prior Permission. - Prior permission shall be obtained from the Environmental Management Commission for the construction of (i) any water well or of well systems with a designed capacity of 100,000 gallons per day or greater; and (ii) of any well in a geographical area where the Environmental Management Commission finds, after public hearings, such permission to be reasonably necessary to protect the groundwater resources and the public welfare, safety and health, taking into consideration other applicable State laws; provided, however, that the Environmental Management Commission shall not reject any application under this subsection for permission to construct a well except upon the ground that the well would not be in compliance with a provision of this Article or with a rule or regulation of the Environmental Management Commission adopted pursuant to the provisions of G.S. 87-87 of this Article. Notification of approval or rejection of an application for permission to construct a well shall be given the applicant within a period of 15 days after receipt of such application. Private drinking water wells (i) with a designed capacity of 100,000 gallons per day or greater or (ii) that are to be constructed in a geographical area where the Environmental Management Commission has found that prior permission is necessary shall be subject to permitting and inspection by the Environmental Management Commission and shall not be subject to permitting and inspection by a local health department. All other private drinking water wells shall be subject to permitting and inspection by the local health department as provided in G.S. 87-97.

(b) Reports. - Any person completing or abandoning any well shall furnish the Environmental Management Commission a certified record of the construction or abandonment of such well within a period of 30 days after completion of construction or abandonment.

(c) Prevention of Contamination. - Every well shall be constructed and maintained in a condition whereby it is not a source or channel of contamination of the groundwater supply or any aquifer. Wells subject to the provisions of subdivision (a)(i) of this section shall be operated in such a way that they shall not cause the violation of applicable groundwater quality standards. Contamination as used herein shall mean the act of introducing into water foreign materials of such a nature, quality, and quantity as to cause degradation of the quality of the water.

(d)   Valves and Casing on Flowing Artesian Wells. - Valves and casing on all flowing artesian wells shall be maintained in a condition so that the flow of water can be completely stopped when the well is not being put to a beneficial use. Valves shall be closed when a beneficial use is not being made.

(e)   Access Port. - Every water-supply well and such other wells, as may be specified by the Environmental Management Commission, shall be equipped with a usable access port or air line and to be a minimum of 0.5 inch inside diameter opening so that the position of the water level can be determined at any time. Such port shall be installed and maintained in such manner as to prevent entrance of water or foreign material.

(f)   Mineralized Water. - Whenever a water-bearing stratum or aquifer that contains nonpotable mineralized water is encountered in well construction, the stratum shall be adequately cased or cemented off as conditions may require so that contamination of the overlying or underlying groundwater zones will not occur.

(g)   Polluted Water. - In constructing any well, all water-bearing zones that are known to contain polluted water shall be adequately cased or cemented off so that pollution of the overlying and underlying groundwater zones will not occur.

(h)   Well Test. - Every water-supply well shall be tested for capacity by a method and for a period of time acceptable to the Department and depending on the intended use of the well.

(i)   Chlorination of the Well. - Upon completion of the well construction and pump installation, all water-supply wells installed for the purpose of obtaining groundwater for human consumption shall be sterilized in accordance with standards for sterilization of drinking water wells established by the U.S. Public Health Service.

(j)   Use of Well for Recharge or Disposal. - No well shall be used for recharge, injection or disposal purposes without prior permission from the Environmental Management Commission.

(k)   Abandonment of Wells. -

(1)   Temporary Abandonment: When any well is temporarily removed from service, the top of the well shall be sealed with a water-tight cap or seal.

(2)   Permanent Abandonment: Any well that is to be permanently abandoned shall be filled, plugged, or sealed in such a manner as to prevent the well from being a channel allowing the vertical movement of water and a source of contamination of the groundwater supply.

(3)   Abandonment of Water Supply Wells for Other Use: Any water supply well that is removed from service as a potable water supply source may be used for other purposes, including, but not limited to, irrigation, commercial use, or industrial use, and such well is not subject to either subdivision (1) or (2) of this subsection during its use for other purposes. For purposes of this subsection only, "water supply well" includes wells constructed by an individual on land which is owned or leased by the individual, appurtenant to a single-family dwelling, and intended for domestic use (including nonpotable household purposes, farm livestock, or gardens). (1967, c. 1157, s. 6; 1973, c. 476, s. 128; c. 1262, s. 23; 1987, c. 496, s. 4; 1989, c. 727, s. 14; 1998-212, s. 14.9B(a); 2006-202, s. 3; 2006-259, s. 50(a); 2011-255, s. 3.)

§ 87-89. Existing installations.

No well or pump installation in existence and in use on July 6, 1967, shall be required to conform to provisions of subsection (a) of G.S. 87-88, or any rules or regulations adopted pursuant thereto not inconsistent with the provisions of this Article; provided, however, that any well now or hereafter abandoned, including any well deemed to have been abandoned, as defined in the Article, shall, within such time as may be specified by the Environmental Management Commission, be brought into compliance with the requirements of this Article and any applicable rules or regulations with respect to abandonment of wells. It is the intention of the General Assembly that if the provisions of this section are held invalid as a grant of an exclusive or separate emolument or privilege, within the meaning of Article I, Sec. 7 of the North Carolina Constitution, the remainder of this Article shall be given effect without the invalid provision or provisions. (1967, c. 1157, s. 7; 1973, c. 1262, s. 23.)

§ 87-90. Rights of investigation, entry, access and inspection.

The Environmental Management Commission or Department shall have the right to conduct such investigations as it may reasonably find necessary to carry on its duties prescribed in this Article, and for this purpose to enter at reasonable times upon any property, public or private, for the purpose of investigating the condition, installation, or operation of any well or associated equipment, facility, or property, and to require written statements or the filing of reports under oath, with respect to pertinent questions relating to the installation or operation of any well: Provided, that no person shall be required to disclose any secret formula, processes or methods used in any manufacturing operation or any confidential information concerning business activities carried on by him or under his supervision. No person shall refuse entry or access to any authorized representative of the Environmental Management Commission who requests entry for purposes of inspection, and who presents appropriate credentials, nor shall any person obstruct, hamper or interfere with any such representative while in the process of carrying out his official duties, consistent with the provisions of this Article. (1967, c. 1157, s. 8; 1973, c. 1262, s. 23.)

§ 87-91. Notice of violation; remedial action order.

(a) Whenever the Environmental Management Commission has reasonable grounds to believe that there has been a violation of this Article or any rule adopted pursuant to this Article, the Environmental Management Commission or Department shall give written notice to the person or persons alleged to be in violation. The notice shall identify the provision of this Article or rule adopted pursuant to this Article alleged to be violated and the facts alleged to constitute the violation. The Environmental Management Commission may also issue an order requiring specific remedial action. An order requiring remedial action shall specify the action to be taken, the date by which the action must be completed, the possible consequences of failing to comply with the order, and the procedure by which the alleged violator may seek review of the order.

(b) The notice may be served by any means authorized under G.S. 1A-1, Rule 4. (1967, c. 1157, s. 9; 1973, c. 1262, s. 23; 1977, c. 771, s. 4; 1989, c. 727, s. 15; 1997-358, s. 7; 1997-443, s. 11A.119(a).)

§ 87-92. Hearings; appeals.

Any person wishing to contest a penalty, permit decision, or other order issued under this Article shall be entitled to an administrative hearing and judicial review conducted according to the procedures established in Chapter 150B of the General Statutes. (1967, c. 1157, s. 10; 1973, c. 1262, s. 23; 1977, c. 771, s. 4; 1985, c. 728, s. 1; 1987, c. 827, ss. 1, 70.)

§ 87-93: Repealed by Session Laws 1985, c. 728, s. 2.

§ 87-94. Civil penalties.

(a) Any person who violates any provision of this Article, Article 7A of this Chapter, any order issued pursuant thereto, or any rule adopted thereunder, shall be subject to a civil penalty of not more than one thousand dollars ($1,000) for each violation, as determined by the Secretary of Environment and Natural Resources. Each day of a continuing violation shall be considered a separate offense. No person shall be subject to a penalty who did not directly commit the violation or cause it to be committed.

(b) Repealed by Session Laws 1997-358, s. 3.

(c) In determining the amount of the penalty the Secretary shall consider factors set out in G.S. 143B-282.1(b). The procedures set out in G.S. 143-215.6A and G.S. 143B-282.1 shall apply to civil penalties assessed under this section.

(d) The Secretary shall notify any person assessed a civil penalty of the assessment and the specific reasons therefor by registered or certified mail, or by any means authorized by G.S. 1A-1, Rule 4.

(e) Repealed by Session Laws 1997-358, s. 3.

(f) Repealed by 1995 (Reg. Sess., 1996), c. 743, s. 2.

(g) The clear proceeds of civil penalties provided for in this section shall be remitted to the Civil Penalty and Forfeiture Fund in accordance with G.S. 115C-457.2. (1967, c. 1157, s. 12; 1985, c. 728, s. 3; 1987, c. 246, s. 2; 1989, c. 727, s. 218(22); 1989 (Reg. Sess., 1990), c. 1036, s. 10; 1995 (Reg. Sess., 1996), c. 743, s. 2; 1997-358, s. 3; 1997-443, s. 11A.119(a); 1998-215, s. 44; 2001-440, s. 1.4.)

§ 87-95. Injunctive relief.

Upon violation of any of the provisions of or any order issued pursuant to this Article, or duly adopted rule of the Commission implementing the provisions of this Article, the Secretary of Environment and Natural Resources may, either before or after the institution of proceedings for the collection of the penalty imposed by this Article for such violations, request the Attorney General to institute a civil action in the superior court in the name of the State upon the relation of the Department of Environment and Natural Resources for injunctive relief to restrain the violation or require corrective action, and for such other or further relief in the premises as said court shall deem proper. Neither the institution of the action nor any of the proceedings thereon shall relieve any party to such proceedings from the penalty prescribed by this Article for any violation of same. (1967, c. 1157, s. 13; 1973, c. 1262, s. 23; 1975, c. 842, s. 1; 1977, c. 771, s. 4; 1989, c. 727, s. 16; 1989 (Reg. Sess., 1990), c. 1004, s. 19(b); 1997-443, s. 11A.119(a).)

§ 87-96. Conflict with other laws.

(a) The provisions of any law, rule, or local ordinance which establish standards affording greater protection to groundwater resources or public health, safety, or welfare shall prevail, within the jurisdiction to which they apply, over the provisions of this Article and rules adopted pursuant to this Article.

(b) Rules relating to public health, wells, or groundwater adopted by the Commission for Public Health shall prevail over this Article, rules adopted pursuant to this Article, and rules adopted by a local board of health pursuant to subsection (c) of this section. This Article shall not be construed to repeal any law or rule in effect as of July 1, 1989.

(c) A local board of health may adopt by reference rules adopted by the Environmental Management Commission pursuant to this Article, and may adopt more stringent rules when necessary to protect the public health. (1967, c. 1157, s. 14; 1973, c. 476, s. 128; 1989, c. 727, s. 17; 1991, c. 650, s. 1; 2007-182, s. 2.)

§ 87-97. Permitting, inspection, and testing of private drinking water wells.

(a) Mandatory Local Well Programs. - Each county, through the local health department that serves the county, shall implement a private drinking water well permitting, inspection, and testing program. Local health departments shall administer the program and enforce the minimum well construction, permitting, inspection, repair, and testing requirements set out in this Article and rules adopted pursuant to this Article. No person shall unduly delay or refuse to permit a well that can be constructed or repaired and operated in compliance with the requirements set out in this Article and rules adopted pursuant to this Article.

(b) Permit Required. - Except for those wells required to be permitted by the Environmental Management Commission pursuant to G.S. 87-88, no person shall:

(1) Construct or assist in the construction of a private drinking water well unless a construction permit has been obtained from the local health department.

(2) Repair or assist in the repair of a private drinking water well unless a repair permit has been obtained from the local health department, except that a permit shall not be required for the repair or replacement of a pump or tank.

(c) Permit Not Required for Maintenance or Pump Repair or Replacement. - A repair permit shall not be required for any private drinking water well maintenance work that does not involve breaking or opening the well seal. A repair permit shall not be required for any private drinking water well repair work that involves only the repair or replacement of a pump or tank.

(d)   Well Site Evaluation. - The local health department shall conduct a field investigation to evaluate the site on which a private drinking water well is proposed to be located before issuing a permit pursuant to this section. The field investigation shall determine whether there is any abandoned well located on the site, and if so, the construction permit shall be conditioned upon the proper closure of all abandoned wells located on the site in accordance with the requirements of this Article and rules adopted pursuant to this Article. If a private drinking water well is proposed to be located on a site on which a wastewater system subject to the requirements of Article 11 of Chapter 130A of the General Statutes is located or proposed to be located, the application for a construction permit shall be accompanied by a plat or site plan, as defined in G.S. 130A-334.

(e)   Issuance of Permit. - Within 30 days of receipt of an application to construct or repair a well, a local health department shall make a determination whether the proposed private drinking water well can be constructed or repaired and operated in compliance with this Article and rules adopted pursuant to this Article and shall issue a permit or denial accordingly. If a local health department fails to act within 30 days, the permit shall automatically be issued, and the local health department may challenge issuance of the permit as provided in Chapter 150B of the General Statutes. The local health department may impose any conditions on the issuance of a construction permit or repair permit that it determines to be necessary to ensure compliance with this Article and rules adopted pursuant to this Article. Notwithstanding any other provision of law, no permit for a well that is in compliance with this Article and the rules adopted pursuant to this Article shall be denied on the basis of a local government policy that discourages or prohibits the drilling of new wells.

(e1)   Notice for Wells at Contamination Sites. - The Commission shall adopt rules governing permits issued for private drinking water wells for circumstances in which the local health department has determined that the proposed site for a private drinking water well is located within 1,000 feet of a known source of release of contamination. Rules adopted pursuant to this subsection shall provide for notice and information of the known source of release of contamination and any known risk of issuing a permit for the construction and use of a private drinking water well on such a site.

(f)   Expiration and Revocation. - A construction permit or repair permit shall be valid for a period of five years except that the local health department may revoke a permit at any time if it determines that there has been a material change in any fact or circumstance upon which the permit is issued. The foregoing shall be prominently stated on the face of the permit. The validity of a construction permit or a repair permit shall not be affected by a change in ownership of the site on which a private drinking water well is proposed to be located or is located if the location of the well is unchanged and the well and the facility served by the well remain under common ownership.

(f1) Chlorination of the Well. - Upon completion of construction of a private drinking water well, the well shall be sterilized in accordance with the standards of drinking water wells established by the United States Public Health Service.

(g) Certificate of Completion. - Upon completion of construction of a private drinking water well or repair of a private drinking water well for which a permit is required under this section, the local health department shall inspect the well to determine whether it was constructed or repaired in compliance with the construction permit or repair permit. If the local health department determines that the private drinking water well has been constructed or repaired in accordance with the requirements of the construction permit or repair permit, the construction and repair requirements of this Article, and rules adopted pursuant to this Article, the local health department shall issue a certificate of completion. No person shall place a private drinking water well into service without first having obtained a certificate of completion. No person shall return a private drinking water well that has undergone repair to service without first having obtained a certificate of completion.

(h) Drinking Water Testing. - Within 30 days after it issues a certificate of completion for a newly constructed private drinking water well, the local health department shall test the water obtained from the well or ensure that the water obtained from the well has been sampled and tested by a certified laboratory in accordance with rules adopted by the Commission for Public Health. The water shall be tested for the following parameters: arsenic, barium, cadmium, chromium, copper, fluoride, lead, iron, magnesium, manganese, mercury, nitrates, nitrites, selenium, silver, sodium, zinc, pH, and bacterial indicators.

(i) Commission for Public Health to Adopt Drinking Water Testing Rules. - The Commission for Public Health shall adopt rules governing the sampling and testing of well water and the reporting of test results. The rules shall allow local health departments to designate third parties to collect and test samples and report test results. The rules shall also provide for corrective action and retesting where appropriate. The Commission for Public Health may by rule require testing for additional parameters, including volatile organic compounds, if the Commission makes a specific finding that testing for the additional parameters is necessary to protect public health. If the Commission finds that testing for certain volatile organic compounds is necessary to protect public health and initiates rule making to require testing for certain volatile organic compounds, the Commission shall consider all of the following factors in the development of the rule: (i) known current and historic land uses around well sites and associated contaminants; (ii) known contaminated sites within a given radius of a well and any known data regarding dates of contamination, geology, and other relevant factors; (iii) any GIS-based information on known contamination sources from databases available to the Department of Environment and Natural Resources; and (iv) visual on-site inspections of well sites. In addition, the rules shall require local health departments to educate citizens for whom new private drinking water wells are constructed and for citizens who contact local health departments regarding testing an existing well on all of the following:

(1) The scope of the testing required pursuant to this Article.

(2) Optional testing available pursuant to this Article.

(3) The limitations of both the required and optional testing.

(4) Minimum drinking water standards.

(j) Test Results. - The local health department shall provide test results to the owner of the newly constructed private drinking water well and, to the extent practicable, to any leaseholder of a dwelling unit or other facility served by the well at the time the water is sampled. The local health department shall include with any test results provided to an owner of a private drinking water well, information regarding the scope of the required and optional testing as established by rules adopted pursuant to subsection (i) of this section.

(k) Registry of Permits and Test Results. - Each local health department shall maintain a registry of all private drinking water wells for which a construction permit or repair permit is issued. The registry shall specify the physical location of each private drinking water well and shall include the results of all tests of water from each well. The local health department shall retain a record of the results of all tests of water from a private drinking water well until the well is properly closed in accordance with the requirements of this Article and rules adopted pursuant to this Article.

(l)   Authority Not Limited. - This section shall not be construed to limit any authority of local boards of health, local health departments, the Department of Health and Human Services, or the Commission for Public Health to protect public health. (2006-202, s. 4; 2006-259, ss. 50(b), 50(c), 51; 2007-182, s. 2; 2007-495, s. 1; 2008-198, s. 1; 2009-124, ss. 1, 3; 2010-31, s. 10.10A; 2011-255, ss. 1, 2; 2012-187, s. 12(a), (b); 2013-122, ss. 2, 3; 2013-413, s. 35(a).)

§ 87-98. Bernard Allen Memorial Emergency Drinking Water Fund.

(a)   The Bernard Allen Memorial Emergency Drinking Water Fund is established under the control and direction of the Department. The Fund shall be a nonreverting, interest-bearing fund consisting of monies appropriated by the General Assembly or made available to the Fund from any other source and investment interest credited to the Fund.

(b)   The Fund may be used to pay for:

(1)   Notification, to the extent practicable, of persons aged 18 and older who reside in any dwelling unit, and the senior official in charge of any business, at which drinking water is supplied from a private drinking water well or improved spring that is located within 1,500 feet of, and at risk from, known groundwater contamination. The senior official in charge of the business shall take reasonable measures to notify all employees of the business of the groundwater contamination, including posting a notice of the contamination in a form and at a location that is readily accessible to the employees of the business.

(2)   The costs of testing of private drinking water wells and improved springs for suspected contamination up to once every three years upon request by a person who uses the well, or more frequent testing if the concentration of one or more contaminants in a private drinking water well is increasing over time and there is a significant risk that the concentration of a contaminant will exceed the drinking water action levels set forth in subsection (c) of this section within a three-year period.

(3)   Additional testing to confirm the results of a previous test.

(4)   The temporary or permanent provision of alternative drinking water supplies to persons whose drinking water well or improved spring is contaminated. Under this section, an alternative drinking water supply includes

the repair, such as use of a filtration system, or replacement of a contaminated well or the connection to a public water supply.

(5) Monitoring of filtration systems used in connection with temporary or permanent alternative drinking water supplies provided pursuant to this section.

(c) The Department shall disburse monies from the Fund based on financial need and on the risk to public health posed by groundwater contamination and shall give priority to the provision of services under this section to instances when an alternative source of funds is not available. The Fund shall not be used to provide alternative water supply to households with incomes greater than three hundred percent (300%) of the current federal poverty level. The Fund may be used to provide alternative drinking water supplies if the Department determines that the concentration of one or more contaminants in the private drinking water well or improved spring exceeds the federal maximum contaminant level, or the federal drinking water action level as defined in 40 Code of Federal Regulations § 141.1 through § 141.571 (1 July 2007) and 40 Code of Federal Regulations § 143.3 (1 July 2007). For a contaminant for which a federal maximum contaminant level or drinking water action level has not been established, the State groundwater standard established by the Environmental Management Commission for the concentration of that contaminant shall be used to determine whether the Fund may be used to provide alternative drinking water supplies. The Fund may also be used to provide alternative drinking water supplies as provided in this section if the Department determines that the concentration of one or more contaminants in a private drinking water well is increasing over time and that there is a significant risk that the concentration of a contaminant will exceed the federal maximum contaminant level or drinking water action level, or the State groundwater standard. A determination of the concentration of a contaminant shall be based on a sample of water collected from the private drinking water well within the past 12 months.

(c1) In disbursing monies from the Fund, the Department shall give preference to provision of permanent replacement water supplies by connection to public water supplies and repair or replacement of contaminated wells over the provision of temporary water supplies. In providing alternative drinking water supplies, the Department shall give preference to connection to a public water supply system or to construction of a new private drinking water well over the use of a filtration system if the Department determines that the costs of periodic required maintenance of the filtration system would be cost-prohibitive for users of the alternative drinking water supply.

(c2) If the Department provides an alternative drinking water supply by extension of a waterline, the Department may disburse from the Fund no more than fifty thousand dollars ($50,000) per household or other service connection. For projects where more than 10 residences are eligible for alternative water supplies under this section, no more than one-third of the total cost of the project may be paid from the Fund. The Department may combine monies from the Fund with monies from other sources in order to pay the total cost of the project.

(c3) The Fund shall be used to provide alternative drinking water supplies only if the Department determines that the person or persons who are responsible for the contamination of the private drinking water well is or are not financially viable or cannot be identified or located and if the Department determines that one of the following applies:

(1) The contamination of the private drinking water well is naturally occurring.

(2) The owner of the property on which the private drinking water well is located did not cause or contribute to the contamination or control the source of the contamination.

(3) The source of the contamination is the application or disposal of a hazardous substance or pesticide that occurred without the consent of the owner of the property on which the private drinking water well is located.

(c4) The Department may use up to one hundred thousand dollars ($100,000) annually of the monies in the Fund to pay the personnel and other direct costs associated with the implementation of this section.

(c5) The Fund shall not be used for remediation of groundwater contamination.

(c6) Nothing in this section expands, contracts, or modifies the obligation of responsible parties under Article 9 or 10 of Chapter 130A of the General Statutes, this Article, or Article 21A of this Chapter to assess contamination, identify receptors, or remediate groundwater or soil contamination.

(c7) In disbursing monies from the Fund for replacement water supplies, the Department shall give priority to circumstances in which a well is contaminated as the result of nonnaturally occurring groundwater contamination in the area over circumstances in which a well has naturally occurring contamination.

(d) The Department shall establish criteria by which the Department is to evaluate applications and disburse monies from this Fund and may adopt any rules necessary to implement this section.

(e) The Department, in consultation with the Commission for Public Health and local health departments, shall report no later than October 1 of each year to the Environmental Review Commission, the House of Representatives and Senate Appropriations Subcommittees on Natural and Economic Resources, and the Fiscal Research Division of the General Assembly on the implementation of this section. The report shall include the purpose and amount of all expenditures from the Fund during the prior fiscal year, a discussion of the benefits and deficiencies realized as a result of the section, and may also include recommendations for any legislative action. (2006-255, s. 5.2; 2007-182, s. 2; 2007-323, s. 12.2(a); 2008-107, s. 12.1; 2013-360, s. 14.14.)

Article 7A.

Well Contractors Certification.

§ 87-98.1. Title.

This Article may be cited as the North Carolina Well Contractors Certification Act. (1997-358, s. 2.)

§ 87-98.2. Definitions.

The definitions in G.S. 87-85 and the following definitions apply in this Article:

(1) Commission. - The Well Contractors Certification Commission, as established by G.S. 143B-301.11.

(2) Department. - The Department of Environment and Natural Resources.

(3) Person. - A natural person.

(4) Secretary. - The Secretary of Environment and Natural Resources.

(5) Well contractor. - A person in trade or business who undertakes to perform a well contractor activity or who undertakes to personally supervise or personally manage the performance of a well contractor activity on the person's own behalf or for any person, firm, or corporation.

(6) Well contractor activity. - The construction, installation, repair, alteration, or abandonment of any well. (1997-358, s. 2; 1997-443, s. 11A.119(b); 2002-165, s. 1.1.)

§ 87-98.3. Purpose.

It is the purpose of this Article to protect the public health and safety by ensuring the integrity and competence of well contractors, to protect and beneficially develop the groundwater resources of the State, to require the examination of well contractors and the certification of their competency to supervise or conduct well contractor activity, and to establish procedures for the examination and certification of well contractors. (1997-358, s. 2.)

§ 87-98.4. Well contractor certification required; exemptions.

(a) Certification Required. - No person shall perform, manage, or supervise any well contractor activity without being certified under this Article. A person who is not a certified well contractor or who is not employed by a certified well contractor shall not offer to perform any well contractor activity unless the person utilizes a certified well contractor to perform the well contractor activity and, prior to the performance of the well contractor activity, the person discloses to the landowner in writing the name of the certified well contractor who will perform the well contractor activity, the certification number of the well contractor, and the name of the company that employs the certified well contractor.

(b) Exempt persons and activities. - This Article does not apply to any of the following persons or activities:

(1) A person who is employed by, or performs labor or services for, a certified well contractor in connection with well contractor activity performed under the personal supervision of the certified well contractor.

(2) A person who constructs, repairs, or abandons a well that is located on land owned or leased by that person.

(3) A person who is employed by a government agency and who performs well contractor activity solely within the scope of the person's government employment.

(4) A person who is licensed as a professional engineer under Chapter 89C of the General Statutes, a geologist under Chapter 89E of the General Statutes, or a soil scientist under Chapter 89F of the General Statutes who uses a hand auger to collect soil or water samples or to measure water levels. This exemption does not include the construction of a monitoring well.

(5) Construction, repair, or abandonment of a well used for a temporary dewatering activity that is associated with, and necessary to complete construction of, a utility distribution or collection system, a building or other structure, or a transportation system, if all of the following conditions are met:

a. The dewatering well is constructed solely for the purpose of removing water from or lowering the water table in the immediate area of the construction activity.

b. The dewatering well is located within 25 feet of the excavation and is not greater than 25 feet deeper than the excavation.

c. The dewatering well is abandoned in accordance with rules governing the abandonment of wells adopted by the Environmental Management Commission pursuant to G.S. 87-87 within 30 days of installation of the well or within 10 days of completion of the project, whichever is later.

(6) Construction, repair, or abandonment of a well used for a temporary dewatering activity that is associated with the construction of a borrow pit if the dewatering activity is located within 15 feet of the proposed perimeter of the borrow pit.

(7) Exploratory drilling for mining-related investigations.

(8) Installation of a water level observation well on property for which a mining permit has been issued under the Mining Act of 1971, Article 7 of Chapter 74 of the General Statutes.

(9) Drilling of a blast hole.

(10) Installation of a cathodic protection anode.

(11) Installation of a wetland monitoring gauge at a depth of eight feet or less for the purpose of monitoring fluctuations in the water table.

(12) Installation of a caisson, piling, or structural pier.

(13) A person who is licensed as a plumbing contractor under Article 2 of Chapter 87 of the General Statutes who installs pumps or pumping equipment; installs, breaks, or reinstalls a well seal in accordance with G.S. 87-85(6); or disinfects a well incident to the installation, alteration, or replacement of pumps or pumping equipment within or near a well. However, the plumbing contractor shall maintain documentation of having attended a continuing education course that covered well seal installation, protection, and sanitation within the last two years prior to the work being performed. The State Board of Examiners of Plumbing, Heating and Fire Sprinkler Contractors shall ensure that continuing education courses covering well seal installation, protection, and sanitation are available to licensed plumbing contractors during each six-month continuing education course schedule. The licensed plumbing contractor shall remain on-site while the work is being performed until the well is disinfected and sealed.

(c) Additional Exemptions. – In addition to the exemptions set out in subsection (b) of this section, the Commission may exempt by rule a geophysical activity, construction activity, or other well contractor activity from the requirements of this Article if the Commission finds that the activity has a negligible impact on the environment; public health, safety, and welfare; and the groundwater resources of the State. (1997-358, s. 2; 1998-129, s. 1; 2001-440, s. 1.1; 2005-386, s. 9; 2009-418, s. 1.)

§ 87-98.5. Types of certification; sole certification.

The Commission, with the advice and assistance of the Secretary, shall establish the appropriate types of certification for well contractors. Each certification type established by the Commission shall be the sole certification required to engage in well contractor activity in the State. (1997-358, s. 2.)

§ 87-98.6. Well contractor qualifications and examination.

The Commission, with the advice and assistance of the Secretary, shall establish minimum requirements of education, experience, and knowledge for each type of certification for well contractors and shall establish procedures for receiving applications for certification, conducting examinations, and making investigations of applicants as may be necessary and appropriate so that prompt and fair consideration will be given to each applicant. (1997-358, s. 2.)

§ 87-98.7. Issuance and renewal of certificates; temporary certification; refusal to issue a certificate.

(a) Issuance. - An applicant, upon satisfactorily meeting the appropriate requirements, shall be certified to perform in the capacity of a well contractor and shall be issued a suitable certificate by the Commission designating the level of the person's competency. A certificate shall be valid for one year or until any of the following occurs:

(1) The certificate holder voluntarily surrenders the certificate to the Commission.

(2) The certificate is revoked or suspended by the Commission for cause.

(b) Renewal. - A certificate shall be renewed annually by payment of the annual fee and proof that the applicant has completed any professional development hours as may be required by the rules of the Commission. A person who fails to renew a certificate within 30 days of the expiration of the certificate must reapply for certification under this Article.

(c) Temporary Certification. - A person may receive temporary certification to construct a well upon submission of an application to the Commission and subsequent approval in accordance with the criteria established by the

Commission and upon payment of a temporary certification fee. A temporary certification shall be granted to the same person only once per calendar year and may not be valid for a period in excess of 45 consecutive days. To perform additional well contractor activity during that same calendar year, the person shall apply for certification under this Article.

(d) Refusal to Issue a Certificate. - The Commission shall not issue a certificate under any of the following circumstances:

(1) The applicant has not paid civil penalties assessed against the applicant under G.S. 87-94 for a violation of this Article, Article 7 of this Chapter, or any rule adopted to implement either of those Articles.

(2) The applicant has not conducted all restoration activities ordered by the Department related to a violation by the applicant of Article 7 of this Chapter.

(3) As determined by the Commission, the applicant has a history of not complying with this Article, Article 7 of this Chapter, or any rule adopted to implement either of those Articles. (1997-358, s. 2; 2001-440, s. 1.2; 2007-495, s. 2.)

§ 87-98.8. Disciplinary actions.

The Commission may issue a written reprimand to a well contractor or, in accordance with the provisions of Article 3A of Chapter 150B of the General Statutes, may suspend or revoke the certificate of a well contractor if the Commission finds that the well contractor has:

(1) Engaged in fraud or deception in connection with obtaining certification or in connection with any well contractor activity.

(2) Failed to use reasonable care, judgment, or the application of the person's knowledge or ability in the performance of any well contractor activity.

(3) Been grossly negligent or has demonstrated willful disregard of any applicable laws or rules governing well construction.

(4) Failed to satisfactorily complete continuing education requirements established by the Commission. (1997-358, s. 2.)

§ 87-98.9. Fees; Well Construction Fund.

(a) Fees. - The Commission may set a fee for certification by examination, an annual fee for certification renewal, and a fee for temporary certification. The fee for certification by examination may not exceed one hundred dollars ($100.00), the annual fee may not exceed two hundred dollars ($200.00) per year, and the temporary certification fee shall not exceed one hundred dollars ($100.00). A well contractor certificate is void if the well contractor fails to pay the annual fee within 30 days of the date the fee is due.

(b) Fund. - The Well Construction Fund is created as a nonreverting account within the Department. All fees collected pursuant to this Article shall be credited to the Fund. The Fund shall be used for the costs of administering this Article. (1997-358, s. 2.)

§ 87-98.10. Promotion of training.

The Commission and the Secretary may provide training for well contractors and cooperate with educational institutions and private and public associations, persons, or corporations in providing training for well contractors. (1997-358, s. 2.)

§ 87-98.11. Responsibilities of well contractors.

All persons receiving certification under this Article to perform well contractor activities in this State shall be responsible for complying with all statutes, rules, and generally accepted construction practices, including all local rules or ordinances governing well contractor activities. (1997-358, s. 2.)

§ 87-98.12. Continuing education requirements.

In order to continue to be certified under this Article, a well contractor shall satisfactorily complete the number of hours of approved continuing education required by the Commission. The Commission shall establish the minimum number of hours of continuing education that shall be required to maintain certification, shall specify the scope of required continuing education courses, and shall approve continuing education courses. (1997-358, s. 2; 1998-129, s. 1; 2001-440, s. 1.3; 2007-495, s. 5.)

§ 87-98.13. Injunctive relief.

Upon violation of this Article, a rule adopted under this Article, or an order issued under this Article, the Secretary may, either before or after the institution of proceedings for the collection of any penalty imposed under this Article for the violation, request the Attorney General to institute a civil action in the superior court in the name of the State for injunctive relief to restrain the violation or require corrective action and for any other relief the court finds proper. Initiating an action shall not relieve any party to the proceedings from any penalty prescribed by this Article. (1997-358, s. 2.)

§ 87-99. Reserved for future codification purposes.

Article 8.

Underground Damage Prevention.

§ 87-100. (Repealed effective October 1, 2014 - see note) Short title.

This Article shall be known as the "Underground Damage Prevention Act". (1985, c. 785, s. 1; 2013-407, s. 1.)

§ 87-101. (Repealed effective October 1, 2014 - see note) Definitions.

As used in this Article:

(1) "Association" means an association, sponsored by utility owners, that provides for receipt of notification of excavation operations and surveyor operations in a defined geographical area, and that maintains the records of the notifications.

(2) "Damage" includes the substantial weakening of structural or lateral support of an underground utility, penetration or destruction of protective coating, housing, or other protective device of an underground utility, and the partial or complete severance of an underground utility.

(3) "Excavate" or "excavation" means an operation for the purpose of the movement or removal of earth, rock, or other materials in or on the ground by use of equipment operated by means of mechanical power and/or an operation by which a structure or mass of material is wrecked, razed, moved, or removed by means of any tools, equipment, or discharge of explosives. This term includes road construction but does not include road maintenance activities within rights-of-way of a highway, including those maintenance activities defined by the rules and regulations of the North Carolina Department of Transportation.

(4) "Highway" has the meaning set out in G.S. 20-4.01 as the same shall be amended from time to time.

(5) "Location of underground utilities" means a strip of land not wider than the width of the underground utility plus two and one-half (2½) feet on either side of the underground utility.

(6) "Person" means a corporation, individual, copartnership, company, association, or any combination of individuals or organizations doing business as a unit, any subdivision or instrumentality of the State, and includes any officer, agent, trustee, receiver, assignee, lessee, or personal representative of any of the above entities.

(7) "Person financially responsible" means that person who ultimately receives the benefits of any completed excavation activities, including a person owning or leasing real property or holding an easement or interest in an easement.

(8) "Public spaces" means any area owned by the State or any of its political subdivisions or dedicated for public use.

(9) "Road construction" means the actual building of a new highway; or the paving, grading, widening, relocation, reconstruction, or other major improvement of a substantial portion of an existing highway.

(10) "Road maintenance" means preservation, including repairs and resurfacing of a highway, not amounting to road construction.

(10a) "Small water or wastewater utility owner" means any person who owns or operates any underground line, system, or facility that is used for producing, storing, conveying, transmitting, or distributing water under pressure or sanitary sewage and that serves 100 or fewer service connections.

(11) "Street" has the meaning set out in G.S. 20-4.01 as the same shall be amended from time to time.

(11a) "Surveyor" means a person who is responsible for surveying underground utilities or requires a general description and location of existing underground utilities in an area, and who has been retained by an engineer, architect, or property owner.

(12) "Underground utility" means any underground line, system or facility used for producing, storing, conveying, transmitting, or distributing communication or telecommunication, electricity, gas, petroleum and petroleum products, coal slurry, hazardous liquids, water under pressure, steam, or sanitary sewage, but not including traffic signal control cables and vehicle detection cables of the North Carolina Department of Transportation.

(13) "Utility owner" means any person who owns or operates an underground utility.

(14) "Work day" means every day except Saturday, Sunday, national legal holidays and State legal holidays. (1985, c. 785, s. 1; 2013-142, s. 1; 2013-407, s. 1.)

§ 87-102. (Repealed effective October 1, 2014 - see note) Notice required prior to excavation.

(a) Except as provided in G.S. 87-106, before commencing any excavations in highways, public spaces or in private easements of a utility owner, a person planning to excavate shall notify each utility owner having underground utilities located in the proposed area to be excavated, either orally or in writing, not less than two nor more than 10 working days prior to starting, of his intent to excavate.

(b)   The written or oral notice required in subsection (a) shall contain:

(1)   The name, address, and telephone number of the person filing the notice;

(2)   The name, address, and telephone number of the person doing the excavating;

(3)   The anticipated starting date of the excavation;

(4)   The anticipated duration of the excavation;

(5)   The type of excavation to be conducted;

(6)   The location of the proposed excavation; and

(7)   Whether or not explosives will be used.

(c)   If the notice required by this section is made by telephone, an adequate record shall be made of the notification by the utility owners or the utility association and the person making the notification, to document compliance with this section. (1985, c. 785, s. 1; 2013-407, s. 1.)

§ 87-103. (Repealed effective October 1, 2014 - see note) Effect of permit on liability.

A permit authorizing excavation operations and issued pursuant to law or ordinance shall not relieve a person of the responsibility of complying with this Article. (1985, c. 785, s. 1; 2013-407, s. 1.)

§ 87-104. (Repealed effective October 1, 2014 - see note) Requirements of person doing excavation.

(a) Except as provided in G.S. 87-106, no person may excavate in a highway, a public space, or a private easement of a utility owner without first having given the notice required in G.S. 87-102 to the utility owners.

(b) In addition to the notification requirements, each person excavating shall:

(1) Plan the excavation to avoid damage and to minimize interference with underground utilities in and near the construction area, to the best of his abilities;

(2) Maintain a clearance between an underground utility and the cutting edge or point of any mechanized equipment, taking into account the known limit of control of that cutting edge or point, as is reasonably required to avoid damage; and

(3) Provide support for the underground utilities in or near the construction area, including backfill, as may be reasonably required by the utility owner for the protection of the underground utilities. (1985, c. 785, s. 1; 2013-407, s. 1.)

§ 87-105. (Repealed effective October 1, 2014 - see note) Requirements of the person financially responsible for the excavation.

The person financially responsible shall provide to the person responsible for doing the excavating, the names of all underground utility owners in the area of the proposed excavation. The names of the utility owners may be obtained from the County Register of Deeds or the Building Inspection Department of the political subdivision in which the excavating is taken place, if there is one. (1985, c. 785, s. 1; 2013-407, s. 1.)

§ 87-106. (Repealed effective October 1, 2014 - see note) Exceptions.

The following excavations are exempted from the notification requirements of this Article:

(1) Tilling of soil for agricultural purposes;

(2) Excavation by a utility owner, by the State or its subdivisions or agencies, or by anyone contracting with any of these entities to perform the excavation, on or within an easement, right-of-way, or property owned or controlled by any of these entities, where:

a. Only the facilities of the utility owner doing the excavating are permitted; or

b. All persons having an interest in the excavation and the underground utilities that may be damaged during the excavation have agreed in writing to provide the equivalent of the notification required by this Article among themselves; or

(3) The replacement of a pole as long as the replacement pole is within three feet of the original pole and within the line of existing poles. This exception shall not apply to poles at highway intersections or at the crossings of highways and permanently marked transmission underground utilities.

(4) In the case of an emergency involving danger to life, health, or property requiring immediate correction, or in order to continue the operation of a major industrial plant, or in order to assure the continuity of utility services, excavations immediately required to repair or maintain the needed service may be made, without using explosives, if notice is given to the utility owner or association as soon as is reasonably possible; except that the prohibition against the use of explosives shall not apply to the North Carolina Department of Transportation. Performance of emergency excavation shall not relieve the excavator of liability for damages. (1985, c. 785, s. 1; 2013-407, s. 1.)

§ 87-107. (Repealed effective October 1, 2014 - see note) Duties of the utility owners.

Each utility owner, or his designated representative including an association, notified of an intent to excavate shall, before the proposed start of excavating (unless another period is agreed to by the person conducting the excavation and the utility owner or their representatives), provide the following information to the person excavating to the extent such information is reflected by records in the possession of and reasonably available to the utility owner:

(1) The location and description of all of the underground utilities which may be damaged as a result of the excavation;

(2) The location and description of all utility markers indicating the location of the underground utilities; and

(3) Any other information that would assist in locating and avoiding damage to the underground utilities, including providing temporary markings when necessary indicating the location of the underground utility in locations where permanent utility markers do not exist. (1985, c. 785, s. 1; 2013-407, s. 1.)

§ 87-107.1. (Repealed effective October 1, 2014 - see note) Surveyor requests; notice required; duties of utility owners; exceptions.

(a) Before surveying an area containing highways, public spaces, or private easements of a utility owner, a surveyor may give notice to each utility owner having underground utilities located in the area to be surveyed or to the utility owner's designated representative or association, either orally or in writing, not less than 10 working days prior to starting, of the surveyor's intent to have a survey conducted. The written or oral notice shall contain all of the following:

(1) The name, address, and telephone number of the surveyor.

(2) The name, address, and telephone number of the person conducting the survey.

(3) The anticipated starting date of the survey.

(4) The anticipated duration of the survey.

(5) The area to be surveyed.

(b) If a surveyor provides oral notice under subsection (a) of this section, the utility owner or designated representative or association and the surveyor shall make an adequate record of the notification to document compliance with this section.

(c) Each utility owner or designated representative or association, other than a small water or wastewater utility owner, notified of an intent to survey under subsection (a) of this section shall, before the proposed start of the survey, unless another period is agreed to by the surveyor and the utility owner or designated representative or association provide at least one of the following to the surveyor to the extent the information is reflected by records in the possession of and reasonably available to the utility owner:

(1) The location and description of all of the underground utilities within the area to be surveyed.

(2) The best available description of all underground utilities in the area of the proposed survey, which may include drawings marked with a scale, dimensions, and reference points for underground utilities already built in the area or other facility records that are maintained by the utility owner.

(3) Allowing the surveyor or any other authorized person to inspect the drawings or other records for all underground utilities within the area to be surveyed at a location that is acceptable to both parties.

(d) The requirements in subsection (c) of this section shall not apply to a notice of intent to survey a single-family residential property given by an engineer or architect. However, subsection (c) of this section shall apply to a notice of intent to survey a single family residential property given by a property owner or a surveyor who has been retained in connection with the development of the property. (2013-142, s. 2.)

§ 87-108. (Repealed effective October 1, 2014 - see note) Absence of utility location.

Should any utility owner who has been given notice pursuant to G.S. 87-102 fail to respond to that notice as provided in G.S. 87-107, or fail to properly locate the underground utility, then the person excavating is free to proceed with the excavation. Neither the excavator nor the person financially responsible for the excavation will be liable to the nonresponding or improperly responding utility owner for damages to that utility owner's facilities if the person doing the excavating shall exercise due care to protect existing underground utilities when there is evidence of the existence of those underground utilities near the proposed excavation site. (1985, c. 785, s. 1; 2013-407, s. 1.)

§ 87-109. (Repealed effective October 1, 2014 - see note) Recording requirements for associations.

An association shall record with the Register of Deeds of each county in which participating utility owners own or operate underground utilities, a notarized document providing the telephone number and address of the association, a description of the geographical area served by the association, and a list of the names and addresses of the utility owners receiving these services from the association. (1985, c. 785, s. 1; 2013-407, s.1.)

§ 87-110. (Repealed effective October 1, 2014 - see note) Recording requirements for utility owners.

(a) Each utility owner having underground utilities in North Carolina shall record a notarized document containing the name of the utility owner and the title, address, and telephone number of its representatives designated to receive the written or oral notice of intent to excavate, with the Register of Deeds of each county in which the utility owner owns or operates underground facilities. This document shall be executed by an officer of the utility owner or in the case of a governmental entity, the authorized official.

(b) Any change or modification of the information recorded by a utility owner, pursuant to subsection (a) of this section, shall be made by recording the corrected information with the Register of Deeds of each county to which the change or modification applies, in the manner required by subsection (a) of this section within five days of the change made to the utilities.

(c) For purposes of the recordings required by subsections (a) and (b) of this section, recordings by an association pursuant to G.S. 87-109 shall satisfy the recording requirements for each utility owner who is a member of the association while that utility owner remains a member of the association.

(d) The registration fee imposed by Chapter 161 of the General Statutes shall apply to these documents. (1985, c. 785, s. 1; 2012-18, s. 1.15; 2013-407, s. 1.)

§ 87-111. (Repealed effective October 1, 2014 - see note) Recorded information filed with inspection departments.

A copy of any document or modification or change in the information in that document recorded pursuant to G.S. 87-109 or G.S. 87-110 shall be filed with any county or municipal inspection department having jurisdiction over any area where the underground utilities are located. Such inspection departments shall maintain these filings in alphabetical order in an accessible form. (1985, c. 785, s. 1; 2013-407, s.1.)

§ 87-112. (Repealed effective October 1, 2014 - see note) Color-coding.

When the location of an underground utility is marked with stakes or by other physical means, pursuant to this Article, the utility owner shall use colored markers following the American Public Works Association Uniform Color Code for Utilities. (1985, c. 785, s. 1; 2013-704, s.1.)

§ 87-113. (Repealed effective October 1, 2014 - see note) Notification required when damage done.

(a) The person doing an excavation that results in any known damage to an underground utility shall, immediately after the discovery of the damage, notify the utility owner of the location and nature of the damage and shall allow the utility owner reasonable time to repair the damage before completing the excavation in the immediate area of the damaged underground utility.

(b) The person responsible for conducting any excavation that results in damage to an underground utility where the damage may endanger life, health, or property shall, immediately after the discovery of the damage, take action to protect the public and property, notify the utility owner, notify the police or fire departments, and take any other actions to minimize the hazards until the arrival of the utility owner's personnel, the police, or the fire department. The excavator shall delay any backfilling in the immediate area of the damaged underground utility until authorized by the utility owner unless it is necessary to prevent injury or property damage to others. Repair of any damage shall be performed by the utility owner or by qualified personnel authorized by the utility owner. (1985, c. 785, s. 1.; 2013-407, s. 1)

§ 87-114. (Repealed effective October 1, 2014 - see note) Homeowners.

This Article does not require utility notification before a property owner digs in any area on his own property with nonmechanized equipment nor prior to tilling the soil for agricultural, gardening or landscaping purposes. Mechanized equipment may be used, without utility notification, in any area on the owner's property with the exception of recorded underground utility easements which describes the location of the easement with specificity. (1985, c. 785, s. 1; 2013-407, s. 1.)

Article 8A.

Underground Utility Safety and Damage Prevention Act.

§ 87-115. (Effective October 1, 2014) Short title.

This Article may be cited as the "Underground Utility Safety and Damage Prevention Act." (2013-407, s. 2.)

§ 87-116. (Effective October 1, 2014) Declaration of policy and purpose.

The General Assembly of North Carolina hereby declares as a matter of public policy that it is necessary to protect the citizens and workforce of this State from the dangers inherent in excavating or demolishing in areas where underground lines, systems, or infrastructure are buried beneath the surface of the ground, and it is necessary to protect from costly damage underground facilities used for producing, storing, conveying, transmitting, or distributing communication, electricity, gas, petroleum, petroleum products, hazardous liquids, water, steam, or sewage. In order to carry out this public policy and to satisfy these compelling interests, the General Assembly has enacted the provisions of this Article providing for a systematic, orderly, and uniform process to identify existing facilities in advance of any excavation or demolition in this State and to implement safe digging practices. (2013-407, s. 2.)

§ 87-117. (Effective October 1, 2014) Definitions.

The following definitions apply in this Article:

(1)   APWA. - The American Public Works Association or its successors.

(2)   Business continuation plan. - A plan that includes actions to be taken in an effort to provide uninterrupted service during catastrophic events.

(3)   Contract locator. - A person hired by an operator to identify and mark facilities.

(4)   Damage. - The substantial weakening of structural or lateral support of a facility; penetration or destruction of protective coating, housing, or other protective device of a facility; or the partial or complete severance of a facility.

(5)   Demolish or demolition. - Any operation by which a structure or mass of material is wrecked, razed, rendered, moved, or removed by any means, including the use of any tools, equipment, or discharge of explosives.

(6)   Design notice. - A communication to the Notification Center in which a request for identifying existing facilities for advance planning purposes is made. A design notice may not be used for excavation purposes.

(7)   Designer. - Any architect, engineer, or other person who prepares or issues a drawing or blueprint for a construction or other project that requires excavation or demolition work.

(8)   Emergency. - An event involving a clear and imminent danger to life, health, or property, the interruption of essential utility services, or the blockage of transportation facilities, including highways, railways, waterways, or airways that require immediate action.

(9)   Excavate or excavation. - An operation for the purpose of the movement or removal of earth, rock, or other materials in or on the ground by use of manual or mechanized equipment or by discharge of explosives, including, but

not limited to, auguring, backfilling, boring, digging, ditching, drilling, directional drilling, driving, grading, horizontal directional drilling, well drilling, plowing-in, pounding, pulling-in, ripping, scraping, trenching, and tunneling.

(10) Excavator. - A person engaged in excavation or demolition.

(11) Extraordinary circumstances. - Circumstances that make it impossible for the operator to comply with the provisions of this Article, including hurricanes, tornadoes, floods, ice, snow, and acts of God.

(12) Facility. - Any underground line, underground system, or underground infrastructure used for producing, storing, conveying, transmitting, identifying, locating, or distributing communication, electricity, gas, petroleum, petroleum products, hazardous liquids, water, steam, or sewage. Provided there is no encroachment on any operator's right-of-way, easement, or permitted use, for the purposes of this Article, the following shall not be considered an underground facility: (i) swimming pools and irrigation systems; (ii) petroleum storage systems under Part 2A of Article 21A of Chapter 143 of the General Statutes; (iii) septic tanks under Article 11 of Chapter 130A of the General Statutes; and (iv) liquefied petroleum gas systems under Article 5 of Chapter 119 of the General Statutes, unless the system is subject to Title 49 C.F.R. § 192 or § 195.

(13) Locator. - An individual who identifies and marks facilities for operators who has been trained and whose training has been documented.

(14) Mechanized equipment. - Equipment operated by means of mechanical power, including, but not limited to, trenchers, bulldozers, power shovels, augers, backhoes, scrapers, drills, horizontal directional drills, cable and pipe plows, and other equipment used for plowing-in or pulling-in cable or pipe.

(15) Nonmechanized equipment. - Hand tools.

(16) Notice. - Oral, written, or electronic communication to the Notification Center from any person planning to excavate or demolish in the State that informs an operator of the person's intent to excavate or demolish.

(17) Notification Center. - A North Carolina member-owned not-for-profit corporation sponsored by operators that will provide a system through which a person can notify operators of proposed excavations and demolitions and submit reports of alleged violations of this Article.

(18) Operator. - Any person, public utility, communications or cable service provider, municipality, electrical utility, or electric or telephone cooperative that owns or operates a facility in this State.

(19) Person. - Any individual, owner, corporation, partnership, association, or any other entity organized under the laws of any state, any political subdivision of a state, or any other instrumentality of a state, or any authorized representative thereof.

(20) Positive response. - An automated information system that allows excavators, locators, operators, and other interested parties to determine the status of a locate request.

(21) Subaqueous. - A facility that is under a body of water, including rivers, streams, lakes, waterways, swamps, and bogs.

(22) Tolerance zone. - If the diameter of the facility is known, the distance of one-half of the known diameter plus 24 inches on either side of the designated center line or, if the diameter of the facility is not marked, 24 inches on either side of the outside edge of the mark indicating a facility or, for subaqueous facilities, a clearance of 15 feet on either side of the indicated facility.

(23) Working day. - Every day, except Saturday, Sunday, or State legal holidays. (2013-407, s. 2.)

§ 87-118. (Effective October 1, 2014) Reserve to the State the power to regulate.

The provisions in this Article supersede and preempt any ordinance adopted by a city or county that purports to do any of the following:

(1) Require operators to obtain permits from a city or county in order to identify facilities.

(2) Require premarking or marking of facilities.

(3) Specify the types of paint or other marking devices that are used to identify facilities.

(4) Require removal of unexpired marks. The removal of expired marks shall be the responsibility of the city or county. (2013-407, s. 2.)

§ 87-119. (Effective October 1, 2014) Costs associated with compliance; effect of permit.

Any costs or expenses associated with an excavator's compliance with the requirements of this Article shall not be charged to any operator. Any costs or expenses associated with an operator's compliance with the requirements of this Article shall not be charged to any excavator. The Notification Center may not impose any charge on any person giving notice to the Notification Center. This section shall not affect costs related to the operation of the Notification Center apportioned to an operator pursuant to G.S. 87-120(b). This section shall not excuse an operator or excavator from liability for any damage or injury for which the operator or excavator would be responsible under applicable law. (2013-407, s. 2.)

§ 87-120. (Effective October 1, 2014) Notification Center; responsibilities.

(a) The operators in the State shall maintain a Notification Center for the sole purpose of providing the services required by this Article. The Notification Center shall maintain information concerning receipt of notification of proposed excavation and demolition activities as provided in this Article and shall maintain information received from operators concerning the location of the operators' facilities and the operators' positive responses to marking of the facilities. The Notification Center shall also receive, maintain, and provide general administration of reports of alleged violations of this Article and responses. The Notification Center is not responsible in any way for identifying or marking facilities for operators. The Notification Center is not responsible in any way for resolving reports of alleged violations of this Article. All operators in the State shall join the Notification Center as provided in subsection (b) of this section, and they shall use the services of the Notification Center to perform the acts required by the provisions of this Article. There shall be only one Notification Center for the State of North Carolina. The Notification Center is not an agency of the State or any of the State's political subdivisions and is not subject to the provisions of Chapter 132 or Chapter 133 of the General Statutes.

(b) Operators who are members of the Notification Center by whatever name that is in existence on October 1, 2013, must remain members. Operators with more than 50,000 customers or 1,000 miles of facilities who are not members on October 1, 2013, must join no later than October 1, 2014. Operators with more than 25,000 customers or 500 miles of facilities who are not members on October 1, 2013, must join no later than October 1, 2015. All operators that do not meet one of the criteria provided in this subsection must join no later than October 1, 2016. Each engineering division of the Department of Transportation established pursuant to G.S. 136-14.1 must join no later than October 1, 2016. The board of directors of the Notification Center shall develop a reasonable method of apportioning the costs of operating the Notification Center among the member operators. Prior to adopting a method of determining such cost allocation, the board of directors shall publish the proposed method of cost allocation to the member operators, and the proposed method of cost allocation shall be approved by the member operators.

(c) The Notification Center shall have the following duties and responsibilities:

(1) Maintain a record of the notices received under subsection (d) of this section for at least four years.

(2) Maintain a record of reports of alleged violations of this Article received under subsection (e) of this section for at least four years, including responses to such reports.

(3) Receive and transmit notices as provided in subsection (d) of this section.

(4) Develop and update, as needed, a business continuity plan.

(5) Notify those persons against whom reports of alleged violations of this Article have been made and receive and maintain information submitted from such persons in defense against the allegations.

(6) Provide a positive response system.

(7) Establish and operate a damage prevention training program for members of the Notification Center. No person may recover damages in any manner or form from the Notification Center arising out of or related to the manner in which the Notification Center conducts a damage prevention training

program or receives, transmits, or otherwise administers a report of an alleged violation of this Article.

(d)   The Notification Center shall receive notice from any person intending to excavate or demolish in the State and shall, at a minimum, transmit the following information to the appropriate operator:

(1)   The name, address, and telephone number of the person providing the notice and, if different, the person responsible for the proposed excavation or demolition.

(2)   The starting date of the proposed excavation or demolition.

(3)   The anticipated duration of the proposed excavation or demolition.

(4)   The type of proposed excavation or demolition operation to be conducted.

(5)   The location of the proposed excavation or demolition.

(6)   Whether or not explosives are to be used in the proposed excavation or demolition.

(e)   The Notification Center shall receive reports of alleged violations of this Article. The Notification Center shall contact persons against whom reports have been filed to inform them of the alleged violation within 10 days of the filing of the report. The Notification Center shall maintain the following information regarding reports of alleged violations:

(1)   The name, address, and telephone number of the person making the report;

(2)   The nature of the report, including the statute that is alleged to have been violated;

(3)   Information provided by the person making the report, including correspondence, both written and electronic, pictures, and videos; and

(4)   Information provided by the person against whom the report has been filed, including correspondence, both written and electronic, pictures, and videos. (2013-407, s. 2.)

§ 87-121. (Effective October 1, 2014) Facility operator responsibilities.

(a)   An operator shall provide to the excavator the following:

(1)   The horizontal location and description of all of the operator's facilities in the area where the proposed excavation or demolition is to occur. The location shall be marked by stakes, soluble paint, flags, or any combination thereof, as appropriate, depending upon the conditions in the area of the proposed excavation or demolition. The operator shall, when marking as provided under this subdivision, use the APWA Uniform Color Code. If the diameter or width of the facility is greater than four inches, the dimension of the facility shall be indicated at least every 25 feet in the area of the proposed excavation or demolition. An operator who operates multiple facilities in the area of the proposed excavation or demolition shall locate each facility.

(2)   Any other information that would assist the excavator in identifying and thereby avoiding damage to the marked facilities.

(b)   Unless otherwise provided in a written agreement between the operator and the excavator, the operator shall provide to the excavator the information required by subsection (a) of this section within the times provided below:

(1)   For a facility, within three full working days after the day notice of the proposed excavation or demolition was provided to the Notification Center.

(2)   For a subaqueous facility, within 10 full working days after the day notice of the proposed excavation or demolition was provided to the Notification Center.

(3)   If the operator declares an extraordinary circumstance, the times provided in this subsection shall not apply.

(c)   The operator shall provide a positive response to the Notification Center before the expiration of the time provided in subsection (b) of this section. The response shall indicate whether and to what extent the operator is able to provide the information required by subsection (a) of this section to respond to the notice from the excavator.

(d) If the operator determines that provisions for marking subaqueous facilities are required, the operator will provide a positive response to the Notification Center not more than three full working days after notice has been provided by the excavator.

(e) If extraordinary circumstances prevent the operator from marking the location of the facilities within the time specified in subsection (b) of this section, the operator shall either notify the excavator directly or notify the excavator through the Notification Center. When providing the notification under this subsection, the operator shall state the date and time when the location will be marked.

(f) An operator shall prepare or cause to be prepared installation records of all facilities installed on or after the date this Article becomes effective in a public street, alley, or right-of-way dedicated to public use, excluding service drops and services lines. The operator shall maintain these records in the operator's possession while the facility is in service.

(g) All facilities installed by or on behalf of operators on or after the date this Article becomes effective shall be electronically locatable using a locating method that is generally accepted by operators in the particular industry or trade in which the operator is engaged.

(h) A locator shall notify the operator if the locator becomes aware of an error or omission in the records or documentation showing the location of the operator's facilities. The operator must update its records to correct any error or omission.

(i) An operator may reject an excavation or demolition notice due to homeland security considerations based upon federal statutes or federal regulations until the operator can confirm the legitimacy of the notice. The operator shall notify the person making the notice of the denial and may request additional information through the positive response system.

(j) Gravity fed sanitary sewers installed prior to the date this Article becomes effective and all storm water facilities shall be exempt from the location requirements provided in subsection (a) of this section. Neither the excavator nor the person financially responsible for the excavation will be liable for any damage to an unmarked gravity fed sanitary sewer line or unmarked storm water facility if the person doing the excavation exercises due care to protect existing facilities when there is evidence of the existence of those facilities near the proposed excavation area.

(k)   An operator who does not become a member of the Notification Center as required by G.S. 87-120(b) may not recover for damages to a facility caused by an excavator who has complied with the provisions of this Article and has exercised reasonable care in the performance of the excavation or demolition. (2013-407, s. 2.)

§ 87-122. (Effective October 1, 2014) Excavator responsibilities.

(a)   Before commencing any excavation or demolition operation, the person responsible for the excavation or demolition shall provide or cause to be provided notice to the Notification Center of his or her intent to excavate or demolish. Notice for any excavation or demolition that does not involve a subaqueous facility must be given within three to 12 full working days before the proposed commencement date of the excavation or demolition. Notice for any excavation or demolition in the vicinity of a subaqueous facility must be given within 10 to 20 full working days before the proposed commencement date of the excavation or demolition. Notice given pursuant to this subsection shall expire 15 full working days after the date notice was given. No excavation or demolition may continue after this 15-day period unless the person responsible for the excavation or demolition provides a subsequent notice which shall be provided in the same manner as the original notice required by this subsection. When demolition of a building is proposed, the operator shall be given a reasonable time in which to remove or protect the operator's facilities before the demolition commences.

(b)   The notice required by subsection (a) of this section shall, at a minimum, contain all of the following:

(1)   The name, address, and telephone number of the person providing the notice.

(2)   The anticipated starting date of the proposed excavation or demolition.

(3)   The anticipated duration of the proposed excavation or demolition.

(4) The type of proposed excavation or demolition operation to be conducted.

(5) The location of the proposed excavation or demolition, not to exceed one-quarter mile in geographical length, or five adjoining addresses, not to exceed one-quarter mile in geographical length.

(6) Whether or not explosives are to be used in the proposed excavation or demolition.

(c) An excavator shall comply with the following:

(1) When the excavation area cannot be clearly and adequately identified within the area described in the notice, the excavator shall designate the route, specific area to be excavated, or both by premarking the area before the operator performs a locate. Premarking shall be made with soluble white paint, white flags, or white stakes.

(2) Confirm through the Notification Center's positive response system prior to excavation or demolition that all operators have responded and that all facilities that may be affected by the proposed excavation or demolition have been marked.

(3) Plan the excavation or demolition to avoid damage to or minimize interference with facilities in or near the construction area.

(4) Begin excavation or demolition prior to the specified waiting period only if the excavator has confirmed that all operators have responded with an appropriate positive response.

(5) If the operator declares extraordinary circumstances, the excavator shall not excavate or demolish until after the time and date that the operator has provided in the operator's response.

(6) If an operator fails to respond to the positive response system, the excavator may proceed if there are no visible indications of a facility at the proposed excavation or demolition area, such as a pole, marker, pedestal, meter, or valve. However, if the excavator is aware of or observes indications of an unmarked facility at the proposed excavation or demolition area, the excavator shall not begin excavation or demolition until an additional call is made to the Notification Center detailing the facility and an arrangement is

made for the facility to be marked by the operator within three hours from the time the additional call is received by the Notification Center.

(7) Beginning on the date provided in the excavator's notice to the Notification Center, the excavator shall preserve the staking, marking, or other designation until they are no longer required. When a mark is no longer visible or is destroyed, but the excavation or demolition continues in the vicinity of the facility, the excavator shall request a re-mark from the Notification Center to ensure the protection of the facility.

(8) When demolition of a building is proposed, the excavator shall give the operator a reasonable time in which to remove or protect the operator's facilities before demolition commences.

(9) An excavator shall not perform any excavation or demolition within the tolerance zone unless the excavator complies with all of the following conditions:

a. The excavator shall not use mechanized equipment, except noninvasive equipment specifically designed or intended to protect the integrity of the facility, within the marked tolerance zone of an existing facility until:

1. The excavator has visually identified the precise location of the facility or has visually confirmed that no facility is present up to the depth of excavation;

2. The excavator has taken reasonable precautions to avoid any substantial weakening of the facility's structural or lateral support, or both, or penetration or destruction of the facilities or their protective coatings; and

3. The excavator may use mechanical means, as necessary, for the initial penetration and removal of pavement or other materials requiring use of mechanical means of excavation but only to the depth of the pavement or other materials. For parallel type excavations within the tolerance zone, the existing facility shall be visually identified at intervals not to exceed 50 feet along the line of excavation to avoid damages. The excavator shall exercise due care at all times to protect the facilities when exposing these facilities.

b. The excavator shall maintain clearance between a facility and the cutting edge or point of any mechanized equipment, taking into account the known limit of control of the cutting edge or point, as may be reasonably necessary to avoid damage to the facility.

c. The excavator shall provide support for facilities in and near the excavation or demolition area, including backfill operations, as may be reasonably required by the operator for the protection of the facilities.

(10) The excavator shall not use mechanized equipment within 24 inches of a facility that is a gas, oil, petroleum, or electric transmission line unless the facility operator has consented to the use in writing and the operator's representative is on site during the use of the mechanized equipment. For purposes of this subdivision, the term "gas, oil, petroleum transmission line" has the same meaning as the term "transmission line" in Title 49 C.F.R. § 192.3, and the term "electric transmission line" has the same meaning as the term "transmission line" in G.S. 62-100(7). (2013-407, s. 2.)

§ 87-123. (Effective October 1, 2014) Training.

(a) Every person who is an excavator, locator, or operator under this Article by virtue of engaging in these activities in the course of a business or trade has a duty to provide education and training to employees and to document such education and training. The training shall include sufficient information, guidance, and supervision such that employees can competently and safely operate the equipment used in the course of the business or trade and complete assigned tasks in a competent and safe manner while minimizing the potential for damage.

(b) When an excavator, locator, or operator under this Article retains an independent contractor to perform activities regulated by this Article, the duty set forth in subsection (a) of this section shall not apply to the excavator, locator, or operator. Independent contractors shall provide training to their employees in accordance with this section.

(c) Excavation shall be conducted in accordance with OSHA Standard 1926 and under the direction of a competent person, as defined therein.

(d) Locators shall be properly trained. Locator training shall be documented. (2013-407, s. 2.)

§ 87-124. (Effective October 1, 2014) Exemptions.

The notice requirements in G.S. 87-122(a) and G.S. 87-122(b) do not apply to the following:

(1) An excavation or demolition performed by the owner of a single-family residential property on his or her own land that does not encroach on any operator's right-of-way, easement, or permitted use.

(2) An excavation or demolition performed by the owner of a single-family residential property on his or her own land that encroaches on any operator's right-of-way, easement, or permitted use that is performed with nonmechanized equipment.

(3) An excavation or demolition that involves the tilling of soil for agricultural or gardening purposes.

(4) An excavation or demolition for agricultural purposes, as defined in G.S. 106-581.1, performed on property that does not encroach on any operator's right-of-way, easement, or permitted use.

(5) An excavation by an operator or surveyor with nonmechanized equipment for the following purposes:

a. Locating for a valid notification request or for the minor repair, connection, or routine maintenance of an existing facility or survey pin.

b. Probing underground to determine the extent of gas or water migration.

(6) An excavation or demolition performed when the Department of Transportation, a local government, special purpose district, or public service district is conducting maintenance activities within its designated right-of-way. Maintenance activities shall include resurfacing, milling, emergency replacement of signs critical for maintaining safety, or the reshaping of shoulders and ditches to the original road profile. Maintenance activities do not include the initial installation of traffic signs, traffic control equipment, or guardrails.

(7) An excavation or demolition performed by a railroad entirely on land which the railroad owns or operates or, in the event of an emergency, on adjacent land. No provision in this Article shall apply to any railroad which owns, operates, or permits facilities under land which the railroad owns or operates.

(8) An excavation of a grave space, as defined in G.S. 65-48(10), the installation of a monument or memorial at a grave space, or an excavation related to the placement of a temporary structure or tent by a cemetery regulated under Chapter 65 of the General Statutes that does not encroach on any operator's right-of-way, easement, or permitted use. (2013-407, s. 2.)

§ 87-125. (Effective October 1, 2014) Notice in case of emergency excavation or demolition.

(a) An excavator performing an emergency excavation or demolition is not required to give notice to the Notification Center as provided in G.S. 87-122. However, the excavator shall, as soon as practicable, give oral notice to the Notification Center which shall include a description of the circumstances justifying the emergency. The excavator may request emergency assistance from each affected operator in locating and providing immediate protection to the facilities in the affected area.

(b) The declaration of an emergency excavation or demolition shall not relieve any party of liability for causing damage to an operator's facilities even if those facilities are unmarked.

(c) Any person who falsely claims that an emergency exists requiring an excavation or demolition shall be guilty of a Class 3 misdemeanor. (2013-407, s. 2.)

§ 87-126. (Effective October 1, 2014) Notification required when damage is done.

(a) The excavator performing an excavation or demolition that results in any damage to a facility shall immediately upon discovery of the damage notify the Notification Center and the facility operator, if known, of the location and nature of the damage. The excavator shall allow the operator reasonable time to accomplish necessary repairs before completing the excavation or demolition in the immediate area of the facility. The excavator shall delay any backfilling in the immediate area of the damaged facility until authorized by the operator. The operator or qualified personnel authorized by the operator shall repair any damage to the facility.

(b) An excavator who is responsible for an excavation or demolition where any damage to a facility results in the discharge of electricity or escape of any flammable, toxic, or corrosive gas or liquid, or that endangers life, health, or property shall immediately notify emergency responders, including 911 services, the Notification Center, and the facility operator. The excavator shall take reasonable measures to protect himself or herself, other persons in immediate danger, members of the general public, property, and the environment until the operator or emergency responders arrive and complete an assessment of the situation. (2013-407, s. 2.)

§ 87-127. (Effective October 1, 2014) Design notices.

(a) A designer may submit a design notice to the Notification Center. The design notice shall describe the tract or parcel of land for which the design notice has been submitted with sufficient particularity, as defined by policies and procedures adopted by the Notification Center, to allow the operator to ascertain the precise tract or parcel of land involved.

(b) Within 10 working days, not including the day the notice was given, after a design notice for a proposed project has been submitted to the Notification Center, the operator shall respond in one of the following manners:

(1) By designating the location of all facilities owned by the operator within the area of the proposed excavation as provided in G.S. 87-121(a).

(2) By providing to the person submitting the design notice the best available description of all facilities in the area designated by the design notice, which may include drawings marked with a scale, dimensions, and reference points for underground utilities already built in the area or other facility records that are maintained by the operator.

(3) Allowing the person submitting the design notice or any other authorized person to inspect the drawings or other records for all facilities within the proposed area of excavation at a location that is acceptable to the operator.

(c) An operator may reject a design notice based upon homeland security considerations pending the operator obtaining additional information confirming the legitimacy of the notice. The operator shall notify the person making the request through a design notice of the denial and may request additional information through the positive response system. (2013-407, s. 2.)

§ 87-128. (Effective October 1, 2014) Absence of facility location.

If an operator who has been given notice as provided in G.S. 87-120(d) by the Notification Center fails to respond to that notice as provided in G.S. 87-121 or fails to properly locate the facility, the person excavating is free to proceed with the excavation. Neither the excavator nor the person financially responsible for the excavation will be liable to the nonresponding or improperly responding operator for damages to the operator's facilities if the person doing the excavating exercises due care to protect existing facilities when there is evidence of the existence of those facilities near the proposed excavation area. (2013-407, s. 2.)

§ 87-129. (Effective October 1, 2014) Underground Damage Prevention Review Board; enforcement; civil penalties.

(a) The Notification Center shall establish an Underground Damage Prevention Review Board to review reports of alleged violations of this Article. The members of the Board shall be appointed by the Governor. The Board shall consist of the following members:

(1) A representative from the North Carolina Department of Transportation;

(2) A representative from a facility contract locator;

(3) A representative from the Notification Center;

(4) A representative from an electric public utility;

(5) A representative from the telecommunications industry;

(6) A representative from a natural gas utility;

(7) A representative from a hazardous liquid transmission pipeline company;

(8) A representative recommended by the League of Municipalities;

(9) A highway contractor licensed under G.S. 87-10(b)(2) who does not own or operate facilities;

(10) A public utilities contractor licensed under G.S. 87-10(b)(3) who does not own or operate facilities;

(11) A surveyor licensed under Chapter 89C of the General Statutes;

(12) A representative from a rural water system;

(13) A representative from an investor-owned water system;

(14) A representative from an electric membership corporation; and

(15) A representative from a cable company.

(b) The Notification Center shall transmit all reports of alleged violations of this Article to the Board, including any information received by the Notification Center regarding the report. The Board shall meet at least quarterly to review all reports filed pursuant to G.S. 87-120(e). The Board shall act as an arbitrator between the parties to the report. If, after reviewing the report and any accompanying information, the Board determines that a violation of this Article has occurred, the Board shall notify the violating party in writing of its determination and the recommended penalty. The violating party may request a hearing before the Board, after which the Board may reverse or uphold its original finding. If the Board recommends a penalty, the Board shall notify the Utilities Commission of the recommended penalty, and the Utilities Commission shall issue an order imposing the penalty.

(c) A party determined by the Board under subsection (b) of this section to have violated this Article may initiate an arbitration proceeding before the Utilities Commission. If the violating party elects to initiate an arbitration proceeding, the violating party shall pay a filing fee of two hundred fifty dollars ($250.00) to the Utilities Commission, and the Utilities Commission shall open a docket regarding the report. The Utilities Commission shall direct the parties enter into an arbitration process. The parties shall be responsible for selecting and contracting with the arbitrator. Upon completion of the arbitration process, the Utilities Commission shall issue an order encompassing the outcome of the binding arbitration process, including a determination of fault, a penalty, and assessing the costs of arbitration to the non-prevailing party. Any party may appeal an order issued by the Utilities Commission pursuant to this section to the superior court division of the General Court of Justice in the county where the alleged violation of this Article occurred or in Wake County, for trial de novo. The authority granted to the Utilities Commission within this section is limited to this section and does not grant the Utilities Commission any authority that they are not otherwise granted under Chapter 62 of the General Statutes.

(d) Any person who violates any provision of this Article shall be subject to a penalty as set forth in this subsection. The provisions of this Article do not affect any civil remedies for personal injury or property damage otherwise available to any person, except as otherwise specifically provided for in this Article. The penalty provisions of this Article are cumulative to and not in conflict with provisions of law with respect to civil remedies for personal injury or property damage. The clear proceeds of any civil penalty assessed under this section shall be used as provided in Section 7(a) of Article IX of the North Carolina Constitution. The penalties for a violation of this Article shall be as follows:

(1) If the violation was the result of negligence, the penalty shall be a requirement of training, a requirement of education, or both.

(2) If the violation was the result of gross negligence, the penalty shall be a civil penalty of one thousand dollars ($1,000), a requirement of training, a requirement of education, or a combination of the three.

(3) If the violation was the result of willful or wanton negligence or intentional conduct, the penalty shall be a civil penalty of two thousand five hundred dollars ($2,500), a requirement of training, and a requirement of education. (2013-407, s. 2.)

§ 87-130. (Effective October 1, 2014) Severability.

If any provision of this Article or the application thereof to any person or circumstance is held invalid, such invalidity shall not affect other provisions or applications, and to this end the provisions of this Article are severable. (2013-407, s. 2.)

Chapter 88.

Cosmetic Art.

§§ 88-1 through 88-30: Repealed by Session Laws 1998-230, s. 1.

Chapter 88A.

Electrolysis Practice Act.

§ 88A-1. Short title.

This Chapter may be cited as the "Electrolysis Practice Act." (1989 (Reg. Sess., 1990), c. 1033.)

§ 88A-2. Purpose.

The purpose of this Chapter is to ensure minimum standards of competency, to protect the public from misrepresentation of status by persons who hold themselves out to be "licensed electrologists" or "licensed laser hair practitioners" and to provide the public with safe care by the mandatory licensing of electrologists and laser hair practitioners. (1989 (Reg. Sess., 1990), c. 1033, s. 1; 2007-489, s. 1.)

§ 88A-3. Definitions.

As used in this Chapter, unless the context requires otherwise:

(1) "Board" means the North Carolina Board of Electrolysis Examiners.

(2) "Electrolysis" means the permanent removal of hair by the application of an electrical current to the dermal papilla by a filament to cause decomposition, coagulation, or dehydration within the hair follicle as approved by the Food and Drug Administration of the United States Government.

(3) "Electrologist" or "electrolocist" means a person who engages in the practice of electrolysis for permanent hair removal.
(4) "Electrology" means the art and practice relating to the removal of hair from the normal skin of the human body by application of an electric current to the hair papilla by means of a needle or needles so as to cause growth inactivity of the hair papilla and thus permanently remove the hair.

(5) "Laser hair practitioner" means a person who engages in laser, light source, or pulsed-light treatments for the removal of hair.

(6) "Laser, light source, or pulsed-light devices" means a device used exclusively in the nonablative procedure for the removal of hair.

(7) "Laser, light source, or pulsed-light treatments" means the use of laser or pulsed-light devices for nonablative procedures for the removal of hair. (1989 (Reg. Sess., 1990), c. 1033, s. 1; 2007-489, s. 2.)

§ 88A-4. Unlawful practice.

(a) It shall be unlawful to engage in the practice of electrolysis or laser, light source, or pulsed-light treatments in this State without a license.

(b) Any person practicing electrology or laser, light source, or pulsed-light treatments for the purpose of hair removal or hair reduction in this State without being licensed by the Board shall be guilty of a Class I felony and may be assessed a civil penalty of up to five thousand dollars ($5,000) for each offense. Any other violation of this Chapter shall be a Class 2 misdemeanor. (1989 (Reg. Sess., 1990), c. 1033, s. 1; 1991 (Reg. Sess., 1992), c. 1003, s. 2; 1993, c. 530, s. 3; c. 539, s. 609; 1994, Ex. Sess., c. 24, s. 14(c); 2007-489, s. 3.)

§ 88A-5. Creation and membership of Board.

(a) The North Carolina Board of Electrolysis Examiners is created. The Board shall consist of five members as follows:

(1) Three electrologists who have engaged in the practice of electrolysis for at least five years, one of whom shall be appointed by the General Assembly

upon the recommendation of the Speaker of the House of Representatives, one of whom shall be appointed by the General Assembly upon the recommendation of the President Pro Tempore of the Senate, and one of whom shall be appointed by the Governor.

(2)   A physician licensed under Chapter 90 of the General Statutes, who shall be nominated by the North Carolina Medical Board and appointed by the Governor.

(3)   A public member, appointed by the Governor, who has not practiced electrolysis, who is not in training to become an electrologist, and who is not related to anyone who would be prohibited by this subdivision from serving on the Board as a public member.

(b)   Legislative appointments shall be made in accordance with G.S. 120-121. A vacancy in a legislative appointment shall be filled in accordance with G.S. 120-122.

(c)   Each member shall be appointed for a term of three years and shall serve until a successor is appointed. Of the members initially appointed, one of the electrologist members shall serve a term of one year. The public member and the second electrologist member shall serve a term of two years. The physician member and the third electrologist member shall serve a term of three years. The terms of all initial appointments shall commence within 30 days of the effective date of this act. No member may serve more than two consecutive full terms.

(d)   Vacancies shall be filled by the appropriate appointing authority within 30 days after the position is vacated. Appointees shall serve the remainder of the unexpired term and until their successors have been appointed and qualified.

(e)   The Board may remove any of its members for gross neglect of duty, incompetence, or unprofessional conduct. A member subject to disciplinary proceedings shall be disqualified from all Board business until the charges are resolved. The Governor may also remove any member of the Board which he appoints.

(f)   Each member of the Board shall receive per diem compensation and reimbursement for travel and subsistence in the amounts the Board votes upon and records in its minutes, provided the amounts do not exceed the amounts specified in G.S. 93B-5.

(g) The Board shall elect a Chairman, a Vice-Chairman, a Treasurer, and such other officers as are deemed necessary by the Board. All officers shall be elected annually by the Board for one-year terms and shall serve until their successors are elected and qualified.

(h) The Board shall hold at least two meetings each year to conduct its business, and shall adopt rules governing the calling, holding, and conducting of regular and special meetings. A majority of the members shall constitute a quorum. (1989 (Reg. Sess., 1990), c. 1033, s. 1; 1995, c. 94, s. 6.)

§ 88A-6. Powers and duties of the Board.

The Board shall have the following general powers and duties:

(1) To administer and interpret this Chapter;

(2) To adopt rules in the manner prescribed by Chapter 150B of the General Statutes as may be necessary to carry out the provisions of this Chapter;

(3) To determine the qualifications of persons who are licensed or certified pursuant to this Chapter;

(4) To issue, renew, deny, restrict, suspend, or revoke licenses and to carry out any of the other actions authorized by this Chapter;

(5) To establish, publish, and enforce rules of professional conduct, and to regulate advertising by licensees;

(6) To maintain a record of all proceedings and make available to persons licensed under this Chapter, and to other concerned parties, an annual report of all Board action;

(7) To collect fees for licensure, licensure renewal, and other services deemed necessary to carry out the purpose of this Chapter;

(8) To employ and fix the compensation of personnel, including an executive director, that the Board determines are necessary to carry out the

provisions of this Chapter and to incur other expenses necessary to effectuate this Chapter;

(9) To conduct investigations for the purpose of determining whether violations of this Chapter or grounds for disciplining persons licensed or certified under this Chapter exist; and,

(10) To adopt a seal containing the name of the Board for use on all certificates, licenses, and official reports issued by it. (1989 (Reg. Sess., 1990), c. 1033.)

§ 88A-7. Applicability of Executive Budget Act; audit oversight.

The Treasurer or the Executive Director shall deposit all fees payable to the Board with the State Treasurer, to be credited to the account of the Board. These funds shall be held and expended under the supervision of the Director of the Budget. The provisions of the Executive Budget Act apply to this Chapter. The Board is subject to the oversight of the State Auditor under Article 5A of Chapter 147 of the General Statutes. (1989 (Reg. Sess., 1990), c. 1033, s. 1; 1993 (Reg. Sess., 1994), c. 755, s. 5.1.)

§ 88A-8. The Board may accept contributions, etc.

The Board may accept grants, contributions, devises, and gifts that shall be kept in the same account as the funds deposited in accordance with G.S. 88A-7 and shall be used to carry out the provisions of this Chapter. (1989 (Reg. Sess., 1990), c. 1033, s. 1; 2011-284, s. 62.)

§ 88A-9. Expenses and fees.

(a) All salaries, compensation, and expenses incurred or allowed for the purpose of carrying out the purposes of this Chapter shall be paid by the Board exclusively out of the fees received by the Board as authorized by this Chapter, or funds received pursuant to G.S. 88A-7. No salary, expense, or other obligations of the Board may be charged against the General Fund of the State.

Neither the Board nor any of its officers or employees may incur any expense, debt, or other financial obligation binding upon the State.

(b)   All fees may be calculated by the Board in amounts sufficient to pay the costs of administration of this act, but in no event may they exceed the following:

(1)   Application for licensure as an electrologist $150.00

(1a)   Initial license 150.00

(1b)   Examination or reexamination 125.00

(2)   Licensure of electrology renewal 150.00

(3)   Application for licensure as an electrology instructor.. 150.00

(4)   Licensure of electrology instructor renewal... 150.00

(5)   Application for certification as a ...... Board-approved school of electrology... 500.00

(5a)   Application for licensure as laser hair practitioner...................................... 150.00

(5b)   Licensure of laser hair practitioner renewal... 150.00

(5c)   Application for licensure as laser hair practitioner instructor...................... 150.00

(5d) Licensure of laser hair practitioner instructor renewal............................... 150.00

(5e) Application for certification as a Board-approved school of ...... laser, light source, or pulsed-light treatments....................................... 500.00

(5f) Certificate of Board-approved school of laser, light source, ... or pulsed-light renewal.. 400.00

(6) Certificate of Board-approved school of ...... electrology renewal 250.00

(6a) Certification of out-of-state schools 150.00

(6b) Certification of out-of-state schools renewal 100.00

(6c) Office inspection or reinspection 100.00

(6d) License by reciprocity 150.00

(7) Late renewal charge 125.00

(8) Reinstatement of expired license or certification... 250.00

(9) Reactivation of license 200.00

(10) Duplicate license or certification... 25.00.

(1989 (Reg. Sess., 1990), c. 1033, s. 1; 2001-176, s. 1; 2007-489, s. 4.)

§ 88A-10. Requirements for licensure as an electrologist.

(a) Any person who desires to be licensed as an "electrologist" pursuant to this Chapter shall:

(1) Submit an application on a form approved by the Board.

(2) Be a resident of North Carolina.

(3) Be 21 years of age or older.

(4) Meet the requirements of subsection (a1) of this section.

(5) Pass an examination given by the Board.

(6) Submit the application and examination fees required in G.S. 88A-9(b).

(a1) An applicant for licensure under this section shall provide:

(1) Proof of graduation from a school certified by the Board pursuant to G.S. 88A-19; or

(2) Proof satisfactory to the Board that, for at least one year prior to the date of application or the date of initial residence in this State, whichever is earlier, the applicant was engaged in the practice of electrology in a state that does not license electrologists.

Subdivision (2) of this subsection applies only to applicants whose residence in this State began on or after January 31, 1994, who do not meet the qualifications of subdivision (1) of this subsection or G.S. 88A-12.

(b) At least twice each year, the Board shall give an examination to applicants for licensure to determine the applicants' knowledge of the basic and clinical sciences relating to the theory and practice of electrology. The Board shall give applicants notice of the date, time, and place of the examination at least 60 days in advance.

(c) When the Board determines that an applicant has met all the requirements for licensure, and has submitted the initial license fee required in G.S. 88A-9(b), the Board shall issue a license to the applicant.

(d) An applicant otherwise qualified for licensure who is not a resident of this State may nevertheless submit a statement of intent to begin practicing electrology in this State and receive a license. The applicant must provide to the Board within six months of receiving a license evidence satisfactory to the Board that the applicant has actually begun to practice electrology in this State. The Board may revoke the license of an applicant who fails to submit this proof or whose proof fails to satisfy the Board. (1989 (Reg. Sess., 1990), c. 1033, s. 1; 1993 (Reg. Sess., 1994), c. 755, s. 1; 2001-176, s. 2; 2007-489, s. 5.)

§ 88A-10.1. Temporary license.

The Board may issue a temporary license to practice electrology to an applicant who meets the requirements of G.S. 88A-10(a)(1)-(4). A temporary license may not be valid for more than six months and may be renewed not more than once. The Board may by rule provide for a shorter duration and may prohibit any renewal of a temporary license. The Board shall adopt rules setting the criteria for any renewals. The Board may by rule require that holders of a temporary license practice under supervision and may specify criteria for supervision in its rules, including the setting, amounts of supervision, and qualifications of supervisors. (1993 (Reg. Sess., 1994), c. 755, s. 2.)

§ 88A-11. Licensure without examination.

The Board may issue a license to practice electrology, without examination, to an applicant:

(1) Who was engaged in the practice of electrolysis in this State or another state prior to July 1, 1993, and who submits an application for licensure to the Board on or before January 31, 1994.

(2) Who is certified or licensed in good standing to practice electrolysis in another state, provided that the other state's educational hours of instruction are

equal to or greater than the hours required in this State. (1989 (Reg. Sess., 1990), c. 1033, s. 1; 1991 (Reg. Sess., 1992), c. 1003, s. 1; 1993, c. 530, s. 4.)

§ 88A-11.1. Requirements for licensure as a laser hair practitioner; limitations on licensed laser hair practitioners.

(a) Any person seeking licensure by the Board as a laser hair practitioner shall have met the following requirements at the time the license is requested:

(1) Be an electrologist licensed under this Chapter.

(2) Completed a minimum 30-hour laser, light source, or pulsed-light treatment certification course approved by the Board and in accordance with rules adopted by the Board.

(3) Be currently using or anticipate using laser, light source, or pulsed-light devices that the person has been certified by a Board-approved school to operate.

(b) When the Board determines that an applicant has met all the requirements for licensure, and has submitted the initial license fee required in G.S. 88A-9(b), the Board shall issue a license to the applicant.

(c) Each laser hair practitioner shall practice laser, light source, or pulsed-light treatments under the supervision of a physician licensed under Article 1 of Chapter 90 of the General Statutes. The physician shall be readily available, but not required to be on site when the laser, light source, or pulsed-light treatments are being performed. However, the authority to regulate laser clinicians shall remain with the Board.

(d) A laser hair practitioner shall not dispense or administer medication or provide advice regarding the use of medication, whether prescription or over-the-counter, in connection with laser, light source, or pulsed-light treatments.

(e) All laser hair practitioners shall use laser, light source, or pulsed-light devices approved by the federal Food and Drug Administration and comply with all applicable federal and State regulations, rules, and laws. Any licensed laser hair practitioner violating this subsection shall have his or her license revoked by the Board.

(f) Only a licensed physician may use laser, light source, or pulsed-light devices for ablative procedures. (2007-489, s. 6.)

§ 88A-12. License renewal.

(a) Every electrologist license or laser hair practitioner license issued pursuant to this Chapter must be renewed annually. On or before the date the current license expires, a person who desires to continue to practice electrology or as a laser hair practitioner shall apply for license renewal to the Board on forms approved by the Board, provide evidence of the successful completion of a continuing educational program approved by the Board, meet the criteria for renewal established by the Board, and pay the required fee. The Board may provide for the late renewal of licensure upon payment of a late fee as set by the Board, but late renewal may not be granted more than 90 days after expiration of the license.

(b) Any person who has failed to renew his or her license for more than 90 days after expiration may have it reinstated by applying to the Board for reinstatement on a form approved by the Board, furnishing a statement of the reason for failure to apply for renewal prior to the deadline, and paying the required fee. The Board may require evidence of competency to resume practice before reinstating the applicant's license. (1989 (Reg. Sess., 1990), c. 1033, s. 1; 1993 (Reg. Sess., 1994), c. 755, s. 3; 2007-489, s. 7.)

§ 88A-13. Continuing education.

(a) The Board shall determine the number of hours and subject matter of continuing education required as a condition of license renewal. The Board may offer continuing education to the licensees under this act.

(b) Upon request, the Board may grant approval to a continuing education program or course upon finding that the program or course offers an educational experience designed to enhance the practice of electrology.

(c) The Board shall maintain and distribute, as appropriate, records of the educational course work successfully completed by each licensee, including the subject matter and the number of hours of each course.

(d) Laser hair practitioners are required to complete a minimum of 10 hours of continuing education annually to maintain their licenses pursuant to rules adopted by the Board. (1989 (Reg. Sess., 1990), c. 1033, s. 1; 2007-489, s. 8.)

§ 88A-14. Inactive list.

Upon request by a licensee for inactive status, the Board shall place the licensee's name on the inactive list. While on the inactive list, the person shall not be subjected to renewal requirements and shall not practice electrology in North Carolina. When that person desires to be removed from the inactive list and returned to an active list, a reactivation application shall be submitted to the Board on a form furnished by the Board and the fee shall be paid for license reactivation. The Board may require evidence of competency to resume practice before returning the applicant to the active status. Any person whose license has lapsed or expired for a period of five years or more shall be required to take and pass the examination for licensure before the license can be reactivated. (1989 (Reg. Sess., 1990), c. 1033, s. 1; 2001-176, s. 3.)

§ 88A-15. Exemptions from licensure.

The following individuals shall be permitted to practice electrology without a license:

(1) Any physician licensed in accordance with Article 1 and Article 11 of Chapter 90 of the General Statutes.

(2) A student at an approved school of electrology when electrolysis is performed in the course of study.

(3) A person demonstrating on behalf of a manufacturer or distributor any electrolysis equipment or supplies, if such demonstration is performed without charge.

(4) An employee of a hospital licensed under Chapter 131E of the General Statutes and working under the supervision of a physician licensed under Article 1 of Chapter 90 of the General Statutes who is certified by the American Board of Dermatology. (1989 (Reg. Sess., 1990), c. 1033, s. 1; 1993 (Reg. Sess., 1994), c. 755, s. 4.)

§ 88A-15.1. Persons and practices not affected.

The requirements of this Chapter shall not apply to any person licensed or approved by the North Carolina Medical Board to practice medicine or perform medical acts, tasks, or functions pursuant to Article 1 of Chapter 90 of the General Statutes or any person employed and working under the direct supervision of a physician licensed to practice medicine pursuant to Article 1 of Chapter 90 of the General Statutes. (2007-489, s. 9.)

§ 88A-16. Permanent establishment required.

(a) Electrolysis shall be practiced by a licensed person only in a permanent establishment, hereafter referred to as an office. The Board may adopt reasonable rules and regulations concerning the sanitation standards, equipment, and supplies to be used and observed in offices. Offices shall be subject to periodic inspection at any time during business hours by members of the Board or its agents or assistants.

(b) Every electrologist shall notify the Board in writing 30 business days prior to, but no later than 10 business days after, any change of address or opening of a new office.

(c) Every electrologist shall display his license in a conspicuous place in the office.

(d) Every electrologist may make calls outside the office. The Board shall adopt rules and regulations concerning the equipment and instruments to be used by an electrologist when treating patients outside the office. (1989 (Reg. Sess., 1990), c. 1033.)

§ 88A-17. Requirements for certification as an electrology instructor.

(a) Any person who desires to be certified as an "electrology instructor" pursuant to this Chapter shall:

(1) Submit an application on a form approved by the Board;

(2) Be a licensed electrologist;

(3) Have practiced electrology actively for at least five years immediately before the application; and,

(4) Pass a written examination given by the Board.

(b) At least twice each year, the Board shall give an examination to applicants for certification as an electrology instructor. The examination shall consist of written and verbal sections testing the applicants' knowledge of the basic and clinical sciences relating to the theory and practice of electrology. The Board shall give applicants notice of the date, time, and place of the examination at least 60 days in advance.

(c) When the Board determines that an applicant has met all the qualifications for certification as an electrology instructor, and has submitted the required fee, the Board shall issue an instructor's certificate to the applicant. (1989 (Reg. Sess., 1990), c. 1033.)

§ 88A-17.1. Requirements for licensure as a laser hair practitioner instructor.

(a) Any person who desires licensure as a laser practitioner instructor pursuant to this Chapter shall meet the following requirements:

(1) Submit an application on a form approved by the Board.

(2) Be an electrologist licensed under this Chapter or a physician licensed under Article 1 of Chapter 90 of the General Statutes.

(3) Have practiced laser and light-based treatments actively for at least five years immediately before applying for licensure.

(4) Have at least 100 hours of training in laser and light-based treatments.

(b) When the Board determines that an applicant has met all qualifications for licensure as a laser hair practitioner instructor and has submitted the required fee, the Board shall issue an instructor's license to the applicant. (2007-489, s. 9.)

§ 88A-18. Renewal of instructor's license.

An electrology or laser hair practitioner instructor's license shall be renewed annually. On or before the date the current license expires, the applicant must submit an application for renewal of licensure on a form approved by the Board, meet criteria for renewal established by the Board, and pay the required fee. Any person whose instructor's license has expired for a period of three years or more shall be required to take and pass the instructor's examination before the license can be renewed. (1989 (Reg. Sess., 1990), c. 1033, s. 1; 2007-489, s. 10.)

§ 88A-19. Requirements for certification as a Board approved school of electrology.

(a) Any school in this State or another state that desires to be certified as a Board approved school of electrology shall:

(1) Submit an application on a form approved by the Board;

(2) Submit a detailed projected floor plan of the institutional area demonstrating adequate school facilities to accommodate students for purposes of lectures, classroom instruction, and practical demonstration;

(3) Submit a detailed list of the equipment to be used by the students in the practical course of their studies;

(4) Submit a copy of the planned electrology curriculum consisting of the number of hours and subject matter determined by the Board, provided that the

number of hours required shall not be less than 120 hours and not more than 600 hours;

(5) Submit a certified copy of the school manual of instruction;

(6) Submit the names and qualifications of the instructors certified in accordance with G.S. 88A-16; and,

(7) Any additional information the Board may require.

(b) When the Board determines that an applicant has met all the qualifications for certification as a Board approved school of electrology, and has submitted the required fee, the Board shall issue a certificate to the applicant.

(c) A school's certification is only valid for the location named in the application. When a school desires to change locations, an application shall be submitted to the Board on a form furnished by the Board and the fee shall be paid for certificate renewal.

(d) A school's certification is not transferrable. Schools must immediately notify the Board in writing of any sale, transfer, or change in ownership or management.

(e) Every school shall display its certification in a manner prescribed by the Board.

(f) All epilators used in the school must be approved by the Food and Drug Administration of the United States Government. (1989 (Reg. Sess., 1990), c. 1033, s. 1; 1993 (Reg. Sess., 1994), c. 755, s. 5.)

§ 88A-19.1. Requirements for certification as a Board-approved school of laser, light source, or pulsed-light treatments.

(a) Any school in this State or another state that desires to be certified as a Board-approved school of laser, light source, or pulsed-light treatments shall:

(1) Submit an application on a form approved by the Board;

(2) Submit a detailed projected floor plan of the institutional area demonstrating adequate school facilities to accommodate students for purposes of lectures, classroom instruction, and practical demonstration;

(3) Submit a detailed list of the equipment to be used by the students in the practical course of their studies;

(4) Submit a copy of the planned laser, light source, or pulsed-light curriculum consisting of the number of hours and subject matter determined by the Board, provided that the number of hours required shall not be less than 30 hours pursuant to rules adopted by the Board;

(5) Submit a certified copy of the school manual of instruction;

(6) Submit the names and qualifications of the instructors certified; and

(7) Submit any additional information the Board may require.

(b) When the Board determines that an applicant has met all the qualifications for certification as a Board-approved school of laser, light source, or pulsed-light treatments and has submitted the required fee, the Board shall issue a certificate to the applicant.

(c) A school's certification is only valid for the location named in the application. When a school desires to change locations, an application shall be submitted to the Board on a form furnished by the Board, and the fee shall be paid for certificate renewal.

(d) A school's certification is not transferable. Schools shall immediately notify the Board in writing of any sale, transfer, or change in ownership or management.

(e) Every school shall display its certification in a manner prescribed by the Board.

(f) All laser, light source, or pulsed-light devices used in the school shall be approved by the federal Food and Drug Administration. (2007-489, s. 11.)

§ 88A-20. Certification renewal.

Every certificate issued pursuant to G.S. 88A-19 or G.S. 88A-19.1 shall be renewed annually. On or before the date the current certificate expires, the applicant must submit an application for renewal of certification on a form approved by the Board, meet criteria for renewal established by the Board, and pay the required fee. Failure to renew the certificate within 90 days after the expiration date shall result in automatic forfeiture of any certification issued pursuant to this Chapter. (1989 (Reg. Sess., 1990), c. 1033, s. 1; 2007-489, s. 12.)

§ 88A-21. Disciplinary authority of the Board.

(a) Grounds for disciplinary action shall include:

(1) Conviction of, or finding of guilt with respect to, a crime in this State or any other jurisdiction, regardless of adjudication, if any element of the crime directly relates to the practice of electrolysis;

(2) Obtaining, or attempting to obtain, a license to practice electrolysis by bribery or by fraudulent misrepresentation;

(3) Malpractice or the inability to practice electrolysis with reasonable skill and safety;

(4) Disseminating false, deceptive, or misleading advertising;

(5) Judicial determination of mental incompetency;

(6) The revocation, suspension, or denial of the person's license or certification to practice electrolysis in any other state or territory of the United States;

(7) A finding, upon investigation by the Board, that the applicant or licensee is guilty of unprofessional conduct. "Unprofessional conduct" includes any act which departs from, or fails to conform to, the minimum standards of acceptable and prevailing electrolysis practice;

(8) Assisting, aiding, abetting, or procuring the practice of a person who is not licensed under this Chapter; and,

(9) Violation of any provision of this Chapter, or any rule or regulation of the Board.

(b) In accordance with Chapter 150B of the General Statutes, the Board may require remedial education, issue a letter of reprimand, restrict, revoke, or suspend any license or certification issued pursuant to this Chapter or deny any application for licensure or certification if the Board determines that the applicant or licensee has committed any of the acts listed in subsection (a).

(c) The Board may reinstate a revoked license or remove licensure restrictions when it finds that the reasons for revocation or restriction no longer exist and that the person can reasonably be expected to practice electrology safely and properly. (1989 (Reg. Sess., 1990), c. 1033.)

§ 88A-22. Enjoining illegal practices.

(a) If the Board finds that any person is violating any of the provisions of this Chapter, it may apply in its own name to the superior court for an injunction or restraining order to prevent that person from further violation. The court is empowered to grant an injunction regardless of whether any other enforcement action has been or may be instituted. All actions by the Board shall be governed by the North Carolina Rules of Civil Procedure.

(b) The venue for actions brought under this Chapter shall be the superior court in the county where the illegal or unlawful acts are alleged to have been committed, in the county where the defendant resides, or in the county where the Board maintains its offices and records. (1989 (Reg. Sess., 1990), c. 1033.)

§ 88A-23. Reports and immunity from suit.

Any person who has reasonable cause to suspect misconduct or incapacity of a licensee, or who has reasonable cause to suspect that any person is in violation of this Chapter, shall report the relevant facts to the Board. Upon the receipt of such charge, or upon its own initiative, the Board may give notice of an administrative hearing or may, after diligent investigation, dismiss unfounded charges. Any person making a report pursuant to this section shall be immune from any criminal prosecution or civil liability resulting therefrom unless such person knew the report was false or acted in reckless disregard of whether the report was false. (1989 (Reg. Sess., 1990), c. 1033, s. 1; 1995, c. 509, s. 36.)

Vision Books Order Form

Fax Orders:	1-980-299-5965
Phone Orders:	1-704-898-0770
E-mail Orders:	www.visionbooks.org
Mail Orders:	Vision Books P.O. Box 42406 Charlotte, NC 28215

Shipp To:
Name_____
Address_____
City_____State_____Zip_____
Phone_____Fax_____
Email_____@_____

Bill To: We can bill a third party on your behalf.
Name_____
Address_____
City_____State_____Zip_____
Phone____(_____)_____Fax_____
Email_____@_____

Pamphlet Number ($15.00 Each)	Qty	Total Cost
_____	_____	_____
_____	_____	_____
_____	_____	_____
_____	_____	_____
_____	_____	_____
_____	_____	_____
_____	_____	_____
Full Volume Set 1-92	92 Pamphlets	1,380.00

Free Shipping Shipping & Handling on Full Volume Orders
Add $1.00 Shipping & Handling per pamphlet $_____

Total Cost $_____

DID YOU ENJOY THIS BOOK?

Vision Books, LLC would like to hear from you! If you or someone you know has been fasely imprisoned, we would like to hear your story. If the 'North Carolina Criminal Law and Procedure' has had an effect in your life or if you have suggestions, we would like to hear from you. Send your letters to:

Vision Books, LLC
Attn: Staff Writers
P.O. Box 42406
Charlotte, NC 28215
Email: staff@visionbooks.org

Order Additional Copies:

Fax Orders: 1-980-299-5965

Phone Orders: 1-704-898-0770

E-mail Orders: www.visionbooks.org

Mail Orders: Vision Books, LLC
                    P.O. Box 42406
                    Charlotte, NC 28215

www.ingramcontent.com/pod-product-compliance
Lightning Source LLC
Chambersburg PA
CBHW051627170526
45167CB00001B/84